A HISTORY OF MODERN TUNISIA

Although a favourite destination for tourists, Tunisia is perhaps one of the least studied and least understood countries in North Africa. Situated halfway between Gibraltar and Suez, Tunisia has two windows on the Mediterranean, one opening towards Europe, the other towards the Middle East. Peoples from both regions have left their imprint on this land, although of all the legacies bestowed on Tunisia, that of the Arabs is unquestionably the most enduring. Kenneth Perkins' book, which is the first English-language history of modern Tunisia, explores these legacies as he traces and explains Tunisia's story from the mid-nineteenth century to the present day. The early years from 1881 to 1956 are taken up with the inauguration and development of French colonial rule, the establishment of the nationalist movement and the struggle for independence. Perkins examines the problems that were created by colonialism and the measures undertaken by Tunisians to win their independence. He then goes on to describe the subsequent process of state-building, including the design of political and economic structures and the promotion since 1956 of a social and cultural agenda. In conclusion he reviews the years since 1987, when a new regime came to power with promises of correcting the most widely perceived faults of its predecessor. Perkins' readable and informed introduction to Tunisia will be a necessity for students of North Africa and the Middle East, and also for anyone travelling to the region who wants a more comprehensive approach than most guidebooks can offer.

KENNETH PERKINS is Professor of History at the University of South Carolina. He has worked extensively on North Africa and his research has taken him across the region. His publications include two editions of *Historical Dictionary of Tunisia* (1989, 1997) and *Tunisia: Crossroads of the Islamic and European Worlds* (1986).

A HISTORY OF
MODERN TUNISIA

KENNETH PERKINS

University of South Carolina

PUBLISHED BY THE PRESS SYNDICATE OF THE UNIVERSITY OF CAMBRIDGE
The Pitt Building, Trumpington Street, Cambridge, United Kingdom

CAMBRIDGE UNIVERSITY PRESS
The Edinburgh Building, Cambridge, CB2 2RU, UK
40 West 20th Street, New York, NY 10011–4211, USA
477 Williamstown Road, Port Melbourne, VIC 3207, Australia
Ruiz de Alarcón 13, 28014 Madrid, Spain
Dock House, The Waterfront, Cape Town 8001, South Africa

http://www.cambridge.org

First published 2004

Printed in the United Kingdom at the University Press, Cambridge

Typeface Adobe Garamond 11/12.5 pt.   *System* LaTeX 2$_\varepsilon$ [TB]

A catalogue record for this book is available from the British Library

ISBN 0 521 81124 4 hardback
ISBN 0 521 00972 3 paperback

Contents

Maps

Illustrations

Acknowledgments

The need to select images to illustrate this book confronted me with the pleasurable task of poring over a collection of photographs, stamps, post cards, and other miscellaneous ephemera gathered in Tunisia over the course of the past thirty-five years. It also prompted me to seek out repositories of older images. I am most grateful for the assistance of Dr. James A. Miller, director of the Centre d'Etudes Maghrébines à Tunis (CEMAT), in locating and securing copies of pictures held by the Institut Supérieur d'Histoire du Mouvement National, as well as for his enthusiastic verbal and visual updates on the state of affairs in Tunis. I am also very much in the debt of M. Fayçal Chérif, of the Institut, who kindly arranged to provide the photographs I requested.

Keith McGraw of the Instructional Services Center of the University of South Carolina supplied the expertise needed to transform postcards, stamps, and slides into images suitable for publication, while the Department of History provided the funding to make that project possible.

A sabbatical leave in 2002–3 greatly expedited the completion of this book. My wife Margaret's appointment as a Fulbright scholar in the Department of English at Ibn Zuhr University in Agadir, Morocco, enabled us to spend the year in North Africa. Living in Morocco while writing about Tunisia may have been unorthodox, but doing so greatly enhanced my appreciation of the similarities and differences between the two countries and I am deeply grateful to Margaret for making that experience possible.

A political who's who of modern Tunisia

Habib ⁣ᶜAchour (1913–)
A union leader and champion of workers' rights. Despite a long record as a party loyalist, he was highly critical of the detrimental impact of Socialist Dustur economic policies on UGTT members in the 1970s. Jailed for a time after the 1978 riots, he resumed his union activities in 1981 but was arrested again in 1985 after attacking the government's sponsorship of a rival labor union. On his release in 1988, he eschewed further activism.

Ahmad Bey (1806–55)
The tenth ruler of the Husainid Dynasty, 1837–55. Westernizing reforms that he introduced with an eye towards protecting Tunisia from foreign encroachment proved ruinously expensive. Although few of his projects survived his death, his reign provided many future Tunisian leaders with their first experiences in international affairs.

Amin Bey (1879–1962)
Nineteenth, and last, ruler of the Husainid Dynasty, 1943–57. He sought to maintain a good relationship with both the Neo-Dustur and the French administration after replacing the deposed Moncef Bey. Nevertheless, the independent Tunisian government, eager to eliminate a rival locus of authority, demanded his abdication as a prelude to the abolition of the monarchy.

ᶜAli Bash Hamba (1876–1918)
A Young Tunisian activist. He founded the Association des Elèves du Collège Sadiqi in 1905, and in 1907 was a cofounder and political director of *Le Tunisien*, the first French-language newspaper published by Tunisians. After organizing a boycott of the Tunis tram system in an attempt to win equal treatment for Tunisian and European employees, he was expelled from the country in 1912 and died in exile in Istanbul.

Zine al-ᶜAbidine ben ᶜAli (1936–)

President of Tunisia since 1987. He held ambassadorial and ministerial appointments after retiring from the armed forces, then became prime minister and, with the removal of Habib Bourguiba, president. His economic policies brought improvements to the quality of most Tunisians' lives, but pledges to implement meaningful political pluralism remain unfulfilled. The regime's Islamist opposition was eradicated in the 1990s and its secular opponents have been systematically excluded from the political arena.

Tahar ben ᶜAmmar (1889–1985)

A political figure who participated in the founding of the Dustur Party, abandoned it in favor of the Parti Réformiste, and then, as a member of the Grand Council from 1928 to 1934 and its president after World War II, eschewed any specific party affiliation. Named prime minister in 1955, he oversaw the negotiations leading first to internal autonomy and then to the termination of the protectorate.

Ahmed ben Salah (1926–)

A political activist and labor organizer. Named minister of planning in 1961, he was given the task of developing the postcolonial economy. His efforts to bring agriculture under state control provoked strong criticisms that, coupled with accusations of corruption and mismanagement, led to his dismissal and arrest in 1969. He formed the Mouvement de l'Unité Populaire while in exile after 1973 and returned to Tunisia in 1988.

Salah ben Yusuf (1920–1961)

A Neo-Dustur militant who challenged Habib Bourguiba for control of the party on the eve of independence. Critical of Bourguiba's willingness to compromise with the French and of his secular orientation and his disdain for pan-Arabism, he precipitated an open revolt that was subdued only with French assistance. He left the country in 1956 but continued to attack Bourguiba from Cairo until his assassination.

Habib Bourguiba (1903–2000)

Nationalist leader, cofounder of the Neo-Dustur Party, first prime minister of independent Tunisia, and president of the country from 1958 until his removal for health reasons in 1987. His pragmatic strategies for ending French rule dominated the anticolonial movement, while his aggressively modernist and staunchly secularist philosophy shaped policy making in the postcolonial state.

Paul Cambon (1843–1924)

The French resident general, 1882–6. As France's first chief executive in Tunisia, he oversaw the implementation of reforms agreed to in the treaty establishing the protectorate. His decision to maintain the appearance of beylical sovereignty while reserving real power for himself and a small cadre of French administrators established a pattern that became the norm for his successors.

Rashid Ghannushi (1941–)

Founder in 1979 of the Mouvement de la Tendance Islamique (MTI), a society dedicated to the restoration of Islamic values. He was imprisoned twice in the closing years of the Bourguiba era, but was freed in 1988 as President ben ʿAli sought to improve relations with Islamic groups. When the government banned his Renaissance Party from standing in the 1989 elections, however, he went into exile. Accused of orchestrating a 1992 wave of violence, he was convicted (*in absentia*) of conspiring to overthrow the government.

Hassan Guellaty (1880–1966)

A Young Tunisian activist expelled from the country for his role in the 1912 Tunis tram boycott. Returning after World War I, he broke with his former colleagues who established the Dustur Party and, in 1921, organized the less militant Parti Réformiste. French liberals hailed his moderate philosophy, but it found little support among Tunisians and the party quickly withered away.

Farhat Hached (1913–1952)

A labor organizer and founder of the Union Générale des Travailleurs Tunisiens (UGTT) in 1945. By mobilizing workers in support of Neo-Dustur political objectives, he added clout to the party's demands and earned the animus of French settlers and administrators. His assassination gave the nationalist movement a prominent martyr and touched off a spate of violence throughout the country.

Khair al-Din al-Tunsi (ca. 1822–1890)

A statesman who held a series of offices until his self-imposed exile to Europe in 1862 as a result of differences with Mustafa Khaznadar. Returning to Tunisia in 1869, he advocated reforms designed to forge a strong, just, and responsible state, many of which he implemented after becoming chief minister in 1873. When associates of Khaznadar drove him from office in 1877, he went to the Ottoman Empire.

Charles-Martial Lavigerie (1825–1892)

A Catholic clergyman who espoused the spread of Christianity along with French political control in North Africa. The White Fathers, a missionary order he founded in 1868, helped advance French interests in Tunisia even before the protectorate. Named cardinal-archbishop of Carthage and Algiers in 1882, he advocated harmonious Church–state relations in the interest of strengthening France's position in Tunisia.

Louis Macheul (1848–1922)

Director of public education, 1883–1908. Convinced that education held the key to viable relations between the races, he organized a Franco-Arab school system blending elements from both cultures. Despite the opposition of many settlers, he remained a strong proponent of educational opportunities for Tunisian students throughout his service in the protectorate.

Ahmed Mestiri (1928–)

A Socialist Dustur politician ousted from the party in 1974 after calling for institutional checks on the power of the president and greater transparency in the transaction of party business. He then founded the Mouvement des Démocrates Sociales (MDS), which he led through several undistinguished legislative election campaigns between its official recognition as a political party in 1983 and his retirement from political life in 1992.

M'hammed ᶜAli (ca. 1888–1928)

A labor organizer and Dustur Party militant. In 1924, he organized the Confédération Générale des Travailleurs Tunisiens (CGTT), believing that the promotion of social and economic justice for the working class would broaden the party's bourgeois base. But the Dustur turned its back on the CGTT in 1925 when a series of strikes raised concerns that repressive measures directed against the union might also be applied to the party.

René Millet (1849–1919)

The French resident general, 1894–1900. Sympathetic with the Young Tunisians' aspirations to act as interlocutors between their countrymen and the West, he supported their educational undertakings and provided government subsidies for their publications. French settlers pressured him to refrain from these practices and ultimately lobbied successfully for his dismissal.

Moncef Bey (1881–1948)

The eighteenth ruler of the Husainid Dynasty, 1942–3. With prominent Neo-Dustur Party figures in jail or in exile because of anti-French activity before World War II, he presented himself as a nationalist spokesperson. He maintained only formally correct relations with German officials during their occupation of Tunisia (1942–3), but his nationalist sympathies alarmed the French and they forced him to abdicate on their return.

Muhammad al-Sadiq Bey (1814–1882)

The twelfth ruler of the Husainid Dynasty, 1859–82. Ill-conceived development projects and bureaucratic corruption marked his reign and produced substantial indebtedness. The inability to repay loans from abroad led to the formation of an international commission to oversee Tunisia's finances. The subsequent collapse of a movement of political and economic reform spearheaded by his prime minister paved the way for the French invasion of 1881.

Muhammad Bey (1811–1859)

The eleventh ruler of the Husainid Dynasty, 1855–9. By distancing himself from many of Ahmad Bey's policies, he hoped to lower government expenditures. To protect their interests in Tunisia, Britain and France pressured him to implement judicial reforms and accept substantial foreign investment in the country.

Mustafa Khaznadar (1817–1878)

Frequently chief minister of the beys from the 1850s to the 1870s. He amassed a personal fortune, much of it from collaborating with Europeans anxious to do business in Tunisia. Widely despised for saddling the country with crippling debts and brutally repressing a rebellion triggered by higher taxes, he fell from power in 1873 while attempting to play the country's creditors off against each other.

Muhammad Mzali (1925–)

Prime minister, 1980–6. His introduction of reforms promoting a more open, plural political environment antagonized conservatives within his own Socialist Dustur Party, while his inability to stimulate the depressed economy alienated Tunisians of the middle and lower classes. When influential critics persuaded President Bourguiba to dismiss him in 1986, he left the country to avoid further political and legal reprisals.

Nasir Bey (1855–1922)

The fifteenth ruler of the Husainid Dynasty, 1906–22. He tried to pressure the French to negotiate with the newly formed Dustur Party in 1922 by threatening to abdicate if the party's demands were not addressed. He backed down when Resident General Lucien Saint surrounded the beylical palace with French troops, making it clear that he would not respond to such threats.

Hedi Nouira (1911–1993)

Neo-Dustur politician. He served as director of the Central Bank of Tunisia from 1958 to 1970, then as prime minister until 1980. His main task while in office was to foster a recovery from the disarray brought on by Ahmed ben Salah's experiments in socialist planning. An economic liberal, he promoted private enterprise and sought out foreign investment, but also left in place many state enterprises created in the previous decade.

Marcel Peyrouton (1887–1983)

The French resident general from 1933 to 1936. Hoping to aggravate differences within the nationalist movement and to marginalize its more radical elements, he opened his administration with an offer to lift a ban on the Dustur Party if it disavowed the views of its most militant younger members. When the latter formed the Neo-Dustur Party in 1934, he ordered their arrest and set about attempting to destroy the new party.

Léon Roches (1809–1901)

The French consul general in Tunis, 1855–63. Charged with strengthening French influence in Tunisia, Roches formed close personal relationships with the beys who facilitated his advocacy of pro-French policies. Just prior to the end of his assignment, he arranged with a Parisian bank for the Tunisian government's first international loan.

Lucien Saint (1867–1938)

The French resident general, 1921–9. Assuming office amid the most articulate and organized opposition to the protectorate since its creation, he rejected the key demands of the Dustur Party, intimidated the bey into distancing himself from the nationalists, and severely restricted journalistic and political activity. Beneath a surface calm, Tunisian resentment of French rule rose significantly during his administration.

Bashir Sfar (1865–1917)

An activist in the Young Tunisian movement. His education at the Collège Sadiqi led to positions in the protectorate administration. He resigned as director of the Habus administration in 1898 in a protest over French use of lands designated as religious trusts. A decade later, his continuing criticism of the protectorate resulted in his reassignment far from the capital, severely diminishing his influence.

ᶜAbd al-ᶜAziz Thaᶜalbi (ca. 1875–1944)

Leader of the Dustur Party from its founding in 1920 until his death. Fearful that a wave of repression would follow the party's opposition to French reform proposals, he fled Tunisia in 1923 and did not return until 1937. In the interim, a new generation of activists had taken control of the nationalist movement. When his efforts to reassert himself foundered, the Dustur remained on the margin of the anti-colonial struggle.

Richard Wood (1806–1900)

The British consul general in Tunis, 1855–79. His work in safeguarding the interests of British subjects and in promoting investments enhancing the British presence there sparked a long-running rivalry with his French counterparts that was further aggravated by his campaign to tie Tunisia more closely to the Ottoman Empire.

Note on spelling and transliteration

Where conventional European forms exist for Tunisian place-names, these have been used in preference to the technically more precise, but decidedly less familiar, formal transliterations of the Arabic. Thus, "Sfax" appears in place of "Safaqis," "Kairouan" rather than "Qairawan," and "Sousse," not "Susa." By the same token, spellings of personal names of political figures that have attained general recognition in Western languages have also been adopted: "Habib Bourguiba" rather than "Habib Abu Ruqaiba," for example. The same rule of thumb applies for Arabic words that appear in standard English dictionaries. Inasmuch as nonspecialists are likely to find orthographic symbols confusing and specialists readily recognize names and words without them, only the symbol "ᶜ" to represent the Arabic letter "*ain*" and an apostrophe (') to represent the glottal stop *hamza* have been utilized.

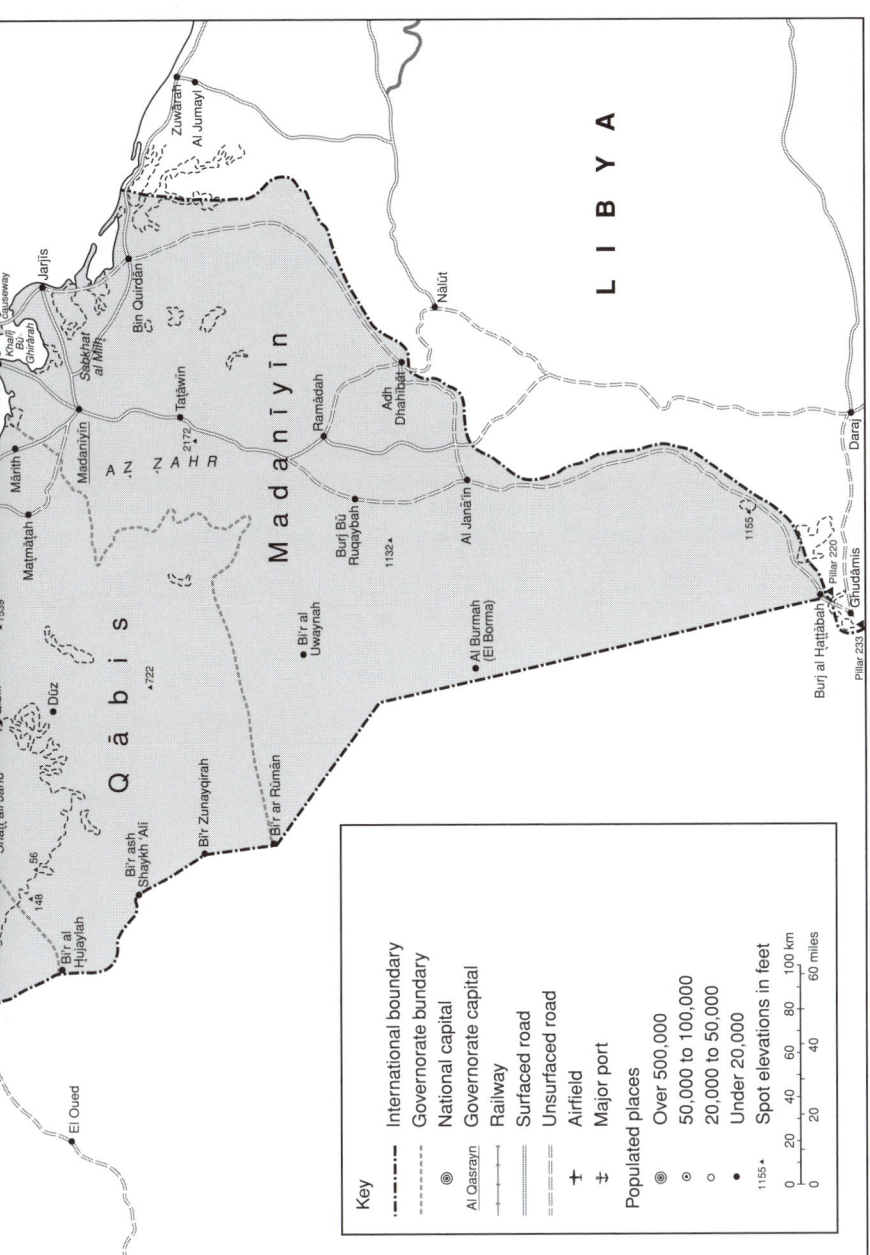

Tunisia

Key

	International boundary
	Governorate bundary
◉	National capital
Al Qasrayn	Governorate capital
	Railway
	Surfaced road
	Unsurfaced road
+	Airfield
✛	Major port

Populated places

◉	Over 500,000
⦾	50,000 to 100,000
○	20,000 to 50,000
•	Under 20,000
1155 ▲	Spot elevations in feet

L I B Y A

Zuwārah
Al Jumayl

Jarjis
Bin Quirdān
Nālūt

Khalīj Bū Ghirārah
Sabkhat al Milh

Mārith
Madanīyīn
Tatāwīn
Ramādah
Adh Dhāhibāt

A Z   Ẓ A H R
2172 ▲

Matmātah
Burj Bū Ruqaybah
Al Janā'in
1132 ▲

Q ā b i s

M a d a n ī y ī n

Bi'r al Uwaynah
Al Burmah (El Borma)

1155 ▲

Dūz
722 ▲

Bi'r al Hattābah
Ghudāmis
Pillar 220
Pillar 233 ▲
Daraj

Bi'r Zunayqirah
Bi'r ar Rūmān

Bi'r ash Shaykh 'Alī

Shaṭṭ al Jarīd
56
148
El Oued
Bi'r al Hujaylah

0	20	40	60	80	100 km
0	20	40	60 miles		

Introduction

For the attentive traveler, a ride on the TGM – the Tunis, La Goulette, and La Marsa, a light railway linking Tunis with a string of suburbs along the Gulf of Tunis – can become an extraordinary trip through the country's history and culture. Not far from the end of the line in La Marsa are the remains of a sixteenth-century palace where Tunisia's rulers passed the summer months to avail themselves of the sea breezes and where, in 1882, the reigning bey signed the document establishing a French protectorate over his country. A mile down the tracks, the train reaches Sidi Bou Said, a village that welcomed Muslims fleeing from the Iberian Peninsula in the fifteenth and sixteenth centuries and that has been, for many years, a favorite haunt of local and European artists. The Museum of Traditional Music and Musical Instruments, located in what was the home of Baron Rudolphe d'Erlanger (1872–1932), honors the work of this French scholar who spent years helping Tunisian musicians preserve the Andalusian melodies and techniques brought to "Sidi Bou" by their refugee forefathers.

The next six TGM stops, spread out over two or three miles, are all in Carthage. Two bear the names of the ancient city's most famous father and son, Amilcar and Hannibal. Down the hill from the Amilcar station is a hotel built in the early days of the campaign to attract European tourists to the newly independent country's beaches. A few hundred yards west of the station, a World War II military cemetery – one of many British, French, German, and US burial grounds scattered across Tunisia along the battle lines of 1942 and 1943 – memorializes the men who fought in North Africa and shelters the remains of almost 3,000 American soldiers.

Just before pulling into the Hannibal station, passengers catch glimpses of Roman Carthage on either side of the railway. Towards the Gulf of Tunis sprawl the Antonine Baths, now an archeological park encompassing the vestiges of a complex of buildings commanding stunning views across the gulf to the Cap Bon peninsula. On the opposite side of the train lies an excavated neighborhood of Roman villas. The station between Amilcar and

Hannibal, Présidence, is close to the official residence of the president of the republic. Perhaps few commuters making their way to or from jobs in Tunis give a second thought to this juxtaposition, but it has no doubt reassured Habib Bourguiba and Zine al-ᶜAbidine ben ᶜAli, the only two chief executives since 1956, to dwell within the symbolic embrace of two such stalwarts of the Tunisian past.

Still another Carthage station, Byrsa, derives its name from the hill where the Carthage acropolis stood and where, by Virgil's anachronistic account, Queen Dido entertained the travel-weary Aeneas. After France established its protectorate over Tunisia, the Catholic Church erected the cathedral of Saint Louis atop the hill to commemorate the saint-king whose ill-fated thirteenth-century crusade foundered on the shores below. From the Byrsa station, an easy walk leads to the twin seaports of Punic Carthage, one for the city's merchant fleet, the other for its warships. A similar walk from the Salammbo station (named for the daughter of Amilcar who also provided Gustave Flaubert, one of many nineteenth-century European writers entranced by Tunisia, with the title for his 1862 novel) ends at the Tophet, a sanctuary at which, some scholars believe, child sacrifices were meant to appease the Carthaginian gods.

A few stops farther on is a station named for Khair al-Din Barbarossa, the sixteenth-century corsair captain whose ships struck fear into the hearts of European sailors – or perhaps for Khair al-Din al-Tunsi, the reform-minded prime minister of the nineteenth century who lived in France for a decade and believed that Tunisia had much to learn about the modern world from the nations of Europe. Inasmuch as the station is on the outskirts of La Goulette, the port from which both Khair al-Dins sailed on their quite different missions, the ambiguity seems appropriate enough.

Situated on the Gulf of Tunis where a break in the coastline provides a passage into the shallow Lake of Tunis – the gullet to which its name refers – La Goulette served for centuries as the port of Tunis. In keeping with its maritime links around the Mediterranean, the city had a cosmopolitan air and, even after independence, remained one of the most ethnically and religiously mixed communities in the country. The TGM passes beneath the massive battlements of the fortress erected in 1535 by the Spanish Hapsburgs to consolidate their conquest of the region. Down the street along the structure's southern wall, far enough away to be difficult to distinguish clearly, is an equestrian statue of Habib Bourguiba that once stood in downtown Tunis but was moved to this less visible location at the end of his presidency in 1987. Leaving La Goulette, the railway tracks turn westward to cross the lake on a causeway built by the Tunis Tram Company in 1905 to replace the longer route along the western shore of the lake which had been laid out by the Italian concessionaires who constructed and initially operated the line in the early 1870s. Arriving at the Tunis-Marine station after a run of some fifty minutes and fifteen miles, the train has passed by sites associated with three millennia of history.

A leisurely walk of an hour or two after exiting the TGM terminus builds upon the ride's introduction to Tunisian history. Just beyond the turnstiles is the main east–west thoroughfare of the "new" city, built in the nineteenth century on the mud flats bordering the lake to accommodate a European quarter outside the walls of the Arab city, the medina. A massive clock tower overlooks the busy Place du 7 Novembre 1987, named in honor of the "Historic Change" of that date when ben ʿAli replaced the ailing Bourguiba as president after the latter had dominated the Tunisian political scene for more than half a century. Before the "Historic Change," the centerpiece of the square was the statue of Bourguiba now consigned to La Goulette.

Nevertheless, the avenue still bears the name of the ex-president. A wide central mall, with towering shade trees on both sides, divides the traffic along the length of the boulevard, creating a pleasant pedestrian space rendered visually attractive and odoriferous by the profusion of flower stalls and the ubiquitous men and boys selling jasmine nosegays. Some three hundred yards up Avenue Bourguiba from the TGM station is the National Theatre. Built in the early twentieth century as part of an entertainment center for European settlers that also included a casino, it became the home of Tunisian drama troupes whose productions fueled nationalist sentiments even as they elevated the level of cultural life. Two blocks farther on loom the most powerful symbols of seventy-five years of French colonial rule: the cathedral of St. Vincent de Paul and, directly opposite, the embassy of France which, before independence, was the seat of the resident general and headquarters of the protectorate administration. Between them, in the median of Avenue Bourguiba, is a statue of the renowned fourteenth-century scholar Ibn Khaldoun, a native of Tunisia. The main point of contact between the downtown business district and the medina lies just slightly more than a hundred yards farther west.

Only a few vestiges of the gates that once pierced the medina's walls remain. By far the best known is the Bab al-Bahr, or Gate of the Sea, which offered the most direct access to the lake. Today, it is more commonly known as the Porte de France. Just inside the gate is the embassy of the United Kingdom, where Her Majesty's consuls once schemed against their French and Italian counterparts in the competition to draw Tunisia into the European orbit. Nearby are the neighborhoods of "Little Malta," a quarter once filled with immigrants from that island, who enjoyed British protection, and the mellah, which once housed the Jewish population. One of two streets plunging into the medina from the Porte de France is rue Jamᶜa Zaituna (Zaituna Mosque Street). It slopes gently uphill past an astounding variety of shops, many of them now specializing in items favored by tourists, to end at the main portal of the mosque. Built in the eighth century, Zaituna served not only as a place of worship, but also as the premier educational institution in Tunisia. Even after modern secular schools began to usurp that role in the nineteenth century, the mosque constituted the locus of Muslim intellectual life until its teaching functions were transferred to a faculty of theology and religious sciences at the University of Tunis in the 1960s. The winding streets and alleys around Zaituna offer numerous diversions, as the mosque is surrounded by the highest quality souks, or markets, in the city. Perfumes, spices, books, jewelry, and fine fabrics create a riot of colors and blend of aromas that set the precincts of the mosque apart as a unique environment. Not far from Zaituna, towards the southern edge of the medina, is the Tourbet al-Bey, which houses the tombs of the monarchs of the Husainid Dynasty (1705–1957).

A second major street traversing the medina from the Porte de France passes close by the mosque but ends at the center of secular, rather than religious, authority in the medina, the kasbah. The former palace of the ruler, the Dar al-Bey, now houses the prime minister's office, while buildings containing other government offices line the Place du Gouvernement at the western edge of the medina. Across the busy avenue that hems in the old city in the absence of its walls is the Collège Sadiqi. This still functioning legacy of Khair al-Din al-Tunsi endowed the sons of the Tunisian bourgeoisie with modern secondary educations and served as a veritable nursery of generations of nationalist leaders.

The final leg of this journey through Tunisian history entails a walk along the perimeter of the medina to the Bab Souika neighborhood, a thirteenth-century suburb of the medina, and from there to the Bab al-Khadra station of the Tunis Metro, a tram system begun in the 1980s to relieve urban traffic congestion and connect the city with its northern, western, and southern suburbs. Line Four, the western route, makes a stop at Le Bardo, the beylical palace where the 1881 treaty, giving France special rights in Tunisia and paving the way for the protectorate, was signed. The National Assembly now occupies a portion of the palace, its entry flanked by soldiers dressed in ceremonial uniforms of the nineteenth century. Other wings of the palace house a world-class museum exhibiting an array of Tunisian artifacts but best known for its collection of mosaics, many from Carthage, others from sites elsewhere in Tunisia: Dougga, El-Djem, Thurburbo Majus, and Bulla Regia. Some experts rate the Bardo holdings as the finest collection of Roman-era mosaics in the world. In a country where layers of history blend so seamlessly, it seems fitting that their twenty-first century home be in a royal palace begun in the fourteenth century.

As extraordinary as is the historical richness and diversity observed in the less than twenty mile trip between La Marsa and Le Bardo, it is by no means unique to the region of Tunis. Although the entire country is only slightly larger than the American state of Florida, equally short journeys of similar diversity could readily be undertaken in such other urban centers as Sousse, Mahdia, Sfax, Gafsa, Kairouan, or Bizerte; among the towns and villages of the Majerda Valley west of the capital; or in Jarid oases of the southwest. How has it happened that the historical experience of what is now Tunisia has unfolded with such density and with so many traces of different cultures?

The southern curve of the African coastline at the Cap Bon peninsula has given Tunisia two windows on the Mediterranean Sea, one opening towards Europe, the other towards the Middle East. Since antiquity, this situation made it easy for peoples from both regions – Phoenicians, Romans, Arabs, Turks, Spaniards, Italians, Maltese, British, and French – to enter, and often take control of, the region. Its name has varied with time – Carthage, Africa (or, in its Arabized form, Ifriqiya), Tunisia – as its population has repeatedly absorbed waves of new arrivals from throughout the Mediterranean basin, all of them leaving their cultural imprints on the landscape and its inhabitants. But of all the rich legacies bestowed on Tunisia, that of the Arabs has unquestionably proven the most profound and enduring. The language, faith, and culture that the Arabs brought to the Maghrib ("the west," which to them meant all the lands beyond the Nile Valley) almost fourteen centuries ago have forged the innermost identity of the region's people ever since.

Nonetheless, the scant eighty-mile width of the Sicilian Channel separating that island from Cap Bon has assured the ready transmission of European influences as well. The rulers of the Mediterranean's northern shores sometimes competed with their counterparts in Tunisia for mastery of the lands bordering the sea. More commonly, however, they imposed their political and economic will on northern Africa, absorbing it into the Roman, and much later the French, empires. Only on rare occasions, such as at the height of the Carthaginian era in the sixth century BCE or during the rule of the Aghlabid Dynasty in the ninth century CE, did political entities based in what later became Tunisia turn the tables and make European territory their own.

But whatever the nature of the relationship between Tunisia and its neighbors at any given historical moment, the land was awash with an array of exogenous influences. Contemporary Tunisians take great pride in their ancestors' skill in blending the many stimuli to which they were exposed into their own distinctive culture. Tunisia's modern history clearly reveals how extensively key challenges confronting the country have elicited responses grounded in concepts and approaches that draw on the full spectrum of the nation's cultural inheritance. An appreciation of the relative strength and popularity of Western versus Arab-Islamic influences at any given moment, of how various segments of the population assessed those influences, and of why they held the views they did, can facilitate our understanding of the country's recent past.

In the modern era, four recurrent themes that have determined the trajectory of Tunisian history well illustrate the interplay of these influences. In the telling of that history, this book weaves together the most salient components of all four – a mix that varied with changing times and circumstances. The themes are (1) the effort to create a political environment deemed acceptable by rulers and ruled alike; (2) the endeavor to modify or, in some cases, eradicate traditional beliefs and practices deemed to impede "progress" while, at the same time, retaining a national identity rooted in the precolonial past; (3) the attempt to foster economic growth sufficiently vigorous to diminish dependence and provide a stable platform for political and social development; and (4) the quest to formulate an artistic tradition mirroring the many divergent inputs the country has undergone.

Modern Tunisia has experienced rule by an indigenous monarchy, colonial control as a French protectorate, and an independent republican government. Early in the protectorate era, Tunisians, many of them veterans of precolonial campaigns to reform the political structure or their protégés, sought a greater voice in their governance. At first, they petitioned for the same rights and privileges enjoyed by European residents of their country. The failure of France to satisfy that appeal led to demands for the termination of French rule altogether. The most successful leaders of the anticolonial struggle utilized ideas and techniques learned as a result of their experiences with Europe and Europeans to build a movement whose insistence on acquiring the assets of the West while still preserving Tunisia's Arab and Islamic cultural inheritance resonated with a broad spectrum of the population. As a result, they were well positioned to mold, and then to dominate, the political system that emerged after independence in 1956.

By the 1970s, however, waning popular enthusiasm for the secular, single-party, authoritarian regime they had put in place produced calls to overhaul the political system with an eye towards restraining executive power and promoting pluralism. But it was not until 1987 that the former nationalist chief Habib Bourguiba, who had been acclaimed "president for life," left office. The extent to which ben ʿAli, his successor as president and party leader, had engineered meaningful and satisfying changes in the political arena remained uncertain as Tunisia entered the twenty-first century.

The most disruptive, unsettling, and far-reaching, but also certainly the most consequential, social debates in modern Tunisian history have centered on the value of traditional beliefs and practices. The enactment of legislation banning or restricting long-established customs and institutions, often in conjunction with other, subtler, forms of governmental pressure, has rendered compliance all but inescapable. From the precolonial era to the present, much of what successive governments have targeted as outmoded, and thus attempted to eliminate or radically alter, has been linked to Islam. Although the state has had the power to secure outward compliance with its will, its approach to religious matters has given a weapon to its opponents and has provoked serious backlashes. The protectorate authorities introduced French courts and schools. Comparable Tunisian (and Islamic) legal and educational institutions remained in place but, over time, lost much of their prestige and relevance in the public arena. Following independence, the nation's new leaders, virtually all of them products of French educations through which they had assimilated the philosophical underpinnings of Western culture, initiated sweeping social reforms allegedly designed to liberate Tunisians from beliefs and practices they saw as obsolete in the modern world and as deterrents to development. In terms of its breadth and impact, only Mustafa Kemal Ataturk's secularization of Turkey in the 1920s and 1930s offered a comparable parallel in the Muslim world. The fact that most Tunisians derived their worldview from different sources than did these Western-educated elites guaranteed that tensions accompanied such reforms. For many years, the power of the government prevented opposition to these policies from crystallizing, but when it did crystallize, it was often very successfully couched in terms of the necessity of preserving Tunisia's traditional Arab-Islamic heritage from an onslaught of imported values and practices.

The rulers of modern Tunisia adopted a variety of strategies as they strove to forge an economy with sufficient strength and stability to support their governments' political and social agendas. During the protectorate era, economic decisions made in Tunis invariably privileged certain segments of the population, facilitating Europeans' acquisition of land and generally promoting the interests of European rural settlers and urban entrepreneurs over Tunisian farmers and merchants. Europeans held the richest, most profitable land in the country and controlled what few manufacturing enterprises emerged. Tunisians pushed to the margins of the economy often found themselves in straitened circumstances, but in singularly hard times, such as the 1920s and 1930s, especially in rural areas, many were unable to survive at all. As a result, economic discontent proved a powerful factor in galvanizing opposition to French control. With independence, the government's key economic objectives became the assertion of Tunisians' control over the economy and the intensification of the process of industrialization. To hasten reaching these goals, the state assumed a prominent role in the planning and management of the economy, as suggested by the 1964 addition of the adjective "socialist" to the name of the ruling party. Serious shortcomings in this arrangement, along with vigorous popular resistance to such policies as the collectivization of agricultural land and the establishment of cooperative farms, compelled the government to rethink its economic philosophy and, at the start of the 1970s, to replace it with another premised on dramatically different tenets. With the restoration of liberal principles and the development of an open, extroverted economy in which petroleum and tourism played major roles, some Tunisian capitalists fared extremely well, but most ordinary Tunisians did not. Class disparities widened as the despair of those experiencing a declining quality of life deepened. Shaken by deadly riots in 1978, 1980, and 1984, the government formulated the economic policy that it has pursued ever since, navigating between the two courses it had previously advocated.

The performing arts, painting, and literature provide a series of relatively little-studied cases revealing the impact on Tunisia of divergent cultural influences. Although theatrical works do not feature significantly in traditional Arab literary expression, Tunisians familiar with productions staged for European settlers began mounting Arabic versions of Western plays early in the twentieth century. In the inter-war years, their repertoires broadened to include more material by Arab authors, including Tunisians. At about the same time and as the result of a similar process, the first Tunisian novels written in Arabic also appeared. To these were added, towards the middle of the century, a flood of new fiction that adopted not only European form, but also European language. Many of the country's most distinguished novelists, whatever their language of expression, have taken as their subject matter the tugs of competing, and often conflicting, cultures that they encounter in their own lives.

Like drama and the novel, painting and sculpting were largely unknown in the traditional Arab-Islamic culture of North Africa. Some European artists lived in the protectorate, however, and many others visited it. Exposure to their work induced a handful of Tunisians to experiment as painters during the 1920s and 1930s. Following World War II, these men became the driving force behind the "School of Tunis." As its first masters, they fostered the creation of an authentically Tunisian artistic personality that valued the country's traditions and symbols but expressed them in modern forms. Tunisian musicians and musicologists manifested a similar respect for authenticity by preserving the nation's vocal and instrumental heritage as the radio and records popularized Western music throughout the world. Following in the footsteps of these pioneers, the post-independence generations of playwrights, actors, authors, musicians, and artists have called upon both Arab-Islamic and European traditions for inspiration, frequently fusing elements from both. Many have won accolades for their work at home, throughout the Arab world, and in Europe. But the facet of Tunisian artistic expression that has achieved the widest international recognition is the cinema. Even in their infancy, motion pictures attracted the interest of a few Tunisians, while foreign producers availed themselves of the country's abundant sunshine and varied landscape to make it a location for filming. More recently, the country's movie industry, which has often combined the talents of Arab and Western writers, producers, directors, actors, and technicians, has evolved into one of the most highly respected and successful in the non-Western world.

The precise point at which Tunisia's "modern" history begins is a matter open to interpretation, but the imposition of French rule in the 1880s unquestionably constituted a turning point of enormous importance. Thus, it is with an account of the environment that set the stage for the protectorate that this book begins.

CHAPTER I

The march to the Bardo, 1835–1881

Fiercely independent tribes with a long history of rejecting outside control inhabited the ruggedly mountainous, heavily forested area of the Tunisian–Algerian frontier. Recurrent feuds, compounded by a border that ignored many traditional tribal boundaries, rendered the region dangerously volatile. During the 1870s, the local Algerian military authorities recorded well over 2,000 incidents, many of them involving incursions across the border.[1] Thus the February 1881 ambush of a Tunisian Khmir tribesman by a group of Algerians might well have faded into oblivion with the arbitration of local notables and the payment of blood money if the confluence of French ambitions in North Africa, the willingness of other European powers to accommodate them, and the inability of the Tunisian government to impede them had not made a pretext for a military campaign in Tunisia highly desirable.

When French military administrators in La Calle, Algeria, hampered negotiations among the tribesmen, their frustrations predictably erupted into new outbreaks of violence towards the end of March. Asserting the need to stabilize the region, units of the French army crossed the border on April 24, capturing the garrison town of Le Kef two days later. At the same time, French warships shelled Tabarka and then sailed east to the larger and more strategically located port of Bizerte. In accordance with orders he had received from Tunis, the city's governor surrendered on May 1 without offering any resistance. Strengthened over the following week by significant reinforcements from France, General Jules-Aimé Bréart prepared to move on Tunis itself. Persistent rain made the march longer and more difficult than anticipated, but Bréart finally reached Ksar Saʿid, the beylical palace at Bardo, on the western outskirts of the capital, on May 12. Anxious to complete his mission, he insisted upon an immediate meeting with Muhammad al-Sadiq Bey, at which he and Théodore Roustan, the French consul general, demanded the ruler's agreement – within three hours – to a document regulating Franco-Tunisian relations. In view of

Figure 1.1. The throne room of the Bardo Palace. The beys formally received Tunisian government officials and foreign dignitaries in this ornately decorated salon.

the overwhelming military power of France, all but one of the notables summoned to the palace as the French approached urged him to comply. The sole objection came from Larbi Zarruk, the mayor of Tunis. The Bardo Treaty acknowledged the bey's sovereignty, but placed Tunisia's external relations under the supervision of a French resident-minister and its army under the command of a French general. Additionally, the treaty allowed France to station troops throughout the country as it deemed necessary to maintain order.

Although ostensibly tied to the recent disturbances in Khmir territory, the constraints embodied in the Bardo Treaty were the culmination of a process whose roots went back half a century. People from every corner of the Mediterranean basin had long been present in Tunisia, often as transients engaged in commerce, but also as residents of diaspora communities that had carved out places for themselves in Tunis and other coastal cities. During the reign of Ahmad Bey (1837–55), however, European persons, commodities, and ideologies flooded into Tunisia in greater numbers and with greater intensity than ever before. At first, these developments primarily affected the upper echelons of Tunisian society, but in short order their impact was discernible everywhere. As happened at more or less the same time in several regions of the Ottoman Empire, the penchant for the things of Europe pushed the government to the brink of bankruptcy even as the ideas of Europe challenged, in extraordinarily unsettling ways, traditional thinking about the most basic concepts of political, social, and economic organization. This debilitating combination of circumstances undermined the country's capacity to cope with a growing European appetite to dominate it politically and economically, although some Tunisian statesmen attempted, almost to the very end, to implement a program of internal reforms that would avert the worst case scenario. As the manifestation of a critical turning point in Tunisia's history, the signing ceremony in the Bardo Palace on the evening of May 12, 1881, confirmed their inability to do so. A full appreciation of the significance of that gloomy occasion requires embedding it within the context of what had been transpiring in Tunisia since the time of Ahmad Bey.

The tenth ruler of the Husainid Dynasty that had governed since 1705, Ahmad came to the throne at a time when his family's historically successful practice of safeguarding its substantial autonomy within the Ottoman Empire appeared threatened. In 1835, Ottoman troops had occupied the adjacent province of Tripoli, where the Qaramanli family had enjoyed similar latitude since 1711. The French conquest of Algeria in 1830 had jolted Istanbul into this dramatic demonstration of its interests in North Africa.

The restoration of direct Ottoman control was intended to deter further losses by emphasizing that this was territory over which the sultan, and not merely a local potentate, held sway, but it registered with Ahmad as a prelude to a similar campaign in Tunisia. Moreover, the easternmost Algerian province of Constantine, with its many political, economic, and social connections to Tunisia, fell to the French in the very year of Ahmad's accession. Thus, at the start of his reign, an army of the power to which he owed allegiance as a faithful Muslim lay just across one of his frontiers, while an army of the power to which he owed considerable money (as the result of an upsurge in French commercial activity in Tunisia since the 1830 invasion of Algeria) lay just across another.

Ahmad believed that he could relieve the discomforting sensation of being in a vise between more powerful neighbors by adopting a bold but deliberate two-pronged strategy. He well understood that France's advocacy of Tunisian autonomy within the Ottoman Empire stemmed from a desire to keep the Turks as far removed from Algeria as possible and to pave the way for the eventual extension of French influence into his country. Appreciative of the French interpretation of Ottoman–Tunisian relations, but wary of the intentions of his powerful new neighbor, Ahmad solicited the support of Britain, which he was confident would thwart any attempt by France to expand its North African holdings at Tunisian expense. British officials received Ahmad's overtures warmly but, to his annoyance, urged him to forge stronger and more overt bonds with the Ottoman authorities, maintaining that such a course of action would help to keep France at arm's length (and facilitate Britain's own economic entrée into Tunisia). Despite this importuning, the bey never lost sight of the danger of smothering in the Ottoman embrace and adamantly refused to act as if he were no more than a provincial governor. Thus he studiously avoided proclaiming the provisions of the landmark 1839 imperial decree (Hatt-i-Sharif) enhancing the rights of the sultan's subjects, although his own edicts abolishing the slave trade and emancipating slaves (in 1841 and 1846 respectively) suggest that his response to the Ottoman reforms had more to do with avoiding the appearance of subordination than with opposition to their substance. Royal displeasure with the bey led to the dispatch of an Ottoman fleet to Tunisia in 1840, prompting France, and then Britain, to send their own warships to Tunisian waters. Only the concurrent outbreak of a more serious crisis in Ottoman Syria averted a showdown. Thereafter Istanbul insisted on retaining practices that symbolized its ultimate sovereignty as diligently as Ahmad sought to dispense with them. These included the payment of tribute and the sending of gifts to the sultan, as well as his issuance of a decree formally confirming the accession of each bey. Despite the ambiguity fostered by Ahmad's elaborate choreography of political relations with the empire, Istanbul, the sultan, and the Ottoman provinces in the Middle East remained powerful religious and cultural poles of attraction for all Tunisian Muslims, as they had been since the arrival of the Turks in the sixteenth century.

Beyond this diplomatic front, Ahmad initiated a program of military modernization designed to enable Tunisian forces to hold their own against challenges from any quarter. In their broad outline, Ahmad's plans paralleled similar undertakings over the previous fifty years by the Ottoman sultans Selim III and Mahmud II and by Muhammad ᶜAli, the viceroy of Egypt. The acquisition of up-to-date weaponry and other military materiel topped Ahmad's agenda, with the equipment coming from several European suppliers, not least France. After 1830 the French government had taken pains to emphasize its opinion that Tunisia was a fully independent political entity, since that status would, in time, permit France to incorporate Tunisia into its North African territories with minimal grounds for objections from Istanbul. This perspective put France and Britain at odds and provided an important ingredient in their bitter rivalry over Tunisia that endured almost until the beginning of the protectorate. It also placed France in the somewhat peculiar position of preparing the Tunisian army to safeguard the very independence that France itself might one day seek to terminate – and, in the process, find French armaments turned against its own troops. Ahmad well knew that all the Europeans with whom he dealt kept their interests, not his, uppermost in the formulation of their policies, but he very much enjoyed the fuss that French officials made over him in according him the trappings of sovereignty. This flattery reached its apex in the bey's 1846 state visit to France, after which he adopted, often at great expense, many of the accoutrements of the French court.

Muskets, cannons, and warships constituted one important aspect of Ahmad's modernization program, but their effectiveness hinged on two requirements: an officer corps familiar with the new military and naval hardware, as well as with the contemporary tactical and strategic thinking it was intended to support, and sufficient numbers of soldiers and sailors to put teeth into the refurbished military establishment. To meet the first of these needs, Ahmad created a military school in the Bardo palace. There, European instructors educated future officers, most of them the sons of mamluks (the prestigious class of state officials purchased by Husainid agents in the slave markets of the Ottoman Empire and trained in Tunis to fill high-level government positions), although some were scions of the *baldiyya*, the socially prominent class of the capital whose traditional bailiwick was commerce. The Bardo school was small and never produced enough officers to staff the revamped armed forces, but its graduates' exposure to an array of new ideas and concepts – in addition to pursuing their military courses, they were the first Tunisians to pursue the systematic study of modern mathematics, engineering, and the applied sciences – instilled in them a sense of cohesiveness and set them apart as a unique elite whose influence in state councils persisted long after Ahmad's military visions had faded.

To provide manpower for the army and navy, Ahmad took the innovative step of conscripting the peasantry. Previously, the Husainid army had consisted only of "Turks" (the descendants of Turkish soldiers and officials or adventurers recruited throughout the Ottoman Mediterranean world), Zouaves (members of an Algerian Kabyle tribe, the Zwawa, renowned for their skill as warriors), Spahis (Tunisian tribal horsemen), and Hambas, mounted units including both "Turks" and Tunisians that performed police functions. An irregular cavalry drawn from tribes receiving tax concessions and other privileges in return for military service supplemented these troops as necessary. Ahmad's significant departure from traditional practice in filling the ranks of his military establishment inevitably triggered a certain amount of popular discontent. Government agents' frequently heavy-handed and capricious application of conscription, not to mention the uncertainties that awaited recruits and the economic distress that their families experienced, heightened opposition and encouraged evasion. In the short term, conscription did little more than add bodies to the ranks of the armed forces, but, in time, the practice contributed to implanting the concept that ordinary Tunisians could have a place in the apparatus of the state and, consequently, a stake in its future.

To finance his extensive plans, Ahmad devised new taxes and increased existing levies. He also imposed a government monopoly on the export of agricultural products, reviving a system that had soured economic relations between the European powers and several of his predecessors. In the wake of its 1830 victory at Algiers, France had pressured Husain Bey (1824–35) to terminate a similar monopoly and grant free access to the Tunisian market. Thus Ahmad's resurrection of export controls was perceived by Europeans as a step backward in their efforts to advance the economic penetration of the country. Despite the vigorous push to increase government revenues, many ancillary projects designed to support the military establishment proved too costly. Small factories producing uniforms and basic supplies rarely operated at maximum potential. Because of the expenses entailed, some projects remained unfinished, while others fell victim to the bey's erratic level of enthusiasm.

Ahmad flirted with financial disaster throughout much of his reign, but it was not until a member of his inner circle absconded with a substantial portion of the state treasury in 1852 that curtailing expenditures received serious consideration. Even then, however, he resisted a retrenchment that might deprive Tunisia of its status (in his own mind at least) as a strong and effective state. Caught between grandiose ambitions and dire financial realities, Ahmad ended his reign on an especially poignant note. Seizing the opportunity to showcase the army he had built and to demonstrate Tunisia's equivalence with the mightiest powers of Europe, Ahmad joined Britain and France in dispatching troops to the Crimea in 1855 to assist the sultan in meeting the threat posed by Russia. To finance the expedition, he sold some of the royal family's jewels, undoubtedly deriving great pleasure from imagining a scenario in which the theoretically subordinate bey helped save his Ottoman master. Ahmad was confident that Tunisian participation in the war would earn it respect and renewed support for ventures he still hoped to initiate. Perhaps it was for the best that he died before learning that his army had sustained enormous losses in the Crimea, not from combat, which it never saw, but from disease. This disaster, so far from home and ultimately to no avail, delivered a final, and fatal, blow to the military modernization program. No subsequent bey showed the slightest inclination to revive it.

Throughout his reign, Ahmad faced a series of exceptional challenges. In the absence of a traditional local paradigm on which to model his responses, he acted much as his earlier counterparts, Muhammad ʿAli in Egypt and the Ottoman sultans Selim III and Mahmud II, had in similar circumstances: initiating pragmatic, ad hoc measures, many of which deviated radically from past practices. Because the bey and the elite coterie around him constituted the sole group articulating the need for major changes, such changes always came from above, where the raw power to impose them existed but was rarely matched by an awareness of (or even an interest in) their impact at the grassroots level. Virtually none of Ahmad's reforms met with unequivocal success, but neither, until the Crimean venture, were any so disastrous as to doom the entire process.

In pursuit of the twin objectives of defending Tunisia and winning respect for the country and for himself in the international arena, the bey forged alliances with European powers that met his immediate needs, which very often entailed offsetting the influence of other Europeans. At the same time, he justified the introduction of innovative, and often unpopular, practices in the name of shoring up the state against increasing foreign influences. That Ahmad's eighteen-year reign was too short a time for the unfamiliar ideas and new technologies that he transplanted to Tunisia to take firm root should in no way devalue his efforts. On the contrary, to have done nothing at the outset of his reign would have courted disaster and to have attempted to address the problems he faced with only the meager resources initially at his disposal would almost certainly have failed.

The most influential and enduring of Ahmad's reforms eroded organizational principles that the Tunisian state had long observed. Allowing the sons of the *baldiyya* class to attend the Bardo military school and conscripting peasants into the armed forces introduced the hitherto unheard-of notion that native Tunisians – the "sons of the homeland" – might play a role in the governance of the country and, therefore, have a genuine stake in its future. In exposing a select group of young men to the material things and intellectual concepts of the European world, Ahmad set in motion a process that profoundly affected the Tunisian state and its society. Within a few years of his death, new efforts to implement fundamental political and social reforms, juxtaposed against the continuing European competition for influence in the country, had created an environment that Ahmad could scarcely have imagined.

Wary of the outcome of the course his predecessor had set, Muhammad Bey would have liked to have distanced himself from the Europeans with whom he believed Ahmad had consorted too freely and spent too lavishly. His plans for a cooling-off period after Ahmad's frenetic reign replicated the hopes of Egyptian and Ottoman rulers who had succeeded dynamic pioneering reformers in those areas, but, like them, Muhammad found very little respite. His accession in 1855 coincided with the arrival in Tunis of two powerful men who lost no time in attempting to bend Muhammad to their will. For most of their tenure, Richard Wood and Léon Roches, the consuls of Britain and France respectively, competed fiercely with each other to gain an economic and political edge in Tunisia, but in their first overtures to the bey they acted in concert. At the end of the Crimean War, Sultan Abdul-Majid complied with his British and French allies' demand that he demonstrate his commitment to tolerance and progressiveness by publicly affirming the rights of his non-Muslim subjects. Whatever concerns the European powers may have had about the well-being of Ottoman Christians and Jews, their underlying calculation was that a more open regime would be more susceptible to Western economic penetration and the empire's integration into the world economy. As the consuls expected, Muhammad declined to apply the 1856 royal decree in Tunisia, just as Ahmad had in 1839, and for precisely the same reasons. Wood and Roches had no intention of letting the bey sidestep the issue so easily, however, and now they could look for support from a group, consisting primarily of mamluks, that concurred with them.

Although these men were protégés of Ahmad Bey, they lamented the surge in imports that had accompanied the former ruler's policies. Extending well beyond military materiel to a wide variety of consumer goods, the foreign products had inflicted severe damage on many small-scale Tunisian craft and artisanal enterprises. Reversing the trend required a thorough overhaul of the Tunisian economy, leading to its integration into the international system – precisely the objectives of Britain and France in the Ottoman Empire. In their European-influenced view, providing ordinary Tunisians with guarantees of protection against arbitrary government was an essential prerequisite for setting such a process in motion. With the people assured of their personal freedom and the security of their possessions, these modernizers envisaged the unfolding of a scenario that included an increase in production, not only in the traditional handicraft sector, but also in agriculture, where cultivation had declined by 80 percent during Ahmad's reign.[2] In time, an expansion of the nascent industrial base Ahmad had created could also be expected. Such growth would encourage capital investment, both domestic and foreign, in those areas of the economy, but also in the development of a modern transportation and communication infrastructure underpinning the whole structure and expediting domestic and international marketing.

An incident in 1857 enabled Wood and Roches to intensify their pressure on Muhammad. The bey sanctioned the execution of Batto Sfez, a Tunisian Jew who had quarreled with a group of Muslims when a cart he was driving killed a Tunisian child. In the heat of the moment, Sfez allegedly committed the capital offense of blaspheming Islam.[3] Expressing indignation over the death sentence, the two diplomats presented Muhammad with a slate of judicial and economic demands. When Muhammad proposed to comply only in part, Roches summoned French warships to the Tunisian coast and Muhammad understood that he had no real options. He met the consul's terms by issuing the ʿAhd al-Aman, or Security Covenant, proclaiming the civil and religious equality of all his subjects. But, as per the pair's original stipulations, the decree went much further, committing the bey to formulate criminal and commercial codes and establish mixed courts to hear cases involving Europeans. It also announced the termination of the state monopolies. To insure the bey's adhesion to these obligations, Roches and Wood insisted that he confer with them as he implemented

Figure 1.2. Worshippers leaving the Zaituna mosque. The oldest and most important mosque in Tunis was not only a place of worship but also the seat of the most renowned insitution of Islamic higher education in the country. The mosque-university lay at the intellectual heart of Tunisian Islam.

the decree. The ʿAhd al-Aman paved the way for sweeping economic and social changes. Like Ahmad's reforms, it was imposed from above but, more ominously than in the past, also from outside.

The mamluks who advocated modernizing the economy recognized the importance of foreign involvement in the process, but most either underestimated the risk of European hegemony or overestimated their ability to prevent it. In some cases, venality dominated their thinking. European entrepreneurs would need middlemen for their Tunisian ventures and the mamluks' familiarity with European culture and languages made them the ideal choice to play, and profit from, such a role. But within another segment of the elite, the ulama, or religious scholars, far greater skepticism prevailed. In accordance with traditional Muslim views about *dhimmis* (monotheists who lived in Islamic lands and enjoyed the protection of the state), the ulama had no objection to the bey affirming the security of his non-Muslim subjects, but they opposed the concept of non-Muslim equality in taxation or in matters of the law. Those who worked as government administrators and clerks tended to mute their criticisms, but others, especially the shaikhs and muftis of the prestigious Zaituna mosque-university, aired their views more candidly. Perhaps to stress the official view of the ᶜAhd al-Aman's conformity with Islam, Muhammad ordered the reading of its preamble, which focused on the welfare of the bey's subjects but glossed over its economic and juridical content, at Friday prayer services. The broad dissemination of such an abridged version of the proclamation suggests that Muhammad knew that its details would meet with disapproval.

Small numbers of European merchants had resided in Tunis since the al-Muwahhid era (twelfth–thirteenth centuries), but the flood of speculators and businessmen who arrived after 1857 raised their profile considerably. As both the Sfez incident and ulama concerns about certain provisions of the ᶜAhd al-Aman reveal, however, the social fabric of the country also included other, more substantial, non-Muslim populations. Batto Sfez belonged to a Jewish community of perhaps 18,000 persons that traced its roots to the Diaspora from Palestine following revolts against Roman rule in the first and second centuries. These Tunisian Jews lived in both rural and urban areas, were generally poor, and exerted little political or social influence. A very different and much smaller group of Jews – only one or two thousand[4] – was descended from sixteenth- and seventeenth-century Spanish refugees and immigrants from Livorno in the eighteenth and early nineteenth centuries. Most of the latter were merchants who made use of their linkages to Mediterranean commercial networks to assume important and remunerative roles in Tunis, at first often as agents for the corsairs and their financial backers. The education and European contacts of some of these Grana (the Tunisian colloquial Arabic for Livorno) enabled them to join the circle of the ruling elite, where they served as advisors, business representatives, or physicians to several beys.

In addition to the Jews, several thousand persons who were neither Arab nor Muslim lived in Tunis and its suburbs during Muhammad's reign. The largest contingent among them, about 7,000, came from the nearby island of Malta and worked on the docks, as carters, and as laborers, usually in unskilled occupations. Speaking a language akin to Arabic, living, for the most part, in a quarter of the medina, or walled city, and adhering to social customs that were variations on themes familiar in Tunisia, the Maltese differed from the country's natives primarily in their Roman Catholicism. Sicilians, Sardinians, and mainland Italians accounted for 4,600 more foreign residents, although political and economic circumstances in Italy caused this number to more than double in the two decades following Muhammad's reign.[5] Their concentration in La Goulette, the port of Tunis, made that town almost as Italian as it was Tunisian as early as the time of Ahmad Bey, whose modernization projects had attracted many skilled and semi-skilled workers and artisans. Other Italians were miners, farmers, and laborers or, like the Maltese, operated small shops, restaurants, and taverns catering to the needs of their compatriots.

Except as purveyors of alcohol, pork butchers, or practitioners of certain skilled trades, Italians and Maltese competed for employment with their Tunisian counterparts at the bottom of the socioeconomic ladder. Nevertheless, by the middle of the century, the immigrants had carved out recognizable niches for themselves in Tunis that made it feasible for wives and children to join what had been an overwhelmingly adult male community. Thereafter, most immigrants arrived as families. Because the Capitulation treaties that had traditionally regulated trade between Muslims and non-Muslims precluded European women from residing in Muslim lands, this unprecedented situation affected social and economic interactions throughout Tunisian society, while the proximity in which immigrants and Tunisians lived further compounded matters. Conflicting notions of appropriate women's behavior exacerbated communal tensions and ultimately required the government to attempt to regulate socioeconomic issues once deemed private matters.[6]

The ʿAhd al-Aman applied to these immigrants as it did to other Europeans, but the Italians and Maltese continued to rely on consular officials (in the case of the latter, British agents, since their homeland was a colony) to protect and advance their interests. The diplomats did not ignore them – the presence of sizeable numbers of their country's citizens or subjects provided potential leverage – but after 1857 they much preferred to concentrate on facilitating the proposals of businessmen and speculators whose Tunisian ventures more immediately advanced the strategy of the governments they represented. In any case, many of the consuls associated the surge of immigration in the 1860s and 1870s with a rise in crime, some petty, but some, such as widespread smuggling that included contraband weapons, far more serious and a threat to their mission. Drawing a connection between criminality and the low socioeconomic status of most immigrants, the diplomats occasionally allowed class interests to supersede national solidarity by colluding with each other and with powerful Tunisians to the disadvantage of subsistence immigrants, and especially women, from the "not-quite-European" shores of the Mediterranean (i.e., Malta and the Italian islands).[7]

The duress under which Muhammad Bey had issued the ʿAhd al-Aman greatly distressed him. He took few steps to implement the decree, but

Map 1.1. Tunis and vicinity, ca. 1898. Founded in 698 by Arab armies advancing from the
Nile Valley, Tunis replaced Carthage as the most important city of the region. Tunis
enjoyed a golden era under the Hafsid Dynasty (1227–1574) and served as the capital of the
Husainid beys (1705–1957) both before and after the La Marsa Convention formalized the

Map 1.1. (*cont.*) French protectorate over Tunisia in 1883. Thereafter, many of the suburbs stretching along the Gulf of Tunis from La Goulette, the city's port, to La Marsa became fashionable communities for European residents of the city.

as European speculators swarmed into Tunisia, their consuls invoked it regularly. Wood and Roches led this chorus, even as they were bringing new pressure to bear on Muhammad to augment the ᶜAhd al-Aman with a full-fledged constitution. Although he had no desire to do so, he knew from experience that he had little choice in the matter. To make the most of an unpalatable situation, the bey formed several commissions to examine possible formats for such a document. In addition to appointing the veterans of Ahmad Bey's entourage, who, as the most outspoken advocates of reform, could hardly be excluded, Muhammad also named a number of ulama to the commissions. Many of the religious leaders had familial and social ties to the city's merchants, who had fallen on hard times as Europeans came to dominate international trade. Consequently they resented the scenario they saw unfolding, associating it with the rampant growth of European influence which, in turn, they linked to the many innovations that had occurred since Ahmad's reign. They feared that the door allowing European penetration of Tunisia, once opened, could never be closed and that Tunisians would have no control over what passed through it. Ulama in Egypt and the Ottoman Empire had expressed similar concerns a few decades earlier that, by the late 1850s, were proving prophetic. Even more importantly, the ulama believed that Tunisia already had a constitution – the Qur'an – and that no other legislation was necessary to ensure the proper ordering of society. The ulama commissioners, however, lacked the political skills and connections of the modernizers. Rather than embarking on a bruising battle they were certain to lose, they opted to retire from the deliberations.

As the constitutional commissions set about their work, Muhammad Bey made a final effort to check European ambitions by embracing what now appeared as the lesser of two evils and identifying Tunisia more closely with the Ottoman Empire. His agents traveled to Istanbul with an offer to acknowledge the rights of the sultan over Tunisia in exchange for his allowing the Husainids a free hand in the running of the country. The Tunisian emissaries stressed that the proposal constituted no more than a formal recognition of the status quo. Knowing that the bey acted from weakness, the sultan refused to countenance any modification of the traditional Ottoman view that Tunisia was simply an imperial province. The sultan's obduracy pushed the most avid Tunisian reformers further towards Europe, but there remained others of the opinion that a good relationship with the world's most powerful Muslim state remained imperative.[8]

Long before the constitutional commissions had concluded their work, the Anglo-French cooperation that had fostered their creation transformed itself into a fierce rivalry over investment opportunities. Wood and Roches regarded Mustafa Khaznadar, the prime minister of both Ahmad Bey and Muhammad Bey, as the most influential figure in the ruling elite and a man who could readily expedite or impede their plans. Roches approached Khaznadar first, in 1858, offering him access to French bankers willing to provide financial support to the beylical government. Sensing a trap, Khaznadar sounded out Wood to determine what sort of counterproposal he might make. The British official seized the opportunity to advocate the establishment of an Anglo-Tunisian Bank jointly underwritten by investors from both countries and controlled by the consulate. In addition to linking Tunisia to the international (or at least the British) monetary system, this institution would also enjoy a monopoly over the issuance of legal tender. Roches, of course, fulminated against this arrangement, but Muhammad sanctioned it, adding the suggestion that the Europeans sort out their differences over the bank. This they failed to do (as the bey assumed they would), but neither did the Tunisian strategy of playing the powers off against each other succeed. Continuing pressure from France, some of it in the form of unsubtle reminders of its strong military presence in Algeria, convinced Muhammad that he could not, in this and in most other matters, defy French wishes with impunity, especially since no such immediate show of military force stood behind Britain's pledges of support. Ultimately, he withdrew his endorsement of the bank, despite incurring a substantial indemnity for this about-face.

Later in 1858 Wood advised the bey of the desire of a group of British entrepreneurs to construct a telegraph line connecting Tunis with La Calle, Algeria, where an undersea cable crossed the Mediterranean to Europe. Even before the bey could respond to this overture, Roches demanded that he reject it and agree, instead, to a French project that not only benefited his countrymen, but had the additional advantage of keeping British economic interests away from Algeria. The proposals differed only in that the French company wanted the Tunisian government to bear a portion of the expenses. Muhammad rebuffed this arrangement, but did accept a modified French tender calling for a more modest Tunisian payment to cover ancillary aspects of the project. Similar investor insistence that the state participate financially in, as well as cede the right of way and provide free labor for, the construction of a railroad linking the port of La Goulette to the capital prevented work from going forward, despite the obvious importance of such a connection for Tunisian integration into the world economy. A few years after Muhammad's death in 1859, a British consortium proposed building the line without a Tunisian contribution in return for a ninety-nine-year concession to operate it. Their intention to extend the line west to the Algerian border disconcerted the French and, as with the telegraph, Roches sabotaged the arrangement before it crystallized.

Even as the greed of potential investors and the Anglo-French rivalry aborted plans that could have advanced Tunisia's economic development, other schemes serving Tunisian needs less well, or only at too high a cost, went forward. This anomaly did not, however, stem exclusively from the ability of the consuls to bring to bear the imbalance of power between Europe and Tunisia, for the ventures brought handsome profits not only to foreign investors, but also to their local intermediaries who, accordingly, promoted them vigorously. Had the Anglo-Tunisian Bank come to fruition, for example, Mustafa Khaznadar would have become its president (ostensibly by virtue of his position as prime minister, but certainly in return for his cooperation with Wood). Other prominent Tunisians engineered partnerships with European investors, while those with access to the corridors of power were well positioned to ingratiate themselves with foreigners by arranging introductions and guiding them through the unfamiliar business environment. Corruption and cronyism, hardly unknown in the past, became ever more pronounced during Muhammad's reign. A prime example was the contract secured by a French company in 1859 through a combination of bribes and pressures exerted by Roches to construct, with government funds, an aqueduct from Zaghouan to Tunis. The expense involved should have been prohibitive, but the weary Muhammad succumbed. His successor, Muhammad al-Sadiq, inherited obligations that the treasury, already depleted by the decline in tax revenues and the abolition of monopolies – both consequences of the ʿAhd al-Aman – simply could not meet. Tunisia's modernization and its dependence went forward hand in hand.

The commissions Muhammad had formed to study the question of granting a Tunisian constitution were just completing their work at the time of his death. Muhammad al-Sadiq expressed enthusiasm for such a step, convinced that adopting this European political model would embed Tunisia in the good graces of the powers and ease the pressure they had exerted during Muhammad's more reactionary reign. In the best-case scenario, such a major reform might prove an important step towards earning Tunisia the parity with European countries that Muhammad al-Sadiq, like his cousin Ahmad, so highly prized. That eventuality would permit Tunisia to keep its distance from the Ottoman Empire and perhaps even to secure its formal sovereignty. A genuine reordering of the Tunisian political system, however, ranked fairly low in the bey's priorities. In light of the traditional

French view of the Ottoman–Tunisian relationship and of France's particularly ardent support for a constitution, Muhammad al-Sadiq showed a draft of the document to Napoleon III, with whose approval he promulgated it in 1861.

The first legislation of its kind in the Muslim world, the fundamental law established a constitutional monarchy whose ministers answered to a sixty-member Grand Council appointed by the ruler. Many of those named to the council were committed proponents of reform, the most prominent of whom was its president, a mamluk named Khair al-Din al-Tunsi. But powerful figures such as Mustafa Khaznadar, who had flourished in the environment of ill-defined responsibility and obligation that had prevailed in the past, also sat on the council and wanted nothing to do with reforms, particularly those stressing accountability. For reasons quite different from Khaznadar's, other Tunisians also had reservations about the process that was unfolding.

To some, the insinuation that Qur'anic teachings no longer sufficed as a sociopolitical frame of reference epitomized the misguided policies of the reformers, turning the constitution into a lightning rod around which a host of grievances coalesced. Having absented themselves from the discussions about its formulation, the ulama largely ignored the proclamation of the constitution, but unrest from other quarters bubbled up in short order. The steady integration of Tunisia into the international economy sharply increased exports of agricultural products such as wheat and olive oil, making these staples more expensive on local markets. In protest, a group of merchants and Zaituna ulama coordinated a demonstration in the Tunis souk (central market) in late 1861, underscoring their action with a march on the Bardo Palace. The beylical response to this confrontation was swift and vigorous: the arrest of many of its secular participants and the cooption of a few moderate ulama into official positions. The government's account of these incidents played down their significance, but it was well known, both in the royal court and the foreign consulates, that the protestors regarded their economic woes as a consequence of the root problem of rampant foreign influence, which the constitution now symbolized.

Strapped for revenue, the bey had begun issuing bonds in 1860, but only the more thorough and systematic collection of taxes from rural regions offered any real prospect of keeping his finances out of the red. Naturally, any such effort met with resistance and was, quite correctly, regarded as a consequence of the government's indebtedness to foreign creditors. The fear that judicial reorganization would lead to the introduction of state courts in areas where tribal shaikhs had customarily dispensed justice produced further antipathy towards Tunis. Again in this instance, the reform process, with the constitution at its apex, was perceived to lie at the heart of a distasteful situation. Roches blamed Khaznadar for sparking this unrest, and while he and his allies no doubt took advantage of the situation, many ordinary Tunisians had been adversely affected, in one way or another, by the course of events since 1857. It seems, therefore, reasonable to conclude that their actions flowed primarily from their perceptions of their self-interest.

The naiveté of Muhammad al-Sadiq's hope that his self-portrayal as an enlightened constitutional monarch would relax European pressures was hammered home by two events in 1863. His decision first to put his financial house in order by arranging a loan with Parisian bankers and then to offset France's augmented clout by granting special privileges to British subjects pushed a pervasive mood of agitation into open rebellion. To meet its international debt of some 30 million francs, the Tunisian government borrowed 35 million, although commissions and discounts reduced the amount actually at its disposal to 29 million. At 12 percent interest, the repayment totaled nearly 65 million francs, with yearly payments set at 7 million, or roughly half the state's average annual income.[9] The bey pledged the revenues generated by the personal tax, or *majba*, to meet this obligation, but made the imprudent decision to double its rate, lest it fail to bring in sufficient funds.

Muhammad al-Sadiq was also discovering that, despite the powers' advocacy of the constitution, members of the Maltese, Italian, and other European communities disliked its declaration of equality for all residents of Tunisia in so far as that concept resulted in the loss of certain of their privileges. Rather than submit to the jurisdiction of Tunisian tribunals, for example, they wanted to retain the consular courts, as well as to continue to enjoy exemptions from certain forms of taxation. Nevertheless, they asserted their entitlement to the protections guaranteed by the constitution. This highly selective interpretation angered Tunisians, further discrediting the reforms. Consequently, the bey looked favorably on the offer of a formal agreement placing British subjects, including the substantial Maltese population, on an equal footing with Tunisians under the umbrella of the constitution. To Muhammad al-Sadiq, the Anglo-Tunisian Convention terminated the extraterritorial status of a large and important foreign community; to the British, its provisions, which confirmed the right of property ownership granted by the constitution, sanctioned their endeavors in the country. Of great importance to both parties, the treaty counterbalanced French weight, which the recent loan had augmented.

To most of the bey's subjects, however, the accord merely represented yet another mechanism for foreigners to insinuate themselves into the country's affairs, almost certainly to the disadvantage of Tunisians.

Fear, anger, frustration, and disgust exploded into full-scale revolt in 1864. Observing the situation from Europe, where he had gone after his failed attempt to dissuade the bey and Khaznadar from borrowing money overseas had marginalized him in Tunis, Khair al-Din painted a grim picture of the situation.

The Arabs, no longer able to support the regime of despotism and injustice that was imposed upon them, rose up from one end of the Regency to the other; this formidable insurrection left the government on the brink of ruin. The Bey was in distress and unable to repress the revolt, waiting from day to day to see the insurgents invade the city and his residence.[10]

The uprising, instigated by ᶜAli ibn Ghdahem, a *marabout* (pious figure, or local saint) and the son of a *qadi* (Muslim judge), originated among tribes in the region between Kairouan and Le Kef. The rebels demanded an end to the crushing taxes, a reversal of the reforms curtailing the prestige of local notables, especially in the judicial arena, and the abolition of the constitution. They laid the blame for all of these undesirable innovations at the doorstep of the palace, denouncing Muhammad al-Sadiq and his mamluks as the perpetrators of their misery. ᶜAli's self-styled title of "bey of the people" brazenly manifested his contempt for a ruler who disregarded his subjects' welfare.

With its ranks decimated by the desertion of long-unpaid troops and no prospect of raising tribal levies, the army could not suppress the rebellion, which quickly spread to the Sahil, the rich plain along the eastern Mediterranean coast. The largely sedentary population of this region shared the tribesmen's grievances, but as producers of the cereals and olive oil that were Tunisia's most valuable exports, they grasped more clearly than the tribesmen the roles played by foreign diplomats, merchants, and speculators in what had been transpiring. Their more sophisticated assessment of the situation led them to the conclusion that Muhammad al-Sadiq no longer acted as a free agent and had lost the capacity to rectify matters even if he wished to do so. Rather than awaiting new policies from Tunis, many Sahilians hoped for the intervention of the Ottoman Empire, particularly as British and French warships, dispatched to protect the interests of their nationals, appeared on the horizon.

From the viewpoint of Istanbul the beylical regime appeared on the verge of going under, taking with it the Ottomans' frayed, but to them still important, connections to Tunisia. Imperial officials harbored no illusions about the outcome of an attempt at intervention along the lines envisioned in the Sahil, but neither could they stand idly by. A senior Ottoman diplomat embarked for Tunis, carrying funds to revitalize the demoralized army and enable it to bring the uprising under control.[11] Even before the Ottomans stepped in, however, Khaznadar had begun to cripple the tribal rebellion by distributing bribes to its leaders, making promises of government employment, and manipulating local rivalries. When autumn plowing required the warriors' presence in their fields, the movement petered out. Ironically, it was in the Sahil, where the rebels had counted on Ottoman support, that the government deployed its Ottoman-financed reinforcements to cow them into submission.

A combination of force and persuasion crushed the uprising, but not before it had achieved a key objective, the revocation of the constitution. In this matter, however, the bey acted more in response to foreign than domestic pressures. The advantageous position Britain had secured by means of the Anglo-Tunisian Convention, in no small part as a result of Prime Minister Khaznadar's close ties to the British consulate, greatly disturbed France. At least by this gauge, the reform movement had gone awry, strengthening its main competitor for influence in Tunisia. French officials linked the constitution and the convention, as General Jean-Baptiste Campenon, the chief of the military mission during the rebellion, made clear: "The English convention is the consequence of the Tunisian constitution; let the constitution become a dead letter, let it fall . . . and it will carry in its wake the English treaty."[12] Towards that end, but under the pretext of ending rampant injustices, France called for Khaznadar's ouster, encouraged the rebels, and demanded that the bey suspend the constitution. As in the past, the credible inference that the French would resort to military means to have their way impelled Muhammad al-Sadiq to accommodate them and dismantle the constitutional system they had so recently insisted he impose. As Campenon had predicted, without the safeguards of the constitution, the Anglo-Tunisian Convention withered. In short order, the status quo ante, with its virulent competition among Europeans and the absence of constraints on Tunisian officials, had returned. On the other hand, the end of the revolt brought about a change, at least on paper, in Tunisia's relationship with the Ottoman Empire. At the bey's request, Khair al-Din reached an understanding with the sultan by which his sovereignty was acknowledged in return for his recognition of hereditary Husainid rule and Tunisia's administrative autonomy. Bearing in mind the events that had precipitated Khair al-Din's mission, the sultan also explicitly retained his right to intervene in any future troubles arising in Tunisia.

The sultan's willingness to come to terms with Muhammad al-Sadiq did not extend to providing him what he needed far more urgently than esteem – money. Having spent the Ottoman emergency contribution to mount the campaign against the rebels, the bey still needed substantial funds to make the repayments on the 1863 loan. Reasoning that the people of the Sahil should pay a price for their disloyalty, Muhammad al-Sadiq approved Khaznadar's orders to Ahmad Zarruk, a trusted retainer, to plunder the region, confiscating real property and crops, imposing extortionate indemnities, and conscripting hapless residents into military service. The ruthlessness with which Zarruk executed his task devastated the Sahil, destroying its economy and depopulating cities, villages, and countryside alike as their inhabitants lost all they had in lieu of the levies they could not pay. Similar, if less remunerative, depredations befell the tribes that had rallied around ʿAli ibn Ghdahem. Even so, the vicious onslaught failed to raise sufficient funds to allow the bey to settle with his creditors, forcing him to suspend reimbursements in 1866. More significantly in the long term, Zarruk's tactics created a reservoir of deep enmity towards the central government, and specifically the bey. In 1881, with the French army on Tunisian soil, Muhammad al-Sadiq reaped the whirlwind he had sown after the rebellion. But his creditors had more immediate humiliations in store.

The derailing of the liberal reforms, resulting from the same external pressures that had imposed them, occasioned little mourning in the inner circles of the Tunisian government. As their brutality in the wake of the rebellion demonstrated, the bey, Khaznadar, and their associates returned reflexively to the exercise of arbitrary power. To preclude a repetition of the rebellion, they purchased substantial quantities of military materiel from Europe, even as they continued to pursue ill-conceived investments enriching themselves and their business associates, both Tunisian and European. By the end of the decade, however, creditors had concluded that they were throwing good money after bad. In 1869, Britain, France, and Italy compelled the Tunisian government to agree to the creation of an International Finance Commission. Hoping to mollify the country's largest creditors, Prime Minister Khaznadar prevailed upon Khair al-Din al-Tunsi, whose advocacy of judicious and responsible government was well known, to end his self-imposed exile and return to Tunisia as the commission's chairperson. The commissioners supervised reforms in fiscal policy designed to protect foreign investments, but their power to allocate government revenues for the repayment of existing debts transferred a crucial aspect of financial management from Tunisian to European hands.

Italy's partnership in the International Finance Commission reflected more the growth in the number of its citizens (particularly Sicilians) living in Tunisia and quickly becoming its largest foreign community than it did a high level of Italian economic engagement, which remained an objective but was not yet a reality. An 1868 Italo-Tunisian treaty expedited the acceleration of economic infiltration by guaranteeing resident Italians privileges similar to those secured five years earlier by Britain for its subjects. These included the retention of Italian citizenship, their right to work, including to fish in Tunisian waters,[13] and their acquisition of property. The treaty also allowed Italians to maintain their own laws and courts in matters solely within their community or involving only other non-Muslims.

No sooner had the commission set to work than Khair al-Din and Khaznadar found themselves at daggers drawn. In an approach entirely consonant with his past behavior, the prime minister's first impulse regarding the commission was to sabotage it altogether or, failing that, to stonewall directives imperiling his lucrative business arrangements or easy access to state funds. Khair al-Din, despite his chairmanship of the commission, had no enthusiasm for foreign interference in Tunisia, but believed that setting the country on an even keel required a housecleaning that no powerful figure, least of all the bey or his prime minister, would willingly countenance. In the face of such determined opposition, no other Tunisian, himself included, could engineer such a process without outside assistance. Britain continued to support Khaznadar, but the French and Italian members of the commission lobbied for his removal on the grounds of fiscal irresponsibility and flagrant corruption. When Muhammad al-Sadiq named Khair al-Din prime minister in 1873, Tunisia's creditors demonstrated that their control extended from the budget to key ministerial appointments.

Khaznadar's cronies and clients vowed to take their revenge. Consul Wood, on the other hand, did not hesitate to abandon his discredited associate and begin cultivating Khair al-Din, lest the new prime minister cite the disreputable Wood–Khaznadar collaboration as reason enough to disregard British interests. Moreover, Wood realized that the French regarded Khair al-Din as something of a protégé – he had spent several years in Paris in the 1850s and returned there when he left Tunisia in 1862 – and welcomed his ascendancy at a time when French prestige was still recovering from the defeat by Prussia in 1871. The astute Khair al-Din intended to make the most of the competition for his goodwill by playing Britain, France, and

Italy off against each other in order to maximize the arena in which he could maneuver with relative freedom.

A book he had published in 1867, *Aqwam al-masalik li maʿrifat ahwal al-mamalik* (*The Surest Path to Knowledge Concerning the Conditions of Countries*), provided the blueprint for his prime ministry. In part a study in comparative politics, in part a political manifesto, *The Surest Path* drew on the three most important components of Khair al-Din's intellectual heritage: Muslim piety, the traditional statecraft incorporated into his training as a mamluk, and the modern culture of the West first encountered in Ahmad Bey's service but comprehended more fully as a result of his residence in France. His experience of the West taught him that its political, social, and economic development had endowed it with countless assets – some concrete, others less tangible – that Tunisia might usefully borrow or imitate, provided it did so selectively and judiciously. However, he also understood that Western institutions had undergone a centuries-long process of maturation within a specific cultural context and that their successful transplantation in societies not embedded in Western culture hinged on laying the groundwork in a similar, albeit telescoped, process.

In Khair al-Din's view, good governance equated with prudent stewardship and conscientious guidance, and was reciprocated by public confidence and trust – a relationship between ruler and ruled analogous to that between a shepherd and his flock. Any mandate for change had necessarily to come from above, but it also had to fall within the parameters of Islamic values, as confirmed by its endorsement by the ulama, the guardians of those values. Because Khair al-Din regretted the widespread abstention of the ulama from the process that had transpired in Tunisia, he targeted them as the key audience for *The Surest Path*. He called on them to join with honorable statesmen in a coalition that would cleanse government of its oppressive character, eschewing abusive and arbitrary practices of any kind. Guided by Islamic precepts, including sharia law, this new order would bestow on its subjects the blessings of justice, security, and prosperity, thereby restoring the public confidence that recent leaders had forfeited by their behavior. On these principles, and with the support of the ulama, Khair al-Din governed until 1877.[14]

At the start of his administration, almost a decade after the 1864 rebellion and its repression, agriculture in the Sahil remained in disarray. Judging its revitalization critical for Tunisia's stability and prosperity, the prime minister canceled unpaid taxes, offered tax exemptions to farmers who planted new olive trees,[15] and lowered export duties. Higher tariffs levied on imports aided artisans and craftsmen, while closer monitoring of tax collectors checked many of the abuses to which they had customarily been prone. Such measures came only at a cost, in terms of their implementation as well as of the revenue lost from lowering taxes and abandoning extortionate methods of gathering them. The continuing work of the International Finance Commission further constricted the funds available to underwrite Khair al-Din's agenda. As a result, he devoted considerable attention to less costly reforms designed to adapt existing institutions, many of them religious in nature, to contemporary needs.

With the goal of introducing contemporary managerial concepts into the hitherto uncoordinated administration of the almost 25 percent of Tunisian land set aside as pious trusts (*habus*), Khair al-Din established a Habus Council in 1874, appointing as its director Muhammad Bairam al-Khamis, one of the country's most respected ulama. He also spearheaded the modification of the Zaituna mosque-university curriculum by the addition of secular disciplines to the traditional religious studies, reflecting his certainty of the relevance of these subjects in the education of Tunisians, including future religious scholars. This conviction also lay behind Khair al-Din's most enduring contribution to his country, the creation of Sadiqi College. The school combined a course of traditional studies, taught in Arabic, with a French-inspired curriculum emphasizing modern languages, mathematics, and science. Sadiqi's bicultural training made its students ideal candidates for positions in a government thrust into wide-ranging contacts with a Western world barely comprehended by most Tunisians. Sadiqi graduates soon began to supplant their counterparts from the Zaituna in government clerkships and secretarial positions. Many advanced rapidly through the ranks of the civil service, forming a tightly knit cadre that preserved and, when possible, acted on Khair al-Din's philosophy well beyond the end of their mentor's ministry. As Tunisia's leading institution of secular education for many decades after its founding, the college produced generations of graduates who figured prominently in the country's subsequent history.

In the realm of international affairs, Khair al-Din achieved an objective as prime minister that he had advocated throughout his career: the strengthening of Tunisia's ties with the Ottoman Empire. In contrast to the beylical view of the sultan as an impediment to Tunisian autonomy, Khair al-Din saw him as the spiritual and temporal head of the world's most important Muslim state and a figure with whom any leader guided by Islamic principles would feel a natural affinity. At the same time, Khair al-Din also believed that the recognition of imperial rights in Tunisia provided the country with "its best safeguard against the covetousness of various European powers."[16] But to calculate that as long as the Ottoman Empire continued to exist a

Figure 1.3. Collège Sadiqi. Founded by Khair al-Din al-Tunsi in 1875, Sadiqi made a secular Western education available to Tunisian students for the first time. Many of its early graduates worked in the protectorate administration; many later alumni were activists in the nationalist movement.

Tunisia formally bound to it would remain free of European control was to assume, quite wrongly, that imperial survival implied the capacity to influence events within its sphere of interest. The sultan's request for Tunisian troops to help repel the Russian invasion of 1877 hinted at this miscalculation. Financial and diplomatic constraints prevented Khair al-Din from obliging, although he urged Tunisians to donate money to the Ottoman war effort. The episode did not shake his confidence in the Ottoman–Tunisian relationship, but it does raise the question of which party stood more in need of the other.

Khair al-Din's attitude towards Istanbul augmented French distress with the course of action he had pursued since taking office. Irritation over his willingness to entertain business propositions put forward by Wood turned to alarm with the conclusion of a new Anglo-Tunisian commercial treaty in 1875. Although Théodore Roustan, who had arrived in Tunis as consul general the previous year, initially met with some success in his vigorous efforts to promote French interests, he was soon calling for Khair al-Din's ouster. The Khaznadar clique, still smarting from its own removal, enthusiastically joined the chorus clamoring for the prime minister's downfall. At the same time, British interests in the Mediterranean were shifting eastward as the

Suez Canal, which had opened in 1869, began to assume a dominant place in imperial thinking. Wood gradually distanced himself from Khair al-Din, thus clearing the way for Muhammad al-Sadiq to dismiss him in 1877. The reformer's strategy of playing the powers off against each other ended with all of them aligned against him. Ottoman loyalist that he was, Khair al-Din retired to Istanbul, where he spent the last decade of his life, which included a brief term, in 1878–9, as the sultan's grand vizier (prime minister). The bitter and ailing Khaznadar returned to the prime ministry, but died less than a year later.

As it happened, his demise came in the midst of a spate of European diplomatic and economic activity that presaged the end of the regime in which he had figured so prominently. Britain's need to safeguard the approaches to the Suez Canal led to its acquisition of Cyprus in 1878, signaling the abandonment of its venerable policy of supporting Ottoman integrity – a shift that led Britain to dissociate itself more or less entirely from Tunisian affairs. In that same year the European powers convened the Congress of Berlin to consider the fate of the Ottoman Empire following its defeat by Russia. The Berlin agenda included negotiations over competing interests and claims regarding Tunisia. Britain remained on the sideline of these discussions as France and Italy presented their cases. Germany, seeing in Tunisia a prize capable of diverting France from its potentially destabilizing obsession with recovering the provinces lost in the Franco-Prussian War, pressed successfully for unrestricted French influence there. Doubts about German motives led France to hesitate to accept such an arrangement, but pressure from business interests and investors heavily involved in Tunisia, along with the emergence of an aggressive Italian campaign predicated on its citizens' fifteen-to-one numerical advantage over French residents of Tunisia, reversed this stance. The distraught, but relatively weak, Italian government had to settle for promises of a similar status in Tripolitania. The endemic unrest in Khmir territory provided France with a bridge from the negotiating table at Berlin to the table in the beylical palace around which Muhammad al-Sadiq, Consul General Roustan, and General Bréart gathered to finalize the Bardo Treaty in May 1881.

Their mission apparently accomplished with the bey's compliance and the stifling of resistance to the invasion, most of the French forces not designated as part of the garrison permitted by the treaty were withdrawn in June. In the following month, however, an uprising erupted across much of the country, revealing that beylical submission did not translate into popular acceptance of the French presence. Frequently justified in the rhetoric of a jihad against an infidel incursion in its early stages, the insurrection ultimately targeted Muhammad al-Sadiq and his entourage as much as it did the French. The bey had lost the respect of his subjects, many of whom seized upon the uprising as a means of avenging grievances nursed over many years. His assertion, albeit probably under French duress, to officials ordered to contain the rebellion that the French had come at his request, and as friends, left him vulnerable to portrayal by his enemies as either a lackey or a fool.[17]

The most prominent instigator of the uprising was ᶜAli ibn Khalifa, a tribal *qaid* from the southeast. He owed his appointment to the government, but, like most agents of beylical authority in rural regions, he recognized that failing to repel the French would lead to the imposition of controls restricting tribal independence in a process parallel to the subjugation of the bey. Rebel hopes for the appearance of an Ottoman *deus ex machina* had even less chance of fulfillment than in 1864. A few days after the French invasion, Ottoman officials reminded the European powers of the empire's rights in Tunisia and subsequently made an ostentatious show of rejecting the Bardo Treaty. But the sultan had no intention of challenging a curt French warning that it would regard the passage of Ottoman naval vessels out of the Dardanelles as an act of war.

As tens of thousands of tribal warriors joined the insurgency, much of the south and west, as well as rural regions of the Sahil, fell to them, but their inability to gain control of the Sahil's cities deprived them of resources crucial for a final victory. Urban defiance stemmed from city dwellers' long-standing mistrust of the volatile, and always potentially destructive, nomads. For the most part, they preferred to cope with whatever liabilities might accompany the imposition of order by the French than to risk the certain instability of tribal dominance. Fear of a reprise of the government's actions after the 1864 revolt further dissuaded urbanites from supporting the rebels. The dispatch of French reinforcements during the summer turned the tide of the uprising. The dissidents fell back on the holy city of Kairouan, where they held out until October before dispersing into fragmented bands, some of which kept up a sporadic resistance in the south until the end of the year. Superior French firepower ultimately doomed the insurrection, but other problems contributed to undermining it. Habitual rivalries often thwarted cooperation among the tribes, while the demands of the approaching harvest distracted many of the warriors. As the rebellion collapsed, more than 100,000 tribesmen and their families sought refuge in Ottoman Tripolitania.

With the revolt extinguished and the Bardo Treaty ratified by the French parliament, Paul Cambon, a senior diplomat, arrived in Tunis in early

1882 as France's first resident general. His mission was to represent the interests of the French government and, as specified in the treaty, to serve as the foreign minister of the bey, from whom he planned to tolerate no obstructive behavior. Muhammad al-Sadiq died only a few months later, however, leaving the new resident general to establish the parameters of the new Franco-Tunisian relationship with a new bey, Muhammad al-Sadiq's younger brother ᶜAli.

CHAPTER 2

Whose Tunisia?, 1881–1912

FRANCE'S TUNISIA: INSTALLING THE FRAMEWORK
OF THE PROTECTORATE

^cAli Bey well knew that the retention of his office hinged on his rapport with Cambon. He had initially condemned the French invasion, but, once the anti-beylical character of the resistance had come to light, he took command of Tunisian forces serving with the French army in Khmir territory. Mindful of rumors that some French officials responsible for planning the 1881 operation had advocated deposing Muhammad al-Sadiq in favor of his brother Taieb, despite ^cAli's designation as heir apparent, he had no reason to doubt that installing Taieb on the throne remained an option. For Cambon, the beylical transition afforded the opportunity to underscore the right of diplomatic supervision France had secured through the Bardo Treaty, as well as to prepare for the extension of its role to the much broader administrative and political oversight endorsed at the Congress of Berlin. It might, if properly managed, also help to put paid to Ottoman political claims in Tunisia. Towards these ends, and without objection from the insecure ^cAli, Cambon orchestrated the October 28, 1882, accession ceremony of the new ruler. The resident general accompanied ^cAli from his seaside residence in La Marsa to the Bardo Palace, where Cambon invested him as bey in the name of France, bestowing on him the *grand cordon* of the Légion d'Honneur. The adroit prior intervention of the French ambassador in Istanbul ensured that this usurpation of the sultan's customary practice of issuing an investiture decree passed without incident in the Ottoman capital. In the evening the resident general, acting as the senior diplomat in Tunis, gathered the foreign consuls together for an audience with the bey.

Confident that ^cAli would toe whatever line he chose to draw,[1] Cambon now prepared to remove the two major obstacles to the exercise of a totally free French hand: the International Finance Commission and the Tunisian government ministries responsible for internal affairs. This he accomplished

on June 8, 1883, when he obtained the bey's signature to the La Marsa
Convention. By its terms France guaranteed the repayment of the Tunisian
debt (thus rendering the International Finance Commission irrelevant)
in return for the execution of administrative reforms stipulated by the
resident general. In depriving ᶜAli of any meaningful sovereignty, the accord
converted Tunisia into a French protectorate. ᶜAli Bey continued to reign,
but he no longer ruled. By the time his son Muhammad al-Hadi (1902–6),
and then his nephew Muhammad al-Nasir (1906–22), came to the throne,
protectorate officials had come to take beylical subservience for granted.

The La Marsa Convention ended a debate, dating from the invasion,
about Tunisia's final status. Many opponents of colonial expansion lobbied
for a total withdrawal, arguing that the deployment of troops in Tunisia
weakened the defenses of metropolitan France. They also feared that the
multitude of international agreements to which Tunisia was a party, many
of them including most-favored-nation clauses, in conjunction with its
substantial Maltese and Italian populations, made for a diplomatic morass
likely to confound the most determined French administration. French military leaders and businessmen already established in Tunisia drew a quite
different lesson from the same set of facts. To them, any approach short of
a declaration of full French sovereignty, suppressing all foreign claims at a
single stroke, would saddle France with the burdens of annexation but none
of its advantages. The protectorate mentality occupied a middle ground.
Its proponents believed that preserving the shell of an indigenous government lessened the likelihood of stimulating the bitterness and hostility that
political assimilation to France had produced among the indigenous people of neighboring Algeria. Moreover, maintaining such a façade allowed
for the Tunisian funding of a French-supervised administration. For the
duration of the protectorate, French officials and residents in Tunisia frequently referred to Algerian policies and practices, occasionally as models
to emulate, but more often as examples of what *not* to do.

By 1883, the Tunisian debt had soared to more than 140 million francs, or
eleven times the government's annual income.[2] As the initial quid pro quo
for guaranteeing the debt, France insisted on placing key agencies, beginning with the ministry of finance, under the leadership of French specialists

———————————————————————————————————→

Map 2.1. Cities and tribes, ca. 1912. With the exception of the desert regions of the
deep south, which were administered by French army officers, the cities and tribal
areas of the protectorate were presided over by *contrôleurs civils*, French officials
whose supervision of local Tunisian authorities replicated the resident general's
oversight of the bey and his ministers.

TUNISIE

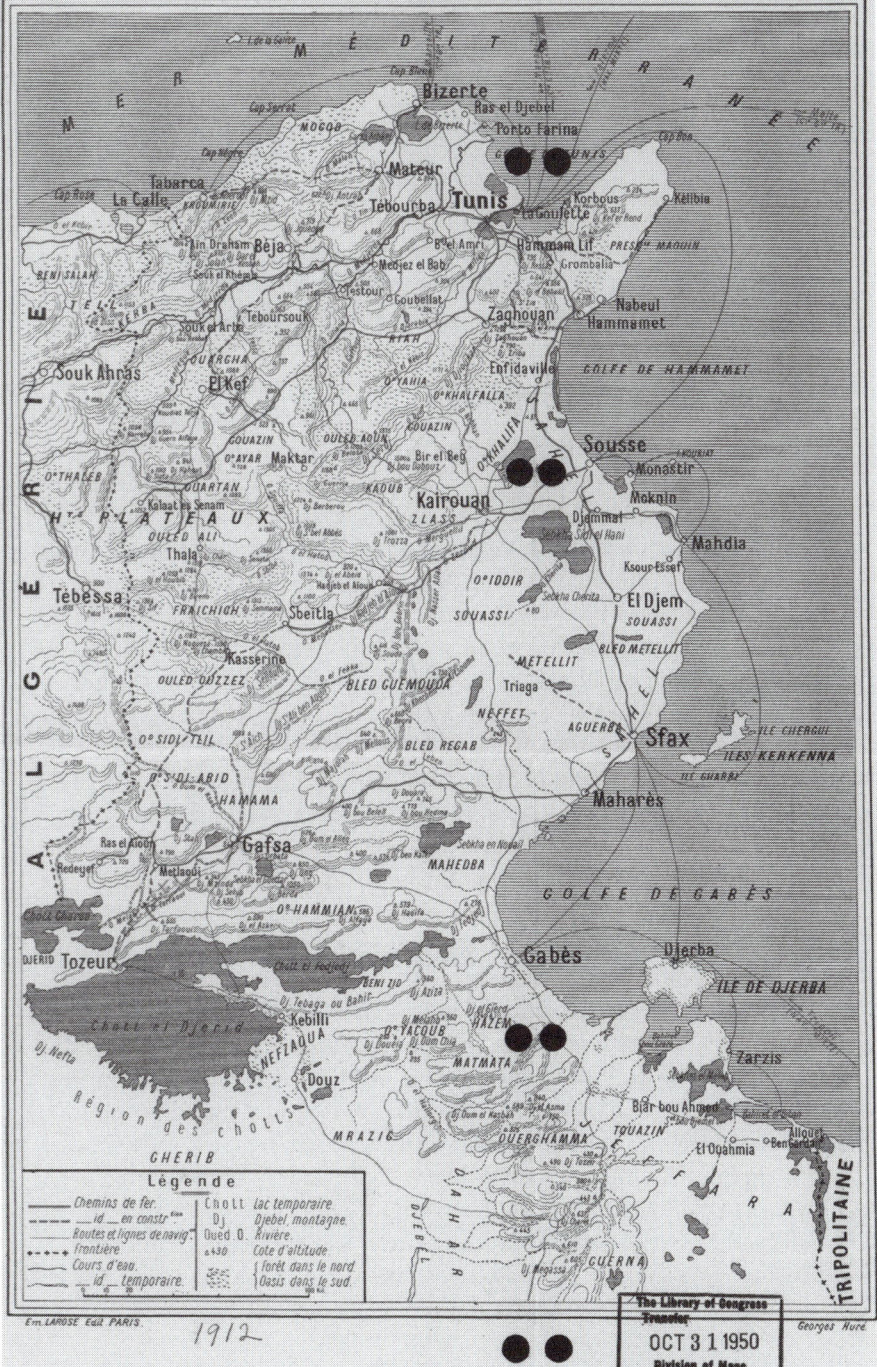

Légende

—— Chemins de fer.	Chott lac temporaire.
— — id — en constr⁻	Dj Djebel, montagne.
— — — Routes et lignes de navig⁻	Oued O. Rivière.
• • • • Frontière	▲+30 Cote d'altitude
—— Cours d'eau.	{ forêt dans le nord.
— — id — temporaire.	{ Oasis dans le sud.

Em. LAROSE Édit PARIS.

1912

Georges Huré

accountable to the resident general. Cambon made this department his first target because the systematic collection and sound management of government revenue were critical both to maintaining the confidence of foreign creditors and to implementing the reforms envisioned in the La Marsa Convention. To satisfy their chronic need for funds, leaders in the pre-protectorate era (with Khair al-Din as a notable exception) had imposed a welter of generally regressive levies on production and commerce. After the restructuring of the ministry into a Directorate of Finances, its French head reduced the rate of many existing taxes and saw to the disciplining of state agents responsible for irregularities in their assessment and collection. These measures, coupled with the protectorate authorities' greater thoroughness and proficiency, increased revenue and placed the government on a solid financial footing that enabled it, in the decade after 1883, to phase out most export duties, lower market fees considerably, and reduce the *majba* by 25 percent.[3] Even with these cutbacks, however, the payment of taxes still occasioned significant hardships for many Tunisians.

Under Cambon and his successors Justin Massicault (1886–92), Urbain Rouvier (1892–4), and René Millet (1894–1900), all but three Tunisian ministries experienced similar reorganizations under the supervision of French officials. Collectively labeled as the technical services of the protectorate, these agencies employed a smattering of Tunisians, but only at the lowest echelons or as interpreters, a practice that embittered the many displaced administrators, clerks, and other officials of the beylical bureaucracy. With the resident general acting as foreign minister and the general commanding French troops as minister of war (as stipulated by the Bardo Treaty), only the minister of the pen (the chief clerk), the minister of justice, and the prime minister were Tunisians and had Tunisian staffs. To advise the prime minister and coordinate the bureaucracy, Cambon created the office of secretary general of the protectorate, to which he appointed Maurice Bompard, a senior French diplomat.

Provincial governance lent itself less well to the displacement of Tunisian office holders. The *qaids* and *khalifas* who represented beylical authority in the cities, towns, and other sedentary regions usually came from powerful local families; in rural areas where the tribe and *qiyada* (the administrative unit headed by a *qaid*) overlapped, they were tribal leaders. Few showed any inclination to change habitual, and sometimes repugnant, practices. In order to standardize administrative units, but also to curb the tribal notables, the protectorate authorities redrew the boundaries of the existing *qiyadas* to form divisions based on geography rather than kinship. Beginning in the 1890s, appointments as urban provincial officials often went to promising graduates of Sadiqi College in the expectation that they would bring an enlightened approach to these positions.

At the start of the protectorate, French consuls and vice-consuls represented the resident general in several of the larger provincial centers, while French soldiers monitored the behavior of *qaids* and *khalifas* in rural areas. Cambon worried that permanently sanctioning such a role for the army would give rise to a destabilizing, Algerian-style "régime du sabre." Throughout his tenure he sought a viable alternative, but was thwarted by the military's insistence that it alone could guarantee security in the countryside. Shortly after becoming resident general in 1887, Justin Massicault, building on Cambon's efforts, created a corps of *contrôleurs civils* (civil controllers) to act as his eyes and ears beyond Tunis. Posted in thirteen *circonscriptions* corresponding to *qiyadas* from La Goulette to Gafsa, the *contrôleurs* provided direction and guidance to *qaids* and *khalifas* and had at their disposal small contingents of Tunisian gendarmes to carry out basic police work. In those cities and towns where the size of the European population warranted the creation of a municipal council, they also monitored the work of that body.[4] This arrangement preserved the façade of Tunisian government, but the *contrôleurs* and the resident general, to whose office they reported directly, expected nothing less than the diligent execution of their suggestions. In a few remote areas of the south and west where tribes had customarily heeded the writ of the government only under duress, a Service des Renseignements (renamed Service des Affaires Indigènes in 1900) based on the Algerian model of military administration of the tribes fulfilled a similar function. Only in 1906, after twenty years of intense efforts by Cambon, Massicault, and their successors did the Residency finally gain control over these officers and dispel the recurrent nightmare of a military role in the administration of the protectorate.

The restructuring of the central and regional governments consolidated French control over the Tunisian population, but Cambon also recognized the need to bring the foreign community, 95 percent of whose 20,000 members in 1883 were not French,[5] within the orbit of the protectorate. The Ottoman-era Capitulations and the more recent treaties negotiated with, or imposed by, European states, accorded foreigners privileges, most notably the maintenance of consular courts, that had limited the beylical government's control over them and now similarly constrained protectorate officials. Cambon ordered their suppression in 1883. Individuals subject to their jurisdiction acquired full access to the French judicial system that was emerging in the protectorate and consisted of local justices of the peace and a court of first instance in Tunis (eventually supplemented by others in Sousse, Sfax, and Bizerte).

Britain, which confronted a similar situation in Egypt, raised no objection to this decision. Italy's acceptance was considerably more grudging, and neither the Italian residents of Tunisia, who constituted more than half of the foreign population, nor the Italian government intended to surrender other dispensations secured in the 1868 Italo-Tunisian Treaty merely at the behest of France. The Italian premier, Francesco Crispi, described Tunisia as "an Italian colony occupied by France," while *L'Unione*, the leading Italian-language newspaper in Tunis, insisted that the situation in North Africa remained "unsettled, that it could not last, and that the rights of Italy in Tunisia were equal to those of France."[6] As Italy stubbornly refused to acknowledge the inevitability of French control, the Italian population of Tunisia mushroomed, increasing by 88 percent during the first decade of the protectorate. By 1896, when France acquiesced to Italian insistence on retaining most of the privileges accorded in the 1868 Italo-Tunisian treaty in return for Italy's recognition of the protectorate, the 55,000 Italians living in the country outnumbered French citizens by a ratio of five to one.[7] Confident that the 1896 settlement had carved out a secure, albeit not dominant, niche for them, Tunisia's Italians began enlarging and refining the numerous political, educational, social, cultural, and religious institutions that already existed within their community in order to underscore and preserve its distinctive identity.

The thin French population in the protectorate led to a search for "demographic allies" to offset the Italians' numerical superiority. Britain's retreat from Tunisia and the absorption of its subjects into the French legal system made the 7,000 Maltese living in the country in 1883 prime candidates for this role. When French Catholics first came into contact with the Maltese in Tunisia, they tended to belittle the traditional, and in their view unsophisticated, Maltese practice of the faith. Among other things, they cited as evidence the blind obedience of the Maltese to their clergy and their exceptionally high birth rate. By the end of the century, however, supporters of the protectorate had come to see its 12,000-strong Maltese community as a fertile source of settlers not only for Tunisia, but for all of French North Africa. In his dealings with the Catholic population, Cambon had an important ally in Cardinal Charles Lavigerie, the archbishop of Carthage and Algiers. Lavigerie fervently advocated linking France's political mission and the Church's spiritual one in North Africa – a connection symbolized in Tunis by the situating of the Residency building and the cathedral directly opposite each other on the Avenue de France. The prelate urged French priests to support the policies of the protectorate and

Figure 2.1. Avenue de France, ca. 1920. The main thoroughfare of the European city ran from the medina to the Lake of Tunis. This view is from the Bab al-Bahr (Porte de France), the most important junction between the old and new cities. The spires of the cathedral of St. Vincent de Paul can be seen in the left background. The headquarters of the protectorate administration were across the avenue.

to foster the assimilation by Maltese and Italian Catholics of France's aims. A concordat between France and the Vatican in 1891 left the See of Carthage a preserve of the French church, much as the Tunisian state had become a preserve of the French government. When the last Italian Capuchin priests, whose order had worked in Tunisia since the seventeenth century, decided to leave in the same year, Lavigerie made no effort to discourage them.[8]

The establishment of French courts endowed Tunisia with two discrete judicial administrations (not unlike the pre-protectorate legal configuration, except for the consolidation of the foreigners' tribunals under a single authority). Justice for Tunisians was dispensed in religious courts (both Islamic and Jewish) or by the ministry of Tunisian justice, referred to simply as *wizara* (ministry), unless they became parties to a dispute involving Europeans, in which case the French courts took precedence. The *wizara* – in essence, the state secular court – derived its authority from the traditional right of the ruler to adjudicate criminal and civil matters. The sharia courts judged personal status cases and property disputes in accordance with Islamic law, while the rabbinical courts applied the Mosaic law to similar issues.

Preserving the sharia courts was essential to virtually all Muslims, but considerable differences of opinion about an appropriate legal structure emerged among Tunisia's 25,000 Jews. In the early years of the protectorate a number of prosperous Grana businessmen requested access to French courts, and even to French citizenship, on the basis of the 1870 Crémieux Decree granting those rights to Jews in Algeria; however, protectorate officials firmly rejected the extension of such privileges. They pointed out that the Bardo and La Marsa protocols precluded the transfer of Tunisians from beylical to French sovereignty, a prohibition that they knew the contingent of politically conscious Tunisians emerging in the late 1880s would defend vigorously. In any event, many Tunisian Jews also opposed assimilation, the desirability of which became the central issue dividing two well-organized and articulate political camps within the Jewish community. In addition to advancing cultural and religious arguments, critics stressed the imprudence of alienating the Muslim majority, with whom Tunisian Jews had generally enjoyed good relations and with whom they had more in common than with the French, particularly after the establishment of the protectorate. Reminding their co-religionists of the virulent anti-Semitism of many settlers, they cast doubts on the alleged benefits of integration and warned of the cool reception its pursuers were likely to encounter.[9]

In 1909 the news that impending French legislation would facilitate the naturalization of Tunisians provoked animated debate in Jewish circles, as well as between Jews and Muslims. Under the final terms of the 1910 Messimy Law, however, very few Tunisian Jews qualified for citizenship. Those whose hopes were dashed by the rigorous conditions of the bill reacted with bitterness to their experiences of rejection by French officials, contempt on the part of many private French citizens in Tunisia, suspicion from their Muslim countrymen, and estrangement from their fellow Jews. The search of these deeply frustrated individuals for a hospitable political environment led some to French socialist circles, others to the Aghoudat-Sion, a Tunisian Zionist movement organized in 1911. These were the ideologies to which they subsequently devoted themselves.

Although French officials refrained from infringing on the operation of the religious courts, they did introduce changes in the *wizara*, most dramatically by in 1896 placing it under the control of a newly created technical service, the directorate of judicial services, headed by a French judge. Over the next few years, this agency established regional tribunals in six large cities, leaving the *wizara* to hear cases from the capital but also to rule on the most serious matters arising in the provinces and to resolve appeals from lower court judgments. A decade later, the directorate attached French representatives, called *commissaires du gouvernement*, to all Tunisian secular courts, creating yet another network of French supervision ostensibly parallel to, but in reality in control of, officials of the beylical government. Not all of these men spoke Arabic – the language of the proceedings they were meant to oversee – and few had any legal background or training, but their negative assessment could result in the destitution of even the most senior Tunisian judge. Between 1906 and 1913, French lawyers and Tunisian *wizara* officials collaborated in drawing up a code of contracts, a penal code, and a code of civil procedures, all of them deeply rooted in French law.

The jurisdiction of sharia courts over property matters had long enabled Tunisians to use their knowledge of Islamic law to obstruct foreigners' attempts to acquire land and to challenge their title to parcels they professed to own. Cambon recognized the importance of sidestepping a procedure certain to inhibit future European settlement, but, in deference to Tunisian sensibilities concerning the sharia, he proceeded cautiously. He began by appointing a Franco-Tunisian commission, a third of whose members were either ministers in the beylical government or high officials of the Islamic legal system, which he charged with the tasks of codifying existing property laws and developing a method for representatives of the protectorate to have a voice in their adjudication. In 1885 the commission formulated a mechanism, available to Tunisians and foreigners alike, for registering privately owned land with the state, which then issued an unassailable title. Disputes involving such land went before a Tribunal Mixte Immobilier (Mixed Real Estate Court), presided over by a French judge and staffed by six other magistrates, half of them French, half Tunisian.[10] The placing of this hybrid court under the aegis of the Directorate of the Interior rather than the Directorate of Judicial Services confirmed its primary purpose of strengthening foreigners' claims to land rather than guaranteeing the equitable dispensation of justice.

THE EUROPEAN SETTLERS' TUNISIA: PROSPERITY AND PENURY

In the early years of the protectorate, French land acquisition followed a pattern that had emerged soon after the 1861 constitution had legalized the purchase of real estate by foreigners. Corporations and wealthy speculators bought large tracts of land, often in the form of *hanashir* (rural estates belonging to the royal family or other notables and usually consisting of a combination of state-owned and *habus* land). In 1880, Prime Minister Khair al-Din had sold one such property near Enfida that comprised more than 100,000 hectares. Five years later, the Enfida and Sidi Thabit holdings of the Société Marseillaise de Crédit, along with 30,000 hectares controlled

by five other investment companies, accounted for 88 percent of all French
property in the protectorate, with the remaining 12 percent divided among
thirty-four other owners.[11] Tunisian peasants continued to work this land,
occasionally as renters but more likely as sharecroppers, since the speculators
drove up its value to a level few Tunisians could afford. Alternatively, the
companies resold smaller parcels to individual buyers, many of whom were
Italians. Much of this land was well suited for growing wheat, but the surge
of Russian and North American cereal exports to Europe over the last two
decades of the century steadily reduced their prices, making it difficult to
export Tunisian wheat profitably. As a result, as much as a third of the
speculators' land sometimes lay fallow.

    Although the French population of the protectorate exceeded 10,000
within a decade, few of the new arrivals chose to settle in rural areas. Some
400,000 hectares had come into French hands by 1892, but the number
of properties had risen only to 333 and no more than 1,500 French citizens were engaged in agricultural work. Only in 1897 did the number of
French-owned properties reach 1,000, although the census of the previous
year placed a mere 22 percent of the French population (just over 2,000
persons) on the land. By contrast, roughly 1,000 Italian families, some of
whose claims predated the protectorate, owned and worked 27,350 hectares
in the early 1890s, at a time when the overall Italian population exceeded
that of the French by a factor of five.[12] This pattern of large French commercial ventures with few settlers and small Italian holdings farmed by their
owners heightened concerns in Tunis and Paris about demographic imbalances in the protectorate and stimulated efforts to attract French *colons*
(settlers).

    In 1890, Resident General Massicault created a Directorate of Agriculture
to facilitate French citizens' purchases of desirable agricultural property.
"Official," or state-promoted, colonization began in the following year,
when the directorate placed on sale thousands of hectares of state-owned
land in the vicinity of Tunis.[13] But the stringent conditions it imposed – cash
payments, a commitment not to resell, and the formal deeding of the land
only after the construction of a house and the start of cultivation on two-
thirds of the plot – deterred many would-be buyers. Not until 1896, when
these obligations were relaxed and the size of the parcels doubled, did sales
reach desired levels. A more immediately successful step entailed simplifying
the land registration process and making it less expensive by transferring
most of the costs incurred from the registrant to the government. In 1893,
the first year of this revised system, more registration applications were filed
than in the previous seven years combined, although many of these claims

originated with Tunisians. By beylical decree *mawat*, or dead land, reverted to the state in 1896, thus also becoming available for French purchase.

Land collectively held by tribes and *habus* land represented two other large and lucrative reservoirs that were also tapped for the benefit of *colons*. The government seized the former in 1901. Three years later, the Tribunal Mixte ruled that tribes did not constitute organized groups and could not, therefore, own property as collectivities. Extensive areas that had always technically belonged to the state, but on which tribes had enjoyed rights of usufruct and pasturage, were now subject to alienation. Even before the inauguration of "official" colonization, a legal ruse had enabled non-Muslims to lease *habus* lands on a permanent basis. Starting in 1898, the government required the Habus Council to sell a minimum of 2,000 hectares of its property to French buyers each year. The Directorate of Agriculture selected the parcels, setting their prices in consultation with the council. Between 1892 and 1914, these and other "official" colonization strategies transferred more than 250,000 hectares from Tunisian to French control and increased French land holdings to approximately 700,000 hectares, or 84 percent of all the land in non-Tunisian hands, by the outbreak of World War I.

The cultivation of vines and olive trees predominated on the property acquired during those two decades as grapes and olives, and their by-products of wine and oil, developed into the most lucrative products of *colon* agriculture. The devastation wrought on French vineyards by phylloxera infestations beginning in the 1860s prompted the extension of viticulture in both Algeria and Tunisia. In the latter, during the 1880s, the area planted with vines quintupled from 1,000 to 5,000 hectares. Although French production revived in the 1890s, the demand for Tunisian wine remained strong, with the area devoted to viticulture covering more than 15,000 hectares by the turn of the century.[14] Small-scale French settlers owned most of the vineyards, which were located in the region of Tunis and in the Majarda Valley, but often hired Italian agricultural laborers to work them. Because Tunisians had no interest in acquiring the skills necessary to produce wine, the profits of viticulture accrued almost entirely to *colons*.

Olives were an entirely different matter. In the Sahil, the focal point of olive cultivation and oil production, small privately owned farms immune to foreign acquisition except through voluntary sales, flourished. But Paul Bourde, the director of agriculture from 1891 to 1895, envisioned the development of *colon* olive plantations in the triangle of steppe land bounded by Kairouan, Gabès, and Gafsa. He knew that the historical and archeological record showed that this desolate region in which nomadic tribes pastured

GOUVERNEMENT TUNISIEN

DIRECTION GÉNÉRALE
DE L'AGRICULTURE, DU COMMERCE
ET DE LA COLONISATION

Propriétés possédées
par des Français à la date
du 1ᵉʳ Juillet 1911

RÉPARTITION
PAR CONTRÔLES CIVILS

Echelle : 1:500000°

Récapitulation des Contrôles
Civils

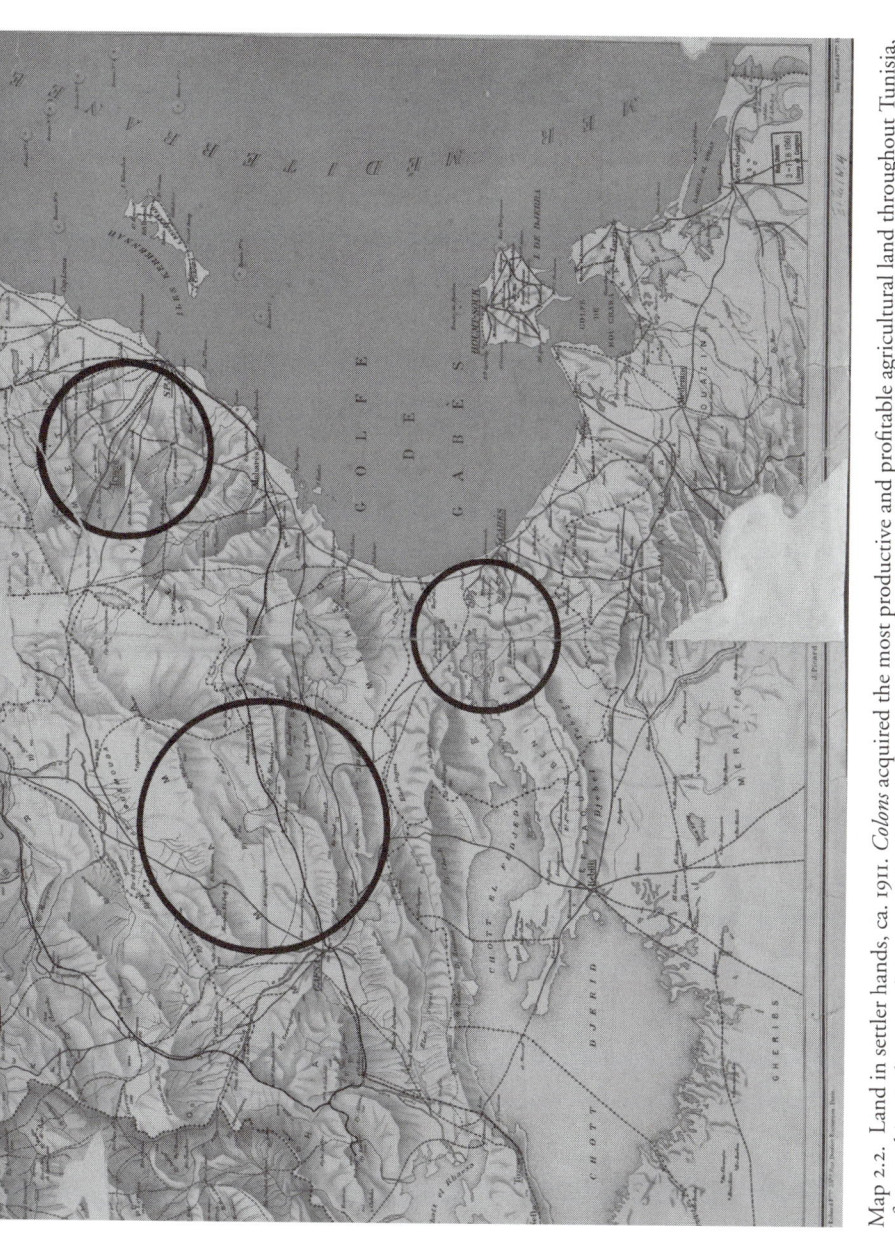

Map 2.2. Land in settler hands, ca. 1911. *Colons* acquired the most productive and profitable agricultural land throughout Tunisia, often pushing indigenous farmers and herdsmen to marginal lands on which they could not survive. Pie charts on this official map indicate the percentage of land held by Europeans in various regions.

their livestock and raised small crops of cereals had been an important olive-producing area in antiquity. In 1892 he used his authority to open state lands for colonization to place on sale, at bargain prices, a vast tract of land west of Sfax that Muhammad al-Sadiq had confiscated from a family of local notables, the Siala, in 1871. Within a year, the directorate received 800 requests to purchase portions of the estate. Most came from the Tunisian bourgeoisie of Sfax, but French settlers also laid claim to more than a third of the land. At Bourde's insistence the new owners negotiated traditional agricultural contracts called *mugharasat* with Tunisian peasants. In this arrangement, the owner leased the land to peasants who planted and cultivated olive trees while raising cereal crops for their own use between them until they bore fruit, at which point the owner and the lessee divided the land equally. The cultivation of the Siala lands made the Sfax region and its hinterland a major *colon* center for the growth and processing of olives, albeit at the expense of the nomadic tribes.

Many French officials in both Paris and Tunis considered strong, mutually beneficial Franco-Tunisian commercial relations to be as important in binding the protectorate to France and marginalizing the interests of other European states as was the acquisition of property by French citizens. Tunisian international trade entailed the export of agricultural products, with olive oil foremost, and the import of manufactured ones. Even after the inauguration of the protectorate, however, more of Tunisia's crops went to Italy than to France, owing to the former's lower tariffs. In order to capture this trade, France removed the duty on many imports from Tunisia and imposed only minimal taxes on the remainder in 1890. Skyrocketing sales to France led to an immediate and massive influx of francs, which had become legal tender in the protectorate in 1888. This glut, in conjunction with a scarcity of piasters, which had begun disappearing from circulation as Tunisians hoarded them to protest the new coinage, diminished the franc's value relative to the piaster. Within months of the new tariff regime taking effect, the Directorate of Finances ordered the withdrawal of Tunisian piasters and their replacement by coins minted in Paris and denominated in francs and centimes. Each had a French obverse and an Arabic reverse, on which the name of the bey, the value of the coin, and the *hijra* date appeared.[15]

The most-favored-nation clauses of several commercial treaties negotiated between Tunisia and European countries prior to the protectorate continued, however, to preclude a reciprocal arrangement for imports from France. Not until 1898, after Italy and Britain had renounced such concessions, were protectorate authorities in a position to cancel duties on goods originating in France while leaving them in place for the products of other countries. As a result, France supplied approximately 60 percent of Tunisia's imports and was the destination for a similar percentage of its exports at the turn of the century.[16] Easy access to the French market served all cultivators well, but particularly advantaged the *colons*. Although agriculture remained an overwhelmingly Tunisian pursuit, the modern methods employed by the relatively small number of European farmers enabled them to produce a disproportionate amount of the harvest in terms both of quantity and value. Assurances of the settlers' ability to import machinery and other supplies inexpensively and of their opportunity to export crops to France at a profit contributed significantly to ensuring the success of "official" colonization.

With that success came the dispersal of Europeans throughout rural Tunisia. In the mid-1880s three-quarters of all European-owned rural property lay within an arc stretching from Bizerte to Nabeul, none of it more than fifty miles from Tunis. Twenty years later, Europeans were farming land in the Majarda Valley, the High Tell, the interior steppes, and even some of the pre-Saharan oases. Furthermore, European shopkeepers, businessmen, bankers, and government officials settled in regional market towns and administrative centers – Béja, Souk al-ᶜArba (now Jendouba), Testour, Le Kef, Maktar, Kasserine, Gafsa, Gabès, and Kebili, among many others – where their work supported the agricultural enterprise with essential goods and services. The settlers' distinctively European houses transformed the landscape, as did, in time, the roads, railroads, and telegraph, telephone, and electricity lines that snaked through the country in their wake. Only in the rural Sahil were Europeans a rarity, although many of them did live in its urban centers on the coast – Sousse, Monastir, Mahdia, and Sfax.

Not surprisingly, however, Tunis and its suburbs remained the preeminent European communities of the country, with some 55,000 foreigners (35,000 Italians, 10,000 French citizens, 8,000 Maltese, and 2,000 others) living there in 1904, along with 80,000 Muslims and 39,000 Jews.[17] This burgeoning European population literally reshaped the capital which, at the start of the protectorate, had consisted of a partially walled medina and two immediately adjacent neighborhoods. In the 1880s and 1890s, a quarter built to European specifications, with broad boulevards, multistory buildings, large retail shops, theatres, and churches, took shape in reclaimed marshland between the medina walls and the Lake of Tunis. Most Muslims and Jews continued to live in the original agglomeration, but virtually all the Europeans who had resided there decamped to the new city, as did some Jews. The creation of a new quarter beyond the walls of the existing city "manufactured" space where Europeans could live and work in a familiar,

Figure 2.2. *Colon* grain storage building. While not as numerous as in neighboring
Algeria, European settlers in Tunisia enjoyed considerable political and economic power.
The caption at the bottom of this inter-war era postcard reads: "The peopling of North
Africa by the French is the national work of France in the twentieth century."

comfortable, and largely segregated setting. Sousse, Sfax, Bizerte, Kairouan,
and other cities imitated the Tunis model, which had itself drawn on urban
practices in Algeria. Because European Tunis was situated on unproductive
land, its construction did not necessitate the displacement of many individuals, although the development of some of the other *nouvelles villes* did
entail the displacement of Tunisians and provoked anger and resentment.

Accommodating rural European settlers posed greater complications.
Unclaimed cultivable land was rare and, unlike urban neighborhoods, new
fields and orchards could not be "manufactured." In the first few years of the
protectorate, however, the European acquisition of rural property hardly
disturbed the Tunisian peasants living on it. They continued to cultivate the
large estates that they themselves had never owned and that had passed into
the hands of corporations, individual speculators, and private proprietors,
all of whom needed their labor to keep the land productive. This situation
changed in the 1890s. "Official" colonization had as its goals the transfer
of smaller parcels of rural real estate from Tunisian to French hands and
the promotion of the personal, physical attachment of French citizens to

Tunisian soil. Thus, as French settlers began to carve out farmsteads from what had been state lands, collective tribal lands, and *habus* lands, the Tunisians who had cultivated them or grazed flocks on them were displaced. Those who opted to continue farming or herding could do so only on the marginal lands that held no interest for the colonizers. Some peasants driven from the land found jobs on the French farms, but their culturally divergent work habits and agricultural practices led *colon* owners, especially those who were mechanizing their operations, to prefer French or Italian laborers, despite having to pay them higher wages. Others who had been uprooted turned to vagabondage and lives of petty crime. Still others drifted to the towns and cities, where their lack of education and skills gave them access only to the least desirable jobs, if they found employment at all.

Bashir Sfar, an early graduate of Sadiqi College, headed the Habus Council until his 1898 resignation in protest at the enforced sale of its land to settlers. Like many other Sadiqi alumni who had benefited from their exposure to Western culture, Sfar initially believed that the French presence, including a thoughtfully managed program of rural colonization, could raise the quality of all Tunisians' lives. A decade of "official" colonization, however, left Sfar frustrated, bitter, and angry. "France," he wrote in 1903, "is wealthy enough to finance the installation of its citizens without having to condemn its protégés to starvation or flight, or turn them into a dangerous proletariat."[18] In the alienation of men like Sfar lay serious troubles for the protectorate.

The displacement of the rural population at the end of the nineteenth and the beginning of the twentieth centuries had adverse economic effects on many Tunisians in the towns and cities. For example, the tribes' loss of good grazing land diminished the size and quality of livestock herds which, in turn, reduced the supply of meat, butter, and other animal products in urban markets. It also deprived weavers and leatherworkers of raw materials, further crippling artisans devastated by decades of European competition. In contrast to urban areas, where the growing taste for European goods had lessened demand for locally produced commodities of virtually every kind, rural regions had shown less enthusiasm for imports and so had provided an important outlet for artisanal production. But the impoverishment of the countryside enervated that market, delivering a near knockout blow to craftsmen all over the country.

As French *colons* shouldered them aside, the productivity of Tunisian peasant farmers and herdsmen declined precipitously. The taxes extracted from them did not. By one estimate, government receipts in 1896 translated into an average tax of 10 francs per person,[19] a considerable burden, particularly in the distressed rural regions. This figure, averaged across the entire population, masks the 20-franc annual personal tax (*majba*) that all rural Tunisian males paid, but from which some urban residents, and all foreigners, enjoyed an exemption. The *istitan*, a personal tax set at 10 francs a year and imposed on all males, including foreigners, replaced the *majba* in 1913, but for many Tunisians, who accounted for 90 percent of the revenue it generated, halving the levy provided very little relief. Other forms of direct taxation weighed far more heavily on rural Tunisians than on their urban countrymen or on foreigners. Without exception, cultivated land was subject to the *ʿushr*, an assessment determined by the area sown, regardless of yield. In 1914, settler farmers controlled 10 percent of Tunisia's agricultural land, but paid just over 1 percent of the *ʿushr* owing to discounts given farmers using machinery and modern techniques to work the land – practices limited almost exclusively to foreigners.[20] The inequitable distribution of the *ʿushr* looms larger in view of the quality and productivity of the tenth of the land in *colon* hands. Tunisians occupied more land, but of marginal value; thus they produced less, but paid more. In a similar vein, grapes, the quintessentially European crop, were not taxed at all, while the harvests of olives and dates, crucial to the economy of the Sahil and the desert oases where few *colons* had penetrated, carried additional levies. That a significant portion of tax receipts financed the colonization projects that were rending the fabric of Tunisian rural society added insult to injury.

Under the circumstances conflict between settlers and Tunisians was inevitable. The incursion of nomads' livestock into sown fields provoked frequent confrontations, but robbery, theft, marauding, and assault all escalated in the 1890s. Tunisians as well as Europeans fell victim to these crimes, which were spawned by the desperate misery permeating the countryside. René Millet, the most liberal resident general since the beginning of the protectorate, did not hesitate to place much of the responsibility for the deteriorating rural situation at the feet of the *colons*. "Colonization," he chided them,

has made the European a competitor of the native, and a formidable one at that. He gains control of land and raises its price, along with the prices of essential goods. Each year he brings more land under his control, encloses it, guards it, and defends it against pasturage and trespass. He introduces new methods of cultivation and upsets the routine of the Muslim laborer.[21]

In 1896, Millet agreed to supplement the gendarmes attached to each *contrôle civil* with village policemen, as the *colons* had requested, but attacks on European property remained a fact of life in the countryside, their frequency rising and falling in a rhythm dictated by local tribes' encounters with bad weather, poor harvests, detrimental government policies, and settler arrogance.

Millet warned the *colons*, whom he knew objected vehemently to any measure calculated to empower Tunisians, not to use the rural turmoil as an excuse to attack protectorate policies, including his collaboration with urban, Western-educated Tunisians (among them, Bashir Sfar). They could not "openly demand that a million and a half Arabs be sacrificed to 20,000 of our nationals" but if their assertion that "the Arab population and its chiefs [are] resolutely hostile to our action and the development of our influence" gained credence in French political circles,

> there would remain no other choice . . . than to inaugurate in Tunisia a regime of reducing and driving back the native population, a regime of exceptional measures, of assigning to the French alone all the budgetary resources. . . . Such a regime existed in Algeria and its results are too well known to be necessary to recall.[22]

Millet's running battle to restrain the settlers led to his recall in 1900, underscoring the power the *colon* lobby wielded by that time and the extent to which settler interests set the agenda of protectorate policy.

The transportation and communication infrastructure developed by the Directorate of Public Works, one of the first technical services set up under the protectorate, exemplifies the privileging of *colons* over Tunisians. In 1884 the Algerian-based Compagnie du Bône-Guelma completed the railroad between Tunis and Algiers for which it had won the concession in 1878. Passing through the Majarda Valley and the High Tell, where Europeans were already acquiring land, the line expedited the movement of agricultural products to market, but also served a military and strategic purpose in binding the new protectorate to the French departments of Algeria. As French settlers spread more widely through the Tunisian countryside in the 1890s, they demanded the construction of new lines, but the company resisted undertaking operations in areas thinly populated by Europeans. To resolve this problem, protectorate officials arranged for the Tunisian government to absorb virtually all the costs entailed in extending the Bône-Guelma's main line to Bizerte, Sousse, Sfax, and Kairouan. The vast majority of state revenues thus expended had come from Tunisian taxpayers, but *colons* profited far more from the railroads than did Tunisians. When the focus of railroad construction shifted in the early twentieth century from supporting agricultural development to facilitating the exploitation of mineral deposits, other European entrepreneurs benefited from the company's receipt of state subsidies to build spurs, and sometimes whole new lines, to mineral-rich regions. Between 1902 and 1912, the Tunisian government borrowed more

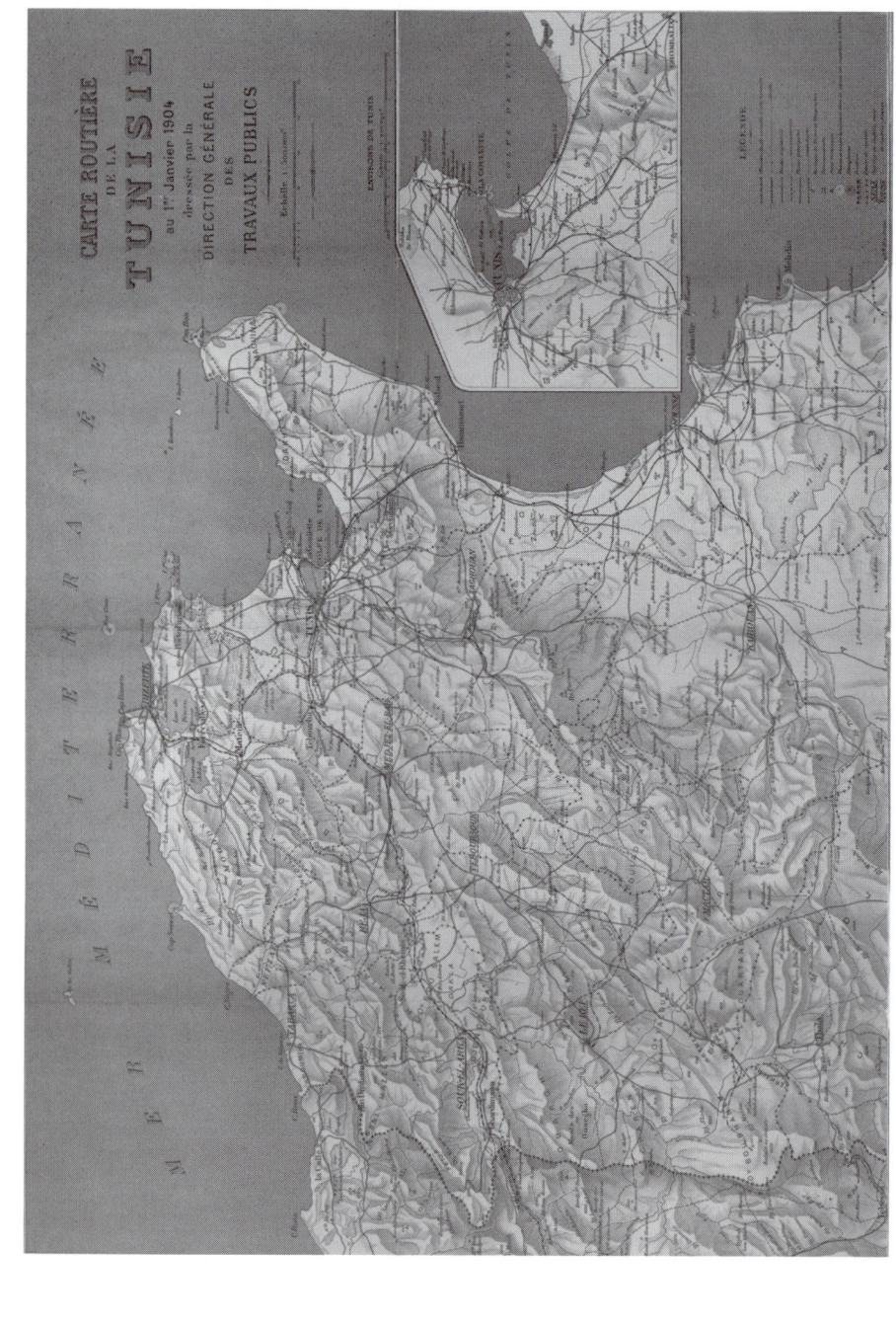

CARTE ROUTIÈRE
DE LA
TUNISIE
au 1er Janvier 1904
dressée par la
DIRECTION GÉNÉRALE
DES
TRAVAUX PUBLICS

Map 2.3. Transportation networks, ca. 1904. Railroad construction after the inauguration of the protectorate primarily served the interests of *colon* farmers and European mine owners. By the start of World War I, a railroad through the rich farmland of the Majerda Valley connected Tunis with Algeria, while other lines extended to Bizerte, Sousse, Sfax, and Kairouan. An industrial railroad carried phosphate ore from deposits around Gafsa to the port at Sfax.

Figure 2.3. A carriage of the Tunis–La Goulette–La Marsa railway. Italian entrepreneurs
operated this railway, built in the 1870s to link Tunis with its coastal suburbs, until 1898.
Thereafter, the Bône-Guelma company ran the line until its incorporation into the
Tunis tram system in 1905.

than 200 million francs to finance infrastructural expansion, of which the
Compagnie du Bône-Guelma received well over half.[23] This growth shifted
the company's main focus from Algeria to Tunisia and enabled it to survive
the Algerian government's 1915 takeover of its assets there.

In addition to the Bône-Guelma system, two other railroads were in service at the turn of the century. The short Italian-owned Tunis–La Goulette–
La Marsa (TGM) route connected the capital with its eastern suburbs; the
Compagnie des Phosphates et Chemins de Fer de Gafsa operated a line
carrying phosphates from mines in the southwest to the Mediterranean.
Following the discovery of major phosphate deposits near Gafsa in 1885, the
government offered a concession for their exploitation, but required that
the concessionaire also develop a port suitable for exporting the ore and
link it with the mines by railroad. These terms elicited no serious response
until the mid-1890s, when a consortium of investors began raising funds
that enabled them to form, in 1897, the Compagnie des Phosphates et

Chemins de Fer de Gafsa. In the interim, the government had dropped its requirement to construct an export terminal in view of expansion and modernization projects then under way at the port of Sfax. The final terms of the concession authorized the company to work the mines and run the railroad for ninety years. Participants in the Compagnie des Phosphates included the St. Gobain Chemical Company (Europe's largest consumer of phosphates), the Mukhtar Hadid Mining Company (an important investor in Algerian mineral development), the Duparchy Company (the firm responsible for the improvements to the port of Sfax, and for which the new company represented an invaluable customer), a number of prominent French industrialists, and thousands of smaller investors. The first shipment of ore reached Sfax on the newly completed railroad in 1899.[24]

The railroads and the Compagnie des Phosphates, which became the single largest employer and one of the largest taxpayers in the protectorate, illustrate the important role of French capital investment, channeled through large, specialized companies, in creating Tunisia's colonial economy. The land speculation in which the earliest of these companies had engaged never diminished appreciably, even after the inauguration of "official" colonization, with its preference for small farmers. From the 1890s on, however, other sectors of the economy, with mining (iron, lead, zinc, and phosphate) in the forefront, began to attract the serious attention of investors. During the four decades from the beginning of the protectorate until the end of World War I, the exploitation of mineral resources, the development of a transportation system (dominated by railroads), the improvement of port facilities (at Tunis, Sousse, and Sfax), the construction of a massive naval base (at Bizerte), and the acquisition of land collectively accounted for three-quarters of all capital investment.[25] Wealthy *colons* joined metropolitan shareholders in reaping the profits of these enterprises, but few Tunisians had the wherewithal to make such investments. Nor did they even participate in these projects as workers. The railroads and the companies developing the ports hired French and Italian laborers and even in the mines migrants from Tripolitania, Algeria, and Morocco were given preference over Tunisians, whom European foremen often characterized as unreliable and incompetent.

THE TUNISIAN BOURGEOISIE'S TUNISIA: FROM HIGH HOPES TO BITTER DISILLUSION

The effective replacement of the beylical government by a French administration, the ascendancy of French interests throughout the country, and the relegation of ordinary Tunisians, in some cases quite literally, to the margins of the economy and the society could not help but provoke deep resentment. The unsophisticated rural population most often manifested its antagonism in inchoate and spasmodic violence, while the modest attempts of a few Tunis ulama to express their discontent early in the protectorate era had sputtered out inconclusively. A small cadre of educated urbanites with training in a European language and an awareness of Western scholarship and technology was, however, learning to articulate grievances with the protectorate in less physically aggressive ways than the tribesmen and in a format and vocabulary that their European interlocutors understood better than they did those at the disposal of the ulama.

Prior to the protectorate, Tunisians had few opportunities to receive such instruction, which was offered only at schools maintained by Christian religious orders for the children of the European community and at specialized institutions like the Bardo military academy that admitted only the sons of the elite. The formal education of Tunisian male Muslims took place in a *kuttab*, whose curriculum revolved around the memorizing of the Qur'an. A select group of young men continued their studies at the renowned Zaituna mosque-university in Tunis. Only after Sadiqi College opened in 1875 did Muslim youths have access to instruction ranging beyond traditional Islamic topics, but admission to Sadiqi was quite limited. The education of most Tunisian Jewish boys went no further than elementary religious studies in schools similar to the *kuttab*. Neither Muslim nor Jewish girls customarily received an education beyond the training in domestic skills acquired in their homes. Louis Macheul, the Director of Public Instruction from 1883 until 1908, understood the risks of intervening directly in Muslim and Jewish education. Instead, he chose to oversee them from a distance and quietly promote select reforms aimed at associating them with a secular education system, designed to encourage the assimilation by Tunisians of French attitudes, that he began implementing at the start of his administration.

The system rested on French-language elementary schools open to Tunisian, and French and other European boys. These Franco-Arab schools employed an appropriately modified French curriculum and included Arabic as a subject of study. From the Directorate of Public Instruction's point of view, the schools enabled it to pose as a guardian of Tunisia's Arab heritage, as befit a protectorate administration, while still promoting assimilation through the spread of French. For the settlers, the schools gave their sons a basic French education, while the study of Arabic, despite having some distasteful overtones, equipped them with a potentially valuable skill that relatively few Europeans possessed. Some Tunisians welcomed the schools as points of access to the European community, but government officials and local notables often enrolled their children only under duress, or to curry favor with the French. Many more Tunisians opposed the Franco-Arab schools, usually on religious grounds, than supported them.

Nevertheless, the realities of life under the protectorate made at least a passing familiarity with the culture and language of the colonizers all but essential, particularly in urban areas. Starting in 1908, liberal Tunisian educators organized "reformed" *kuttabs* that provided such an introduction to Muslim students who rejected the secular Franco-Arab schools in favor of a religious education. Within the Jewish community, the Westernized Grana gravitated to French public schools, an environment that most Jews of Tunisian origin found uncomfortable. Teachers working for the French Alliance Israélite exposed this more tradition-bound community to the rudiments of Western education.

The first elementary school to offer a modern curriculum to Muslim girls opened in 1900 with the enthusiastic backing of Louise Millet, the wife of the resident general. The school took as its objective the dissemination of progressive ideas that would "ameliorate the lot of [Tunisian women] and provide a direct opportunity for French influence to be exercised on them."[26] To alleviate parental anxieties about sending their daughters to the school, its headmistress, the French widow of a protectorate official who knew Tunisian society well, observed traditional social standards, even hiring elderly instructors from the Zaituna mosque-university to teach the Islamic component of the curriculum. The Habus Council provided funds that sustained the school through several years of low enrollments, while its moral support constituted an invaluable imprimatur in the Muslim community. In 1905, enrollment reached 100, and by 1912, when its relocation led to its designation as the Ecole Rue du Pacha, almost 500 young women were attending the school. The Directorate of Public Instruction did not establish public primary schools for Muslim girls until 1908. In them Muslim women assisted French instructors with a curriculum that combined academic studies with vocational and domestic training.

Beyond the elementary level a few other public schools included both Arab and European students. The Collège Alaoui, established in 1884 at Macheul's prodding, but officially by order of the bey, prepared young men to teach in the Franco-Arab schools. Although intended primarily for Tunisians at its inception, the college also enrolled the sons of settlers and protectorate officials. By the early twentieth century, some 20 percent of its students were Europeans.[27] The Lycée Carnot presented a mirror image of Alaoui College. French missionaries founded the school for young men under the name Collège Saint Louis in 1875, but when it later proved to be a financial burden, Cardinal Lavigerie handed it over to the Directorate of Public Instruction in 1889. Renamed Lycée Carnot in 1894 in honor of the French president assassinated in that year, it stood at the pinnacle of French public education in Tunisia. Accordingly, it had a predominantly European clientele, although it always included a handful of the best Muslim and Jewish students to have gone through the Franco-Arab schools. A corresponding institution for women, the Lycée Armand Fallières, trained female teachers and was overwhelmingly European.

Alaoui College and Lycée Carnot also attracted those Sadiqi College graduates capable of continuing their education, but the Sadiqi curriculum did not adequately prepare most students to compete successfully for admission to the post-elementary institutions with young men trained in the Franco-Arab schools. Recognizing Sadiqi's value as a source of clerks and translators for their administration, French officials had acted quickly to bring the college under their control. In 1882, even before the La Marsa Convention formalized the protectorate, Resident General Cambon's appointment of an administrative council to oversee the school undercut the authority of its director, a protégé of Khair al-Din who did not welcome the French presence. Thereafter, the Directorate of Public Instruction had no interest in altering the nature of the college, but only in introducing changes in the course of studies to better serve French needs.

Thus, in the first decade and a half of the protectorate, thousands of Tunisian men and a much more modest number of women were receiving an education that exposed them to an array of new ideas and brought them into direct contact with the French population. For most, the experience ended at the primary level, but hundreds went farther. By the 1890s, those who had completed the highest levels of the public education system were assuming positions in the protectorate government. There they joined Sadiqi College graduates of the pre-protectorate era who had studied in France and returned to launch careers in public service. Macheul and other officials saw in these Western-educated Tunisians, and especially in the nucleus of Sadiqi graduates, bridges to the broader Tunisian society and, therefore, invaluable allies in the campaign to secure broad public acceptance of the protectorate. Many of the Tunisians shared this view and were prepared to act accordingly. Attuned to the principles of 1789, they believed that the application of those ideals in Tunisia would benefit the entire society. Their country would become a modern state, as France had; technology would bind the country together as never before; and republican rule would replace arbitrary monarchical power.

For all that, these men were not deracinated and they continued to care deeply about their Arab-Islamic heritage. For most of them, a second

intellectual concept, *Salafiyya* (Islamic reform), exerted at least as strong
a pull as did European progressivism. Its advocates preached a renewal
of the core values of their ancestors (*al-salaf*), arguing that Muslims had
abandoned or distorted them over the centuries. The ensuing ignorance and
neglect weakened the Muslim community, ultimately leaving it vulnerable
to the ills plaguing it in the nineteenth century, not the least of which was
European imperialism. Adherents of the *Salafiyya* did not necessarily reject
all things non-Islamic and many approved of the adaptation of Western
cultural features capable of enhancing Muslims' lives. The thinking of
Khair al-Din embodied *Salafiyya* ideals, which had naturally taken their
place in the Sadiqi College curriculum. In 1883, a follower of Khair al-Din,
Muhammad al-Sanusi, founded in Tunis a chapter of the most prominent
Salafiyya organization of the time. At al-Sanusi's invitation, Muhammad
ᶜAbduh, the movement's leading light, visited Tunis in 1885 and again
in 1903. ᶜAbduh understood that Tunisians lacked the capacity to break
the French hold on their country. Under the circumstances, he counseled
his audiences to work for reforms in the protectorate system embodying
Muslim principles of equity and justice – advice modeled on his own
engagement with the British in Egypt.

Three years later, a group of *Salafiyya* adepts including al-Sanusi, ᶜAli
Bu Shusha, Muhammad al-Qarwi, and Bashir Sfar established an Arabic
newspaper, *al-Hadira*, to publicize their call for modernization and social
change that respected the centrality of Arabic and of Islam in Tunisian
culture. These men all had links to the Khair al-Din era of reforms, either
as collaborators of the former prime minister or as Sadiqi students of the
pre-protectorate era. *Al-Hadira* particularly targeted the two most literate
Arabic-speaking components of Tunis society, the *baldiyya* and the ulama.
Its appeals met with some success among the former and among the more
progressive ulama, for both of whom the message echoed the words of *The
Surest Path*, Khair al-Din's treatise on government. But the more conservative ulama showed themselves stubbornly resistant to innovation. The
paper survived for twenty-two years, thanks in no small part to a subsidy
paid by protectorate officials who considered it a useful tool in reconciling
Tunisians of a certain persuasion with the French presence.

The appointment of René Millet in 1894 brought a sympathizer with the
reformist strain of Islam to the office of resident general. Millet reinforced
the status of the men associated with *al-Hadira* as the most apt interlocutors between Western and Arab-Islamic culture by discussing with them
their expectations as summarized in an article that appeared on his arrival.
He indicated his broad support for their objectives, which addressed the
issues of greatest concern to urban, educated Tunisians: the respect of the

protectorate authorities for Muslim practices and institutions, the engagement of Muslims in government service, the expansion of public education, and the institution of tariffs to protect domestic craftsmen. He further encouraged the reformers to explore additional methods of disseminating their message. In 1896 Sfar and Muhammad Lasram took the lead in founding the Khalduniyya, an educational society that opened a window to the West for Arabic-speaking Tunisians. With the goal of "expanding among Muslims a taste for the sciences . . . destroy[ing] once for all their prejudices and . . . open[ing] to them, in the practical and commercial domain, many horizons which were totally unknown,"[28] its members offered free instruction in a variety of subjects not taught in the Islamic schools. Any Tunisian could study at the Khalduniyya, but the organization made a special effort to attract students from the Zaituna mosque-university, where a highly traditional Islamic curriculum remained in place. As one of the few venues where young men from the different school systems interacted, the Khalduniyya focused not on building bridges between Tunisians and Europeans but on familiarizing Tunisians of divergent educational backgrounds with each other.

Millet's positive approach to Tunisians prepared to reach an accommodation with the government under certain circumstances distressed the *colons*, who deemed the competition for political and economic power in the protectorate a zero sum game. By the turn of the century, Western-educated Tunisians represented a threat to settler hegemony. Despite their modest numbers – in any given year between 1885 and 1900, less than 0.5 percent of the Tunisian population attended a school with a Western curriculum, while only about 3 percent of the entire Tunisian population in 1900 had ever followed such a course of studies – they induced a splenetic rage among the many settlers who abhorred the thought of educating the colonized population. They insisted that Tunisian children did not belong in the Franco-Arab schools, where they slowed the progress of European students, but should learn only the skills needed for employment as agricultural workers on *colon* properties.

Victor de Canières, the publisher of *La Tunisie Française*, the journalistic voice of extremist settler opinion from 1892 until the 1950s, insisted upon the limitations of the Tunisians, who were, "after all, just Arabs." Misguided French officials who believed that "Arabs are men like any others and ought to have rights equal to those of the French," failed to understand that "they constitute a race that a depressing religion and a long atavism of laziness and fatalism have rendered manifestly inferior."[29] Modern education raised Tunisians' expectations and even promoted competition for certain kinds of jobs between them and settlers at the lower end of the economic ladder. Their expectations could obviously not be fulfilled at the European population's expense, but ignoring them ensured Tunisian enmity. "... [S]cholarly familiarity kills the respect," thundered de Canières, "without which hundreds of *colons* embedded in the midst of a hostile population cannot enjoy full security."[30] Educating Tunisians simply endangered the privileged position the settlers had monopolized since the start of the protectorate. These views could not have been at greater variance with the thinking of leading figures in the Directorate of Public Instruction, as a comment by the headmaster of Alaoui College clearly revealed. While harboring no doubts about the superiority of his own culture, he bemoaned the inability of so many of his compatriots to appreciate that they lived

in the midst of a civilization – other than ours, it is true; let us hasten to add, inferior to ours . . . but, in a word, a civilization. Let the burnous and the chechia not create any illusion: it is with very cultivated people that we have business here.[31]

In this fundamental policy disagreement, the *colons* prevailed, persuading the ministry of foreign affairs to order the protectorate to scale back education for Tunisians. Reluctantly, between 1898 and 1901 the Directorate of Public Instruction closed ten Franco-Arab schools that had only a few French students. For the first time since the inauguration of the system more than a decade earlier, Tunisian enrollments declined steadily over the same period. The directorate responded to another aspect of the settlers' educational agenda by establishing a vocational school in 1898. Most of its students were European, however, and those Tunisians who did attend were pushed into training as traditional craftsmen rather than receiving an opportunity to learn more modern, and better remunerated, skills.

The *colons'* success in this campaign demonstrated their effectiveness in articulating a shared perception, presenting it with conviction and persistence, and pressuring key organs of government to accept it. *La Tunisie Française* played an important part in this process, as did the settlers' participation in the Consultative Conference, a body formed in 1892 to advise the resident general, principally on budgetary matters. Originally consisting of two colleges that were extensions of the settlers' chambers of agriculture and commerce, the Conference expanded to include a third, for government officials and members of the liberal professions, in 1896. Although it had no power to legislate, and could not compel the resident general to follow its recommendations, the Conference afforded a forum for the airing of *colon* opinions and grievances. Tunisians had no parallel official forum, nor were any appointed to the Consultative Conference for more than a decade.

In 1907, the addition of sixteen Tunisians brought the total membership of the Conference to fifty-two. Even this obvious under-representation of Tunisians (30 percent of the Conference as opposed to more than 90 percent of the total population) incensed the settler delegates, who succeeded in segregating the Tunisians in 1910 by recasting the Conference's three chambers into two, one for the "natives," the other for the French *prépondérants*.

The curtailing of educational opportunities for Muslims, which the reformers had always seen as a *sine qua non* for the society they envisaged, profoundly disappointed and frustrated them. Their encounters with widespread and overt racism compelled them to acknowledge that the settlers would never accept them as equals, no matter how far down the road to assimilation they traveled, simply because of their "otherness." Their confidence in both the will and the ability of protectorate authorities to persevere in implementing policies that improved the lot of Tunisians also diminished. Even specialists like Macheul answered to Parisian ministries that came under intense pressure from colonial lobbyists whose ear the Tunisian settlers had. Western educations detached Tunisians from the mainstream of their society and underscored their minority status. As a result, they risked falling between two stools, credible neither to their fellow Tunisians nor to the Europeans. Finally, as they took stock of the setbacks to their agenda, they realized that similar, and even more tragic, misfortunes had befallen many of their countrymen in the 1890s. For years, the reformers had focused on articulating the desires of the urban educated class, downplaying criticisms of the government to stay in its good graces, but the devastatingly pervasive effects of "official" colonization and all that had followed from it could no longer be ignored.

These realities encouraged the reformers to adopt a more aggressive, more political position, and one with a broader outlook. In the transition from advocacy of social change to engagement in political activism, Bashir Sfar, who had already crossed swords with the French over the sale of *habus* land, led the way. In a 1906 speech he called attention to the pauperization of Tunisian society, noting that the quality of virtually all Tunisians' lives had deteriorated in the quarter-century of French control. To reverse this trend, Sfar demanded that the government introduce measures protecting rural land from the grasp of the settlers, reviving artisanal production but also developing new industries, and expanding the number of academic, vocational, and agricultural schools for Tunisians.

Later that year, Sfar's Khalduniyya colleague Muhammad Lasram embarked on the first of three endeavors to publicize the reformers' views to a more extensive audience when he spoke before the Congrès Colonial in Marseille. Appealing to the French to treat Tunisians as equals, not subordinates, he emphasized the imperative of building an education system that prepared Tunisians for the widest possible range of employment, not merely to work as "interpreters for the police or subaltern agents of the administration."[32] Lasram assured his listeners that he and his associates were not calling for the end of the protectorate, but only that its administrators redirect their attention to their original charge of implementing beneficial reforms. With that in mind, he advocated the association of French and Tunisian citizens in a genuine partnership putting the genius of both to work for the development of the country, while acknowledging that important differences of perspective and interest separated the two peoples. Authorizing Tunisians to sit in the Consultative Conference constituted, in Lasram's view, the most logical initial step towards engaging them in public life.

The reformers took advantage of the 1908 Congrès de l'Afrique du Nord in Paris to communicate for a second time with an audience drawn from France and its dependencies. No fewer than six prominent figures in the movement now widely referred to as the "Young Tunisians" addressed the congress. They hammered away at familiar themes and unveiled new initiatives, including one to replace the *majba* with a universally applied levy assessed on ability to pay. This time, however, de Canières and other *colons* were in attendance, and their public derision of the Tunisians sparked a verbal brawl. The disgusted response of one Tunisian to the settlers' defense of "official" colonization epitomizes the feeling of bitterness and futility that enveloped the entire delegation.

No doubt you wish to drive us back to the zone where scarcely any rain falls. Go and colonize it yourselves: you have the financial means and technical knowledge to modify its hydraulic regime.[33]

The third example of the Young Tunisians placing their ideas before new audiences was the publication, beginning in 1907, of *Le Tunisien*. In this instance, however, a new type of activist presented the message. The newspaper's editor, thirty-one-year-old ʿAli Bash Hamba, was the product of an exclusively Western education, culminating with a French law degree. He showed little interest in the *Salafiyya* precepts that had influenced his older colleagues, deriving his inspiration from the ideology of pan-Islam and the campaign of the Young Turks (whose intellectual backgrounds so closely resembled his own) to breathe new life into the Ottoman Empire (whose moribund condition so closely resembled his country's). Bash Hamba wanted to explain the Young Tunisians' objectives directly, and in their own language, to French centrists and leftists – the right-wing *colons* immediately dismissed the paper as "dogmatic . . . a screen behind which war against the French is prepared"[34] – in order to correct misunderstandings about the movement, assuage concerns, and perhaps even win allies. The strategy met with very limited success, but *Le Tunisien* did fill an important niche by giving bilingual Tunisian sympathizers of the movement news and information presented with a far more secular and cosmopolitan outlook than that of *al-Hadira*. To make the same perspective available to all literate Tunisians, Bash Hamba supplemented *Le Tunisien* with an Arabic counterpart, *al-Tunisi*, in 1909. Its editor, ᶜAbd al-ᶜAziz Thaᶜalbi, was an atypical graduate of the Zaituna mosque-university whose modernist and controversial views had involved him in several clashes with the establishment ulama.

The divergence of viewpoint between Bash Hamba and the *al-Hadira* group reflected the influence of the Khair al-Din era on the first generation of reformers and the impact of education under the protectorate on the second. The activity of an alumni association that Bash Hamba helped to create at Sadiqi College in 1905 further manifests this difference. A key objective of the Association des Anciens Elèves du Collège Sadiqi was to advocate the transformation of the school into a genuine lycée on the French model. Five years later, their efforts resulted in government approval of a major curriculum revision that far better equipped Sadiqi students to pursue higher education leading to a career in the liberal professions. The organization also sponsored public classes similar to those at the Khalduniyya. But in contrast to its predecessor's philosophy of fostering the coexistence of traditional Islamic and modern educations, the Association des Anciens Elèves focused on instruction that subordinated the former to the latter, in keeping with the school's evolving course of studies. Bash Hamba's high profile meant that when the government named Bashir Sfar to a post in Sousse in 1908 (primarily to remove him from the hub of Young Tunisian activity in the capital), the editor of *Le Tunisien* effectively assumed the leadership of the movement.

Virtually all of the Young Tunisians came from *baldiyya* families in Tunis or their counterparts in provincial cities. This shared social background underscores the importance of different educational experiences in accounting for their varied assessments of the centrality of *Salafiyya* principles to their objectives. The Young Tunisians' bourgeois origins inevitably distanced them from the bulk of the population. Although they began to close that gap to some degree after 1906, the concepts of appealing directly to a mass audience or mobilizing popular demonstrations in support of their demands remained alien to them until the closing days of their activities. Nor could most of them ever bring themselves to endorse measures potentially harmful to the class with which they identified. A case in point was the dissipation of Young Tunisian support for tax reforms that they themselves had sought once they realized that the Directorate of Finance's proposed solution, while easing the plight of the most impoverished of their countrymen, had costly consequences for the more prosperous.

Despite his secular education and modern outlook, Bash Hamba never lost sight of the importance of positioning the Young Tunisians as defenders of the traditional Muslim social and cultural values that continued to form the core of most of his countrymen's lives. This image sat well with the Tunisian public, but it also had the advantage of making it difficult for the non-Muslim protectorate authorities or the conservative ulama to criticize the movement. In 1911 Bash Hamba invoked a combination of contemporary pan-Islamic political rhetoric and traditional concepts of Muslim identity to raise money and collect supplies to support the resistance of the people of neighboring Tripolitania to Italy's invasion. Amidst the fervor generated by this solidarity campaign, an incident in Tunis, at the Muslim cemetery of Jellaz, seemed to reveal a threat to Islam much closer to home.

The municipal council had scheduled a survey of the cemetery for autumn 1911, but abandoned the plan when ᶜAbd al-Jalil Zaouche, a council member and prominent Young Tunisian, warned of Muslims' resentment at such an intrusion. Although word of the impending survey had spread through the city, the news of its cancellation did not, and a crowd gathered at Jellaz on the appointed day. After clashes between the protesters and the police, French soldiers, brought in as reinforcements, opened fire on the demonstrators and drove them into a nearby Italian quarter. Shooting from houses there touched off a riot that left dozens of Europeans and Tunisians dead.[35] French officials strongly suspected the Young Tunisians of orchestrating this outbreak of urban mob violence – the first of its kind, and a terrifying event for *colons* and protectorate officials alike. Bash Hamba's journalistic and oratorical exploitation of European infringements on Islamic sensibilities undoubtedly inspired some protesters, but he had not yet decided to advance his agenda by popular recruitment. Despite a dogged attempt by French investigators to link the Young Tunisians to the Jellaz events, none of the thirty-five men found guilty of participating in the riots held leadership positions in the movement.

Tunisian antipathy towards Italians, already quite strong owing to the competition between them for jobs, escalated after the Jellaz incident and increased still further a few months later, when an Italian streetcar driver ran down a Tunisian child. Bash Hamba took advantage of the public's acute outrage to plunge, at last, into broad political mobilization by organizing a boycott of the city transportation system. Two conditions for its termination – limiting employment on the streetcars to French and Tunisian staff and adopting an equal pay for equal work rule – directly concerned the system's workers, but a third – the election rather than appointment of the Tunisian members of the Consultative Conference – had a far broader political thrust. Protectorate officials who had supported the early *Salafiyya* reformers and then the Young Tunisians regarded the strike as a betrayal. More worryingly, Bash Hamba's success in galvanizing the previously inert masses contained within it the germ of full-scale rebellion, and the government ordered an immediate end to the boycott. The Young Tunisians refused to give in until their demands were met, but after a month of defying the authorities Bash Hamba, Tha'albi, and Hassan Guellaty, all of whom had been instrumental in mounting and sustaining the boycott, were arrested and expelled from the country. Several other key organizers were sent to internal exile in the southern town of Medenine.

Decapitated before belated efforts to broaden its base had produced an entity strong enough to survive such a loss, the Young Tunisian movement never recovered from this blow. The state of emergency imposed by the nervous government, and kept in place until 1920, prevented the appearance of any new leadership cadre. French officials, thwarted in their efforts to reconcile Tunisians to the protectorate through the mediation of elites with modern educations, executed an about-face in the aftermath of the Jellaz incident and the streetcar strike. Although they had little use for the conservative, and in their view retrograde, ulama, they quickly began to cultivate them lest public sympathy for the Young Tunisians push the religious leadership into opposition to the protectorate. The ulama naturally welcomed this attention, as they did the apparent failure of their nemeses, the reformers. When the Ottoman sultan urged a jihad against the Allies at the start of World War I, the Tunisian ulama's expressions of loyalty to France neutralized the appeal from distant Istanbul. Despite the dispatch of many French troops to the front, the forces that remained suppressed the single serious incidence of opposition during the war, a tribal uprising in the south. Tunis, which the Young Tunisians had threatened to turn into a battleground, remained calm, but it was the calm before the storm. By the end of the war, Sfar and Bash Hamba were dead, but Tha'albi, Guellaty, and their comrades in exile were reassembling in Tunis, reenergizing old networks of sympathizers, and awaiting an opportune moment to return to the political arena.

CHAPTER 3

Squaring off, 1912–1940

Their pan-Islamic sentiments and affinity with the Young Turks made Istanbul a logical place of refuge for many Young Tunisian exiles, but they regarded the Ottoman capital as merely a temporary haven. They were anxious to return to Tunisia at the earliest opportunity in order to continue their drive to reform the protectorate. Those who still resided in Istanbul at the outbreak of World War I contributed to the Ottoman and German war effort, often by writing anti-French propaganda. They hoped that the victory of the Central Powers would strip France of its North African holdings, enabling Tunisia to reclaim its earlier political identity as an autonomous region of the Ottoman Empire. Another group of Tunisians, led by Muhammad Bash Hamba, ʿAli's brother, spent the war in Switzerland, where they published the political journal *La Revue du Maghreb* from 1916 to 1918. Bash Hamba warned that by crushing the Young Tunisian movement in 1912, France had destroyed any prospect of a fruitful association between Muslims and Europeans. Without such collaboration, future stability would hinge on the promulgation of a constitution explicitly defining the powers of the protectorate and the rights of Tunisian citizens. As the likelihood of an Allied victory increased, *La Revue du Maghreb*, basing itself on the concept of self-determination included in Woodrow Wilson's Fourteen Points, called for a postwar referendum to determine the political future of Tunisia. At the same time, the paper also encouraged the Young Tunisians to make use of the impending peace conference as a forum for presenting their grievances.

With the defeat of Germany and the collapse of the Ottoman Empire, Tunisians who had cast in their lot with the Central Powers or who had taken advantage of the war to try to shift the political agenda from reforming the protectorate to ending it had neither financial support nor political alternatives. The activity of the expatriates ground to a halt in early 1919, after two formal appeals to address the peace commissioners fell on deaf ears. In reality, their wartime efforts had almost no impact in Tunisia, since the protectorate authorities invoked their exceptional powers under the state of emergency to block the importation of *La Revue du Maghreb* and other publications they judged inflammatory. Perhaps even more to the point, however, a wave of prosperity swept over Tunisia during the war years, severely blunting the appeal of anticolonial rhetoric.

The departure of French citizens for military service benefited Tunisians in every region of the country and every sector of the economy. Because the government took very little property for "official" colonization during the war, peasant and tribal fears of losing their land eased for the first time since the 1890s. Moreover, some 80,000 hectares of existing *colon* farmland went on sale when its conscripted owners were unable to work it or meet mortgage payments. Tunisians, many of them middle-class urban merchants whose enterprises had flourished when their French competitors were drafted, acquired almost three-quarters of this land. They invested the increased profits of their businesses in mechanizing their farms and employing other modern techniques that enhanced productivity. Italians purchased another 15,000 hectares of the forfeited land, planting most of it with vineyards that strengthened their dominance over viticulture.[1] The combination of high agricultural prices attributable to shortages in Europe and a succession of remarkably good harvests during the war years brought farmers in the protectorate substantial profits that more than offset the increased cost of living.

In the cities, lawyers and other professionals, many of them former Young Tunisian activists, expanded their practices as their French counterparts left for the front. The unprecedented levels of personal success they enjoyed during the war diverted their attention from political issues and contributed to a damping down of expressions of anti-protectorate sentiment. The disruption of imports from Europe provided a much needed boost for craftsmen, as did the rising fortunes of the rural areas on which they depended for both suppliers and customers. Unemployment, which had long plagued unskilled and semi-skilled Tunisian laborers, ended as they moved into jobs vacated by conscripted working-class settlers and others in new industries created to manufacture commodities previously imported. The shortage of labor assured them of higher wages than they had earned in the past.

In contrast to their countrymen who remained at home and prospered as a result of the war, 80,000 Tunisians served in the French army. With some exceptions based on educational level and family status, Tunisian young men were subject to conscription, which accounted for more than 85 percent of these Tunisian troops. Most of them went to the Western Front, where 20,000 lost their lives or were wounded. Another 5,000 fatalities occurred among Tunisian troops assigned to Morocco and Syria. In addition to those in combat and support units, 15,000 conscripts and an equal number of volunteers worked in France, on farms, in mines, and in factories, where they took the place of French workers serving in the armed forces.[2] Tunisians welcomed the 1917 promise of Prime Minister Georges Clemenceau that France would remember and reward the sacrifices made by the people of its dependencies when the war had been won.

In view of this pledge, the dramatic deterioration of the economy in 1919 and 1920 angered many Tunisians. Imports soared as French industries aggressively sought to recover their prewar markets, much to the detriment of local producers and businessmen. This resurgence of imports, aggravated by inflation, prolonged an upward trend in consumer prices that had had little effect in the midst of wartime prosperity, but caused great hardship as the economy faltered. An array of new taxes to support an ambitious program of infrastructural development, including building dams, roads, and new railway lines, imposed a similar burden. These levies weighed heavily on Tunisians from all walks of life, although the settlers had the most to gain from the projects they financed. Perhaps the most galling use of tax revenues, however, was the payment of the "colonial third," a salary supplement first given to French officials in 1919. By making employment in the protectorate administration more attractive to Frenchmen, it reduced the number of posts available to Tunisians, even as it widened an already significant gap between the compensation of French and Tunisian employees of the protectorate.

The return of demobilized *colons* cost Tunisian merchants their privileged position in commerce and Tunisian workers their jobs precisely at a time when each group could least afford such a blow. Tunisian veterans found the state of affairs that greeted them on their homecoming particularly reprehensible. Their discontent contributed to the politicization of their families, neighbors, and fellow workers, all of whom regarded postwar conditions in the protectorate as poor recompense for the misery their countrymen had endured for the sake of France. Strikes and popular demonstrations erupted in Tunis and a few provincial cities on several occasions in 1919 and 1920. To compound the country's woes still further, dreadful harvests in those two years brought famine and disease in their wake.

As the protectorate's most valuable resource, agricultural land remained a bone of contention in the difficult days following the war. With much of its own farmland devastated, France expected Algeria, Tunisia, and Morocco (which had become a protectorate in 1912) to supply more of its food needs than ever before. In 1920, as he was preparing to leave office, Resident General Etienne Flandin (1918–20) issued a directive calling for the cultivation of all unplanted arable land. In no mood for charity to France, Tunisians judged Flandin's initiative as nothing more than a ploy to gain control of those *habus* lands still beyond the protectorate's grasp, in furtherance of its intention to revive "official" colonization. The allocation to land purchases of some 10 percent of a loan of 255 million francs contracted by the government in 1920,[3] with most of the rest earmarked for the augmentation of the rural infrastructure, reinforced their assessment.

THE DUSTUR

Amid universal disgust with economic conditions, and inspired by events that they interpreted as presaging a new era for colonized people – the Paris Peace Conference and the Fourteen Points, Egyptians' campaign for independence from Britain, and Italy's promise to install a liberal, representative political system in Tripolitania and Cyrenaica (which, in fact, it never implemented) – the Young Tunisians reorganized. Resident General Gabriel Alapetite (1906–18) had permitted ᶜAbd al-ᶜAziz Thaᶜalbi to reenter Tunisia even before the war had begun. Other exiles who had kept their distance from the Central Powers were authorized to return in late 1918 and early 1919; those confined within Tunisia received their liberty at the same time. In March 1919, Khairallah ben Mustafa, who had worked at *Le Tunisien*, convened a meeting to consider the adaptation of prewar activism to postwar circumstances. Encouraged by the attendance of several dozen persons, he, Thaᶜalbi, Hassan Guellaty, and Ahmad al-Safi established the Parti Tunisien. The party attracted young men eager to seize the place in shaping Tunisia's future to which they believed their Western education entitled them, but it also appealed to those who feared that their traditional training, once the hallmark of the cream of society, would now make it difficult for them to figure in the same process. Recalling a demand enunciated in *La Revue du Maghreb*, Thaᶜalbi struck a note that resonated with both groups and focused the party on its key goal: the promulgation of a constitution. The widespread conviction that France's role in the collapse of the postwar economy represented a monstrous injustice in view of its debt to Tunisians for their war services, as well as the absence of other vehicles of protest, expanded the party's potential audience well beyond the Tunis bourgeoisie who participated in its creation.

When their petition for an audience with the peace commissioners elicited no response, party leaders chose the French left as an alternative milieu for the presentation of their protests. At their request, Ahmad Sakka, a lawyer familiar with leftist circles, moved to Paris in April. Before joining him in the summer, Tha‘albi pored over Young Tunisian documents dating as far back as the 1908 Congrès de l'Afrique du Nord. He concluded that events since 1912 had invalidated the moderate positions of an earlier time and asked his associates to develop a tougher position for his and Sakka's mission to take. Thus armed, the two Tunisians courted Parisian liberal opinion in the autumn, encountering sympathy but making little political headway. The major achievement of their stay was the anonymous publication, at the end of 1919, of *La Tunisie Martyre*, a diatribe drawing heavily on the material developed in Tunis, but even less accommodating. Tha‘albi subsequently claimed sole authorship of the book, ignoring the invaluable work of his collaborators in Tunis and the crucial contribution of Sakka, who knew French far better than the Zaituna-educated Tha‘albi.[4]

La Tunisie Martyre handed down an unqualified indictment of the protectorate administration. By contrasting an array of specific social, economic, and political conditions before and after the inauguration of the protectorate, the book purported to demonstrate the willful destruction of a prosperous, progressive society experiencing a "golden age" made possible by the ‘Ahd al-Aman and the 1861 Constitution. Ending the abuses introduced by the protectorate required restoring an organic law originally passed in the nineteenth century. The book stopped short of making the politically unrealizable demand for the termination of the protectorate, but it did denounce cooperation with its administration as treasonous, thereby definitively discarding the prewar philosophy of association. As bitter as its invective was, *La Tunisie Martyre* attacked neither France nor the French people, carefully placing the blame for the ills it described on the settlers and officials of the protectorate. Its highly idealized interpretation of the past discredited it in the eyes of all those who knew the realities of the precolonial period and of Tunisians who had benefited from aspects of the French presence, especially educational opportunities. Although a founding member of the Parti Tunisien, one such person, Hassan Guellaty, labeled Tha‘albi's thesis "unjust and maladroit."[5] He and other party moderates also viewed the rejection of cooperation with France as a serious error.

While it was officially banned, hundreds of copies of *La Tunisie Martyre* were smuggled into the protectorate and it soon acquired the status of the quintessential statement of the country's grievances. Among French readers, who were the book's primary target, it had a positive reception only

Figure 3.1. ᶜAbd al-ᶜAziz Thaᶜalbi. The refusal of the Dustur leader to accept the primacy of the young men who bolted from the party and founded the Neo-Dustur in 1934 made him anathema for decades. The 1999 issuing of this postage stamp in his honor indicated his rehabilitation.

among leftists. The limited value of the support available from this quarter was further reduced by a decided swing to the right in the parliamentary elections of 1919. With few effective allies in France or, as the closure of the peace conference with no reference to North Africa showed, anywhere else on the international scene, the redoubling of activity at home assumed critical importance. In February 1920, the Parti Libéral Tunisien supplanted the Parti Tunisien, which had done little more than sponsor the mission of Sakka and Thaᶜalbi. When word of the new party's creation reached Thaᶜalbi in Paris, he urged the inclusion of an additional word in its title, which became Parti Libéral Constitutionnel Tunisien (in Arabic, *al-Hizb al-Dusturi al-Hurr al-Tunisi*), or simply the Dustur (constitution).

The new party differed from the old in more than just name, however. Secretary General Ahmad al-Safi headed an executive committee consisting primarily of government clerks, artisans, progressive ulama, and business-men and land owners (often one and the same after the war). Although some committee members had had some exposure to the French school system, and a handful held degrees from French universities, the Western-educated individuals so prominent in the Young Tunisian movement were less in evidence in the Dustur's leadership cadre. A common thread did, however, run through many of the career patterns represented on the committee: traditionally well respected, they were particularly hard hit by protectorate policies, with their practitioners suffering a dramatic loss of power, income, and prestige. Naturally, they had bridled at the concurrent ascendancy of the Young Tunisians, whom they disdained as upstart social climbers and lapdogs of the French. Through the Dustur they intended to promote polit-ical measures enabling them to hold the line against any further erosion of their status. Residents of the capital dominated the executive committee, but the Dustur broke important new ground by recruiting outside Tunis. Thaᶜalbi's claim of 100,000 members in 1922 undoubtedly exaggerated the strength of the party, but its geographical expansion clearly alarmed the authorities.

As early as 1921, protectorate Secretary General Gabriel Puaux acknowl-edged that he was "frightened by the progress made by the nationalists in the interior in the past year," ominously adding that the time had come "to stop this propaganda."[6] Puaux's "propaganda" consisted of the extremely popular and (as he was among the first French officials to admit) nationalist program Dustur officials had developed from *La Tunisie Martyre*. Its objective was "the emancipation of the Tunisian country from the bonds of slavery"[7] and its core demands included the issuance of a constitution and the formation of a parliament, elected by universal suffrage, with both Tunisian and French representatives, and to which the government answered. The party platform also called for the full access of qualified Tunisians to administrative positions, equal pay for equal work, the popular election of municipal councils, freedom of the press and of association, Tunisians' right to acquire land sold by the state, and the institution of compulsory primary education in Arabic, with instruction in French at higher levels.

To prove that its proposals enjoyed the support of most Tunisians, the Dustur devoted considerable effort to gathering signatures on petitions seeking their enactment. Party leaders hoped to make formal presentations of these appeals, along with copies of the Dustur agenda, to the bey and the resident general in Tunis, and to agents of the government, politicians, and the general public in France. Al-Safi led a delegation to Paris in June 1920, but its visit ended on a thoroughly sour note when Thaᶜalbi was arrested, deported to Tunisia, and imprisoned. In any event, al-Safi and his colleagues had made no progress towards reversing the widely and firmly held conviction that a constitution was not compatible with the protectorate. Even when another Tunisian envoy marshaled sufficient evidence in the following year to persuade two eminent University of Paris jurists to issue a public statement that the constitution and protectorate were not inherently contradictory, the ministry of foreign affairs simply ignored their conclusion, which did, however, help change the opinion of some French socialists and other liberals.

A second delegation, headed by a Dustur moderate, Tahar ben ᶜAmmar, secured a meeting in December 1920 with officials of the ministry of foreign affairs, including the recently appointed resident general, Lucien Saint (1920–9). The session seemed, in itself, a significant achievement, especially in view of growing *colon* insistence on curbing the Dustur, which they persistently conflated with international communism. However, only a few weeks later Saint expressed his definitive refusal to sanction a parliament, although he did promise to take other steps to improve relations with the nationalists. Shortly afterwards, the state of emergency in effect since 1912 was terminated and Thaᶜalbi was released from prison. However much the party may have welcomed these actions, they did not address its key demands.

Dustur efforts to woo the bey succeeded far better than their overtures to the French. In an audience with Nasir Bey (1906–22) in June 1920, party leaders outlined their position and assured him of their loyalty. Gauging the monarch's role in the political system envisioned by the Dustur as more substantial than his current ineffectual status, Nasir encouraged his interlocutors. Protectorate administrators took a dim view of the linkage between the nationalists and the bey, with the particularly apprehensive Puaux encouraging Saint to deal sternly with Nasir. So long as the bey did not overplay his hand, however, Saint preferred to concentrate on undermining the Dustur.

Accordingly, he welcomed Hassan Guellaty's decision to break with the Dustur mainstream and found the Parti Réformiste in early 1921. Guellaty harbored a visceral resentment of Thaᶜalbi, whose provocative polemics had driven a wedge between the French and moderate Tunisians, such as himself, who clung to the prewar notions of association and collaboration. Behind this disagreement over political tactics lay the highly Westernized Guellaty's arrogant confidence in his superiority to the likes of Thaᶜalbi, whose more modest social and more traditional educational background did not (in his view) equip them to grasp the complexities of the modern world. Guellaty had no qualms about abandoning the quest for a constitution and parliament that would fundamentally alter the protectorate's political environment in favor of seeking piecemeal concessions that raised the small, Westernized elite to a level of equality with the colonizers. The Dustur caustically dismissed the affiliates of the Parti Réformiste as traitors, but never regarded them as a particularly serious threat, since the sycophancy of the party attracted almost no support among the increasingly radicalized masses. Despite his satisfaction with Guellaty's challenge to the Dustur's political monopoly, Saint had "no illusions about [the party's] value."[8] As the need arose, he pointed to it as evidence of Tunisian acceptance of protectorate policy, but evinced no interest in working with Guellaty in ways that might have broadened his credibility.

The visit of the French president, Alexandre Millerand, in spring 1922 provided an ideal occasion for the resident general to showcase the Parti Réformiste, particularly since he suspected that Dustur leaders were encouraging Nasir Bey to use his meeting with Millerand as an opportunity to acquaint him with the party's program. To make it difficult for Nasir to act on the Dustur's behalf, Saint arranged for a French journalist who interviewed the bey in advance of Millerand's arrival to portray him as a critic of the nationalists. Nasir, who spoke no French and had not approved the content of the interview prior to its publication, threatened to abdicate when he realized what had happened. The Dustur rallied behind the bey, organizing demonstrations in Tunis and at the beylical palace in La Marsa. Buoyed by this expression of his subjects' support, Nasir prepared to confront the resident general.

When they met, the bey offered to remain on the throne if Saint agreed to a list of demands based on, but even more far-reaching than, the Dustur's

announced stance. He further insisted on the sacking of Puaux, the aggressive secretary general, and several Tunisian officials whose recent behavior
suggested a stronger loyalty to the French authorities than to the bey. Saint
expressed indignation at Nasir's presentation of an ultimatum, but con-
sented to take the proposals and grievances under advisement. On Saint's
return visit to La Marsa he agreed to the dismissals Nasir had sought but
refused to satisfy the remainder of his conditions. These might remain on
the table, he intimated, but he ordered Nasir to withdraw his abdication
threat. The deployment in the palace grounds of a contingent of French
troops made clear Saint's unwillingness to tolerate a negative response. With
Nasir and the Dustur finessed, Millerand's trip proceeded smoothly and,
thereafter, Saint made no attempt to revisit the bey's demands. This episode
demoralized the Dustur, and Nasir's death a few months later deprived it of
a valuable ally and a symbol of French duplicity. His cousin and successor,
Muhammad al-Habib (1922–29), assured the French, apparently with all
sincerity, that he had no use for the Dustur and no objection to protectorate
administrators taking whatever measures they deemed appropriate to deal
with the party.

As the abdication crisis subsided, the arrest of a number of particularly vocal Dusturians served notice that a resident general with no qualms
about employing the stick in his relations with the bey would not hesitate
to apply it to the nationalists, particularly after Guellaty's defection had
narrowed the Dustur's membership to the most obdurate opponents of the
protectorate. Even so, Saint saw merit in the carrot and, in July 1922, he
announced the creation of elected councils for Tunisians in the *qiyadas* and
the *contrôles civiles* districts that lacked municipal commissions. These bodies made non-binding recommendations on budgetary and other economic
matters, but exercised no legislative authority in any field. They also selected
Tunisian delegates to a Grand Council, which superseded the Consultative Conference and, like its predecessor, consisted of separate French and
Tunisian chambers. Carefully crafted voter qualifications enfranchised primarily local notables and others linked to the government. French delegates
to the Grand Council, unlike the members of the "native section," were
elected directly. Forty-four of them represented the protectorate's 54,000
French citizens (roughly one for every 1,200 settlers); eighteen Tunisians
represented 1,865,000 Muslims and 50,000 Jews (roughly one for every
106,300 persons). The concurrence of the two sections on matters before
them obligated the government to accept their advice, although the French
minister of foreign affairs, on the recommendation of the resident general, held an absolute veto over the Council's decisions. In the more likely

event of a disagreement, the mechanism for resolving the difference insured victory for the French point of view.

Although the protectorate authorities introduced these reforms with great fanfare, they merely gave the appearance of complying with the demand for representation, while producing impotent assemblies incapable of compromising French control. The Parti Réformiste accepted them, but the Dustur did not, urging eligible Tunisians to boycott the elections. Despite the disapproval of party leaders and the obvious shortcomings of the councils, their inauguration provided timid Dusturians, worried about what might happen if, as seemed increasingly likely, the French lost patience, with an excuse to break ranks. Others, craving the forum the councils provided, stood for election. To induce important party members to defect, protectorate officials promised them seats on the Grand Council. Whether precipitated by fear, greed, ambition, or conviction, these desertions devastated the Dustur at a time when even its few French friends were reassessing their support in the belief that Nasir Bey, prodded by the Dustur, had gone too far. Lethargy enveloped all but the most ardent Dusturians. In 1923, Habib Bey and Resident General Saint both pointedly informed Tha'albi that he would be well advised to leave Tunisia if he intended to persist in advocating the rejection of the reforms. Fearing a crackdown reminiscent of 1912, he left for the Middle East. Saint had correctly identified Tha'albi as a central figure in the Dustur, but just as his presence failed to energize the party after the abdication crisis, his absence also had little effect. Al-Safi and the assistant secretary-general, Salah Farhat, kept the Dustur afloat at home and tried to regain support in France.

The Morinaud Law (1923) and the emergence of a Tunisian labor union, the Confédération Générale des Travailleurs Tunsiens (1924), provided the Dustur with fresh ammunition against the protectorate, while the advent of a left-wing coalition government in Paris (1924) held out the hope of a sympathetic hearing in France. Implicitly aimed at the Italian population of the protectorate, which in the 1920s outnumbered the French by two to one, the Morinaud Law facilitated the naturalization of non-French residents of Tunisia. Since 1921, children born in Tunisia to non-French European parents automatically received French citizenship, but this legislation enabled any foreigner to claim French citizenship after three years of residence. It also eased some of the restrictions on, and lowered the educational requirements for, the naturalization of Tunisians, although few Tunisian Muslims ever showed any interest in taking this step, which removed them from the jurisdiction of the sharia. During the 1920s about 10,000 Italians (10 percent of that community) and 5,000 Tunisian Jews (a comparable 10 percent) opted

for French citizenship, whereas only 1,000 Tunisian Muslims (fewer than
0.5 percent of their total number) made the same choice.[9] Most of those
who did were government employees eager to increase their incomes with
the "colonial third" or to gain access to positions available only to French
citizens. Despite the Morinaud Law's minimal impact on Tunisians, the
foundering Dustur seized upon it, condemning its intentions to assimi-
late the protectorate to France, marginalize Tunisians further by endowing
foreigners with privileges enjoyed by the French but denied to them, and
undermine Islam.

Declining membership in the party and a government ban on fund-
raising, imposed after the rejection of the 1922 reforms, made financing
this campaign a challenge. But the leadership regarded it as crucial to the
Dustur's revitalization and developed a novel approach to raising money
and, at the same time, spreading their message. Most Tunisian actors and
playwrights had begun their careers in the five or six years prior to the
war, when members of the Young Tunisian movement were among the
few Tunisians drawn to the theatre. Hassan Guellaty and ᶜAbd al-ᶜAziz
Thaᶜalbi had served on the board of directors of al-Adab al-ᶜArabiyya (Arab
Culture), a troupe that flourished at that time. Both men envisioned the
stage as a vehicle not only for entertainment, but also for the expression
of political views and public edification, and both remained involved with
the theatre until political activities became their full-time pursuits. One
of the most successful plays in al-Adab al-ᶜArabiyya's post-war repertoire
was *Huwa Am!* (*What a Year!*), which reminded audiences of the suffering
visited on Tunisia by the war. In 1922 the troupe merged with another
established Tunis company, al-Shahama al-ᶜArabiyya (Arab Pride), whose
European board members had resigned rather than agree to a program
with political overtones, to form al-Tamthil al-ᶜArabi (The Arab Theatre).[10]
It was to sympathizers and party faithful affiliated with these, and other
smaller troupes, that the Dustur executive committee appealed in 1923,
asking them to stage benefit performances for the party, particularly of
productions that emphasized Tunisia's Arab-Islamic identity and history –
concepts that reflected the party's philosophy and underscored its criticisms
of naturalization in an indirect way that avoided confrontation with the
government.

As high-level Dustur leaders made use of the decidedly bourgeois
medium of the theatre, a few party members were developing connections with working-class Tunisians. One such activist, M'hammed ᶜAli,
spent much of 1924 organizing consumer cooperatives as tools for fighting
poverty and winning support for the party in the lower-class neighborhoods

that remained a mystery to most Dusturians, few of whom interacted with workers or understood their problems. In that same summer, the refusal of European longshoremen to endorse their Tunisian coworkers' demands for wage parity, despite their common affiliation with the French Confédération Générale du Travail (CGT), exemplified the kind of discrimination Tunisian workers faced, even in a socialist union. The Morinaud Law aggravated this particular situation. By facilitating the naturalization of Italian and Maltese workers and, consequently, their acquisition of salaries and working conditions comparable to those of other French citizens, it deprived Tunisian laborers, now the sole victims of a two-tier system, of potential allies in the workforce.

Since the Dustur, and the Young Tunisians before it, advocated equal pay for equal work, the isolated longshoremen turned to the party for help. M'hammed ᶜAli saw their appeal as an opportunity to strengthen the links he had begun forging between workers and the nationalist movement. More with an eye towards the usefulness of large numbers of workers in bringing pressure to bear on the protectorate than from any sense of solidarity with their cause, the Dustur leaders supported M'hammed ᶜAli's decision to make the striking dockworkers the core of a new Tunisian union, the Confédération Générale des Travailleurs Tunisiens (CGTT). Along with M'hammed ᶜAli, a handful of Dustur radicals and several Tunisians prominent in the Parti Communiste Tunisien (PCT) played leading roles in organizing the new union, which very quickly drained almost all Tunisian workers away from the CGT. During late 1924 and early 1925 the CGTT orchestrated a wave of strikes in Tunis, Bizerte, and Sfax, but in February the authorities determined to halt the unrest by crushing the union. The CGTT leaders were arrested and the nascent labor movement collapsed.

The Dustur made no effort to sustain the CGTT, from which it had, for a variety of reasons, begun to distance itself well before the repression. Taking their own generally docile and circumspect approach of dispatching delegations and presenting petitions as the most suitable form of political activism, party leaders considered the confrontational tactics of the union – noisy street demonstrations and strikes, both of which often ended in violent clashes with the police – as vulgar and dangerously provocative. Unlike CGTT activists, whose prison sentences became badges of honor, the prospect of incarceration intimidated most Dusturians, who saw it only as a shameful and humiliating experience to be avoided. In working with the PCT to develop the CGTT, M'hammed ᶜAli had provided ammunition to Dustur critics who had tried, since the party's creation, to discredit it by demonstrating a link between it and the communist movement. Until

1924, the Dustur had kept its distance from the PCT, while the communists were, in turn, contemptuous of leading Dusturians, whom they regarded as ineffectual, arrogant, and out of touch with the true sentiments of ordinary Tunisians. In the hands of Resident General Saint, evidence of Dustur–PCT collaboration in the emergence of the CGTT could prove extremely damaging, if not fatal.

Apart from these powerful anxieties, Dustur hopes of cultivating allies in France also pushed it away from the union. The victory of a leftist coalition in French parliamentary elections in 1924 brought to office politicians whose beliefs and values might be expected to incline them to give the party's program a sympathetic hearing. But the Dustur's enemies in Tunisia sabotaged its attempts to open lines of communication. Habib Bey, Saint and other protectorate officials, and spokespersons of the settlers all hastened to warn the new government in Paris that Dustur claims of moderation and its recent acceptance of the 1922 reforms as an initial step towards reaching their goals were a smokescreen camouflaging the party's unwavering hostility to the protectorate. In the face of so concerted a campaign to malign it, one way for the Dustur to demonstrate its receptivity to dialogue and cooperation was to disassociate itself from extremists like the communists, which it unequivocally did, and the CGTT, on which it turned its back without directly denouncing it. Thus the party's abandonment of the union made a virtue – portraying itself to potential supporters in France as an organization eschewing radicalism – out of the necessity of adopting a position that safeguarded it against being swept up in the union's destruction. As further evidence of its restraint, the Dustur joined French socialists living in Tunisia, as well as the Parti Réformiste and Tunisian members of the Grand Council, both of which groups it had previously denounced as traitors, in a moderate political bloc promoting structural reforms in the protectorate. In the end, however, this expedient came to naught.

French Prime Minister Edouard Herriot convened a Consultative Commission for the Study of Tunisian Reforms, but the appointment of Resident General Saint as chair of a key subcommittee insured that its work would result in no substantive changes. When the commission released its proposals in March 1925, the Dustur, the Parti Réformiste, and the Socialists all dismissed them as superficial and tangential to the most pressing political issues in the protectorate. Disillusioned Dusturians realized that they had left the CGTT, with its potential for greatly enhancing the strength of the party, in the lurch, in return for a slap in the face from Paris. Embittered and embarrassed, Dustur leaders reacted in predictable ways, but the impact on the party of M'hammed ᶜAli, his creation (the CGTT), and his following (the working class) gave the round of protests that followed a more highly charged atmosphere than ever before.

During spring and summer 1925, crowds of nationalists regularly took to the streets of Tunis in imitation of the belligerent tactics of the CGTT. In the autumn, the sentencing of the union organizers and the unveiling of a statue marking the centenary of the birth of Cardinal Lavigerie, roundly despised by Tunisians for his missionary efforts, set the stage for particularly raucous scenes. Given the furor over the Morinaud Law, which had revived when the bill's sponsor visited Tunis earlier in the year and encouraged Jews to adopt French citizenship, paying homage to a colonial figure committed to converting Muslims to Christianity inevitably offended public opinion. The stodgy Dustur leaders were coming to recognize the lower-class Tunisians who swelled the ranks of these demonstrations as an asset, but they remained uncomfortable interacting with them. As a result, they exercised less and less control over the protests, even as their frequency, magnitude, and virulence increased.

Other aspects of the Dustur's strategy also changed during 1925. No longer did it focus on persuading the French that its case had merit. Instead, it lashed out at its enemies, determined to extract a price for their refusal to satisfy Dustur demands. In speeches and newspaper articles, party leaders expressed support for anti-French movements elsewhere in the Arab world, most notably those of ᶜAbd al-Krim in Morocco and the Syrian nationalists. This particularly galled the French authorities. When Ahmad Tawfiq al-Madani, a distinguished intellectual and member of the Dustur executive committee, arranged for al-Saᶜada (Good Fortune), a theatrical company with which he was affiliated, to produce a play about the seventh-century hero of the Arab conquest of North Africa, Tariq ibn Ziyad, that was actually a thinly veiled encomium to ᶜAbd al-Krim, they closed the theatre, banned performances of the play, and arrested al-Madani. Its overt enthusiasm for anticolonialists of whatever stripe cost the Dustur the support of the Socialists and the Parti Réformiste, both of which held considerably more nuanced views on the subject of overseas territories. France responded to the radicalization of the Dustur with a campaign of repression that included the arrest of party leaders and participants in the demonstrations, as well as the closure of the Arabic newspapers through which the Dustur spread its views. Only the Parti Communiste Tunisien stood with the Dustur during 1925, but this solidarity only served to reinforce the perception of a connection between the two organizations, such as the French authorities had persistently alleged and the Dustur just as persistently denied.

With the nationalists on the brink of total disarray, Saint moved deci-
sively against them. In January 1926 he issued a series of decrees severely
constraining basic freedoms. The ordinances forbade criticism of French or
Tunisian government officials, whether in public or private; criminalized a
wide range of political activities legal under the existing penal code; transferred all trials involving matters deemed to affect the security of the protectorate to the French courts, regardless of the nationality of the accused; and
brought the French-language press, which had until then escaped restrictions imposed on Arabic newspapers, under close government scrutiny.
The resident general did not foreclose the possibility of future reforms,
but did insist that none could receive consideration before calm had been
restored. Most *colons* applauded Saint's actions, but the liberal minority
among them decried "*les décrets scélérats*" (the villainous decrees), which
impinged on their freedoms no less than on Tunisians'. The Dustur, reel-
ing under the repression that had preceded the decrees, could barely muster
any response to them. Saint had sidelined the party and, although it continued to recruit new adherents, it maintained a low profile for the duration
of his tenure.

In addition to the hostility of the resident general, Dustur leaders confronted new problems within the party after 1926. Tahar Haddad, a professor at the Zaituna mosque-university and a prominent Dustur activist,
wrote *al-ʿUmmal al-tunisiyyun wa zuhur al-harakat al-niqabiyya* (*Tunisian
Workers and the Emergence of the Trade Union Movement*) in 1927. This
wide-ranging essay attacked the growing taste for European goods that had
proven so detrimental to Tunisian craftsmen, but also faulted the Dustur
for its failure to embrace the CGTT and its general lack of interest in the
working class. In the following year Haddad authored a series of articles in
a Tunis journal that were subsequently published as *Imra'tuna fi'l-shariʿa
wa'l-mujtamaʿ* (*Our Women in Islamic Law and Society*). Based on his bold
and innovative interpretation of Qur'anic teachings, he advocated greater
rights for Tunisian women and encouraged them to take a more active
role in public affairs, thus implicitly criticizing the Dustur's tendency to
cling to traditional practices, in this and other matters, merely for their
own sake. Haddad's works irritated party leaders, but their anger paled
in comparison with the rage of Zaituna officials, who labeled Haddad a
heretic and expelled him from the faculty. Nevertheless, the ideas of the
youthful social critic – he was not yet thirty when he wrote these books –
struck a responsive chord with younger Dusturians who were troubled by
the party's docility in the wake of Saint's crackdown.

Many provincial youths with a modern education often capped by a French university degree had joined the Dustur in the 1920s because it was the only viable outlet for political activism. Its lack of success disturbed them, however, and they viewed the post-1926 retrenchment as a surrender in which they were loathe to participate. The personal and professional achievements of these young men flowed from their familiarity and comfort with Western culture and their capacity to function as effectively in such an environment as in their own native milieu. While the Dustur hierarchy yearned for the revival of an idealized past and detested the transformations wrought in Tunisia by the West, the members of this younger generation harbored no such animus – association with the West had, after all, made them what they were – although they took exception to many French policies. Based on their understanding of contemporary political processes and ideologies, frequently gleaned from personal experience in France, they believed that the eventual triumph of the party hinged on more vigorous activism and broadening the movement to include the full spectrum of the Tunisian population.

THE SPLIT IN THE DUSTUR'S RANKS AND THE EMERGENCE OF A NEW PARTY

A nationwide demographic trend gave added weight to the views of this younger generation: in 1930 more than a quarter of Tunisia's population was under twenty-five years of age (an increase of 50 percent in the size of that group since the end of World War I).[11] The expression of reservations about the principles and strategies of the Dustur leadership constituted a subset of this rapidly growing segment of the population's widespread questioning of old norms, not only in the political arena but in virtually every aspect of daily life. The older Dusturians' rigidity and their resistance to accommodating the ideas of the increasingly numerous younger generation within the party's ranks encouraged the latter to push themselves and their ideas to the forefront. A downturn in the economy in the early 1930s and several ill-considered French decisions played into their hands.

The decision of the Catholic Church, with the approval of the French and Tunisian governments, to convene an international Eucharistic Congress at Carthage in May 1930 gave the Dustur mavericks an opportunity to assert themselves. Writing in the party newspaper *La Voix du Tunisien*, men like Habib Bourguiba, a twenty-seven-year-old lawyer who had returned from his studies in France in 1927, condemned as an affront to Tunisia's Muslim personality the celebration on Tunisian soil of a religion they and their countrymen associated with the Crusades and colonialism. Parades of Catholic youths dressed as crusaders, the distribution of pamphlets in Arabic promoting conversion, and the rhetoric of the papal legate, who characterized the Islamic era in North Africa as "fourteen centuries of desolation and death,"[12] revealed congress organizers' ignorance of, and insensitivity to, the very core of Tunisian identity, providing the nationalists with a surfeit of ammunition. In conflating the defense of the nation with the defense of Islam, the militant Dusturians, most of whom were quite secular, put forward a concept with broad mobilization possibilities. Longshoremen launched wildcat strikes as congress participants arrived in Tunis and a protest rally of students from both the Zaituna mosque-university and the elite secular schools – the first such student political alliance – brought opponents of the government into the streets for the first time since 1925.

La Voix du Tunisien also noted economic and political issues raised by the congress. Despite obvious Muslim distaste for the event, the Tunisian government's contribution to its funding of 2,000,000 francs derived primarily from their taxes. This illustration of the ease with which protectorate authorities could sidestep the Grand Council in budgetary matters reinforced the nationalist demands for a constitution and an elected assembly controlling state expenditures. The paper also urged Ahmad II Bey (1929–42) to resign his honorary presidency of the congress and for other Tunisian officials who had lent it their support to distance themselves from it. The leaders of the nationalist campaign claimed that those who ignored this call, including the bey, revealed their subservience to France, abdicating to the Dusturians the role of defenders of Tunisian interests.

Just as the furor over the Eucharistic Congress was subsiding, the commemoration of the fiftieth anniversary of the French presence in 1931 gave Dustur activists a new cause enabling them to sustain the momentum gained in the previous year. In a remarkable repetition of recent errors of judgment, the Tunisian government again allocated substantial sums to an event Tunisians could hardly be expected to applaud, and a high official, this time the French president, Gaston Doumergue, described a period of Tunisian history in terms bound to give offense when he observed that the protectorate had embodied only the highest humanitarian principles. *La Voix du Tunisien* again served as the vehicle for the expression of nationalist anger, but the French attempted to short-circuit this round of protest by arresting several of its most outspoken contributors. The suspension of their trials in the face of public demonstrations appeared to confirm the effectiveness of this tactic, favored by the younger militants but with which their elders remained uncomfortable. Indeed, wary Dustur leaders chastised the activists for putting the movement at risk. Frustrated with the old guard, and anxious to preserve their ability to denounce the authorities, Bourguiba and several of his associates created a paper of their own, *L'Action Tunisienne*, in 1932.

Eager to identify controversies around which it might rally the Tunisian masses, the *Action* group recognized in certain consequences of the Morinaud Law problems they could exploit to the detriment of the protectorate administration. The small number of Tunisian Muslims who had opted for French citizenship had generally been treated as pariahs on the grounds that their abjuration of the sharia amounted to apostasy. For that reason, they were customarily denied burial in Muslim cemeteries. An attempt to contravene this practice in Bizerte in 1932 precipitated a spontaneous protest that thwarted the burial, while another similar interment proceeded only with police intervention. In the hope of preventing an escalation of the situation, Resident General Joseph Manceron (1929–33) instructed the chief Muslim jurists of the capital, the Maliki and Hanafi muftis, to issue a ruling (fatwa) on the subject, but their carefully constructed rationalization satisfied no one.

Portraying the French as again meddling with Islam, and summoning Tunisians to defend the faith that lay at the heart of their identity, Bourguiba and his colleagues assailed both protectorate officials and the collaborationist ulama in the pages of *L'Action*. In a similar vein, other articles and editorials implored readers to ignore French encouragement to abandon traditional forms of dress, including the veil for women, but, instead, to regard such attire as a facet of Tunisia's Arab and Islamic cultural legacy to be safeguarded from colonial subversion. Thus the secular, modern-educated young Dusturian radicals positioned themselves as defenders of religion and tradition – including some traditions, like veiling, that most of them considered backward but which they knew were impervious to assault from any quarter – while the far more traditional, but timid, party leadership, fearful of the repercussions attendant on a bold public stand, hovered ineffectually in the background. The *Action* group alienated conformist religious leaders by articulating a stand on the controversial issue of the burials that reflected the public mood more faithfully than did their own. On the other hand, many forward-thinking Zaituna faculty members and their students, not at all displeased to see their eminent but hidebound superiors challenged, supported the Dustur dissidents, providing them with an entrée to the mosque-university.

Fanned by the rhetoric of *L'Action*, which was disseminated through Dustur branches that by then existed in most parts of the country,[13] protests beginning in Tunis spread far and wide during 1933, as each new attempted burial of a naturalized French citizen in a Muslim cemetery rekindled the flames. Manceron recognized his inability to impose the solution embodied in the muftis' fatwa, particularly after the Dustur campaign acquired support from Muslim leaders in Egypt and Palestine – the first time the nationalists had attracted backing elsewhere in the Arab world. Aware that party militants were pushing the Dustur in dangerous directions, the resident general sought to defuse the immediate crisis before tackling the general radicalization of the movement. To do so, he ordered that enclaves for the naturalized be set aside in Muslim cemeteries, a compromise that *L'Action* accepted. Although the proposal failed to satisfy La Ligue des Musulmans Français, Manceron declined to reopen the case. Following these events, many of the so-called "*musulfrancs*," feeling abandoned and vulnerable, renounced French citizenship and initiated appeals for reintegration into the Muslim community. Their status, however, remained a matter of contention for the duration of the protectorate.

Manceron's anxiety was well founded. In May 1933 Bourguiba and three of his *L'Action* colleagues, Bahri Guiga, Mahmud Matari, and ᶜAli Bouhajib, won election to the Dustur executive committee. Flushed with the success of their incitement against naturalization, the militants were crystallizing a somewhat modified version of the Dustur political platform. Demands for a constitution and a government responsible to an elected assembly remained at its core, but with some new twists: an emphasis on the constitution's function of protecting the national character – a concept that had served them so well as a mobilization technique – along with an insistence that the parliament be solely Tunisian and that all officials, including the resident general, answer to it. The last two provisions symbolized the rejection of the Dustur's willingness to accept political arrangements based on the equality of Tunisians and Frenchmen (but which necessarily implied the prolongation of the protectorate) in favor of demands couched simply in terms of Tunisians' rights. Of greater consequence, the program expounded by the *Action* group put forward a call for independence.

The explicit reference to terminating the protectorate provoked a harsh response from Manceron, one of whose last acts as resident general was to approve decrees authorizing the bey to detain Tunisian subjects accused of political acts deemed inimical to France or the protectorate. The apparent empowerment of the bey shielded these "*super-scélérats*" edicts from the interference of metropolitan parliamentarians. The regulations also limited the latitude of the French-language press, leading to the suspension of *L'Action*. Finally, Manceron ordered the dissolution of the Dustur. Party leaders responded, as they had to Saint's repressive measures in 1926, by hunkering down to await the passing of the storm. In keeping with their efforts not to call attention to themselves, they chastised Bourguiba for leading a delegation of protesters from his home town of Monastir to Tunis for an audience with the bey in August, prompting his resignation from the executive committee. Resident General Marcel Peyrouton (1933–6) tried to further the rift in the party by hinting at the party's revival if the radicals could be restrained. When Guiga alerted his colleagues to the attempted cooption of the executive committee, the remaining members of the *Action* group left the Dustur.

Their skill in identifying issues evoking a visceral response with the Tunisian public, their willingness to defy the French authorities, and their control of an effective information medium in *L'Action* all helped Dustur militants to advance their agenda and begin to construct a support base independent of the mainstream party. That their emergence as an identifiable group coincided with an economic crisis highlighting weaknesses in the economic structure, the protectorate authorities' lack of concern for Tunisians' problems, and the incapacity of the Dustur chiefs to demonstrate effective leadership – all topics enthusiastically tackled by *L'Action* – unquestionably contributed to attracting many of their disgruntled countrymen into their camp. Infestations of locusts and a severe drought, broken only by equally destructive floods, wrought havoc on agriculture and herding in 1930 and 1931, particularly in central and southern Tunisia. Just as this dreadful situation eased, the effects of the Great Depression rolled over Tunisia, converting a crisis of underproduction into one of overproduction. France and other European countries closed their doors to Tunisian agricultural exports even as increased quantities of French manufactured goods poured into the protectorate, disrupting local artisanal output. The other mainstay of the economy, mining, also experienced severe setbacks. At mines throughout the country, including the lucrative phosphate deposits around Gafsa, production levels, profits, and the number of workers all declined precipitously in the early 1930s.

Small farmers, both Tunisian and European, were particularly hard hit, with many losing their property and others having to seek work on the larger *colon* farms that had been better able to weather the storm. Tunisian peasants abandoned the desolate countryside in droves. Unable to find accommodations or jobs in the cities – estimates of unemployment in the mid-1930s reached 30,000 in Tunis and 100,000 nationwide[14] – they joined indigent urbanites in the shacks and tents of spontaneously constructed slums (*bidonvilles*) on vacant land, in cemeteries, and in garbage dumps. In the all but complete absence of sanitary facilities, medical services, or any forms of social assistance, such neighborhoods became breeding grounds of physical disease and social malaise, raising the twin specters of epidemic and revolution. The imposition of regulations to prevent rural people from traveling outside their regions, campaigns to drive inhabitants of the *bidonvilles* back to the countryside, and the creation of government camps for the homeless and unemployed all failed to eliminate this desperate problem.

Government relief efforts in the agricultural sector focused on shoring up the price of wheat, authorizing the entry of Tunisian wines into France, and offering incentives to vintners to replace grape vines with fruit trees – all measures advantaging the export crops at the center of the rural settler economy. Conversely, olive growers, whose crop supported, directly or indirectly, a third of the Tunisian population, received no comparable aid. This emphasis on rescuing European farmers particularly galled Tunisians, who paid a disproportionately high share of agricultural taxes, which were calculated on the area sown rather than the amount produced. The creation of a farm credit bureau to consolidate debts and lend money also benefited *colons* more than Tunisians, since the bank required loan recipients to produce the title to their land, which not all Tunisians could do.

Although peasant farmers lacked leverage with the protectorate authorities, a few Tunisians hit hard by the deteriorating economy were in a position to bring pressure to bear. One such person was M'hammed Chenik, a wealthy businessman and landowner. Chenik had cast in his lot with the French in the 1920s, creating with their financial backing the only truly Tunisian bank, the Coopérative Tunisienne de Crédit, in 1922. Ignoring Dustur calls to boycott the Grand Council, he rose to the presidency of its Tunisian section. Chenik's dispatch of delegations to France in 1931 and 1932 to warn metropolitan officials of the gravity of the situation, along with his calls for more effective responses from the protectorate authorities, earned him the enmity of Manceron, who orchestrated a smear campaign accusing the magnate of financial malfeasance in connection with the bank.

Habib Bourguiba and M'hammed Chenik had little in common, but their mutual scorn for the Dustur leadership and the resident general proved sufficient to engender a profitable alliance. Bourguiba courted Chenik, whose substantial contributions made possible the emergence of *L'Action*. The paper defended Chenik but also, more importantly, pointed to his case as proof that "sincere, loyal collaboration with the government has been shown to be impossible."[15] In 1933, the Tunisian section of the Grand

Council voted not to cooperate with the government. In the crucible of the Depression, relations between the minority of Tunisians who had prospered under the protectorate and the colonial regime were being redefined. Race was trumping class.

By the end of 1933 the Dustur was in shambles. As its official leaders and the more militant *L'Action* group traded mutual recriminations, the gulf between them regarding tactics and long-term goals on both the political and economic fronts so widened as to preclude any prospect of being bridged or of a coordinated policy emerging. Early in 1934 Bourguiba and Tahar Sfar, an especially articulate ally, crisscrossed the Sahil, explaining their views at local Dustur branches and calling for a party congress whose delegates would chart a course for future activism. In a region teeming with olive growers, many of them being crushed by the Depression, in which the native son Bourguiba enjoyed great popularity and in which M'hammed Chenik had numerous business associates, they encountered broad support. The Dustur executive committee flatly refused to endorse such a session, lest it legitimate its rivals, but it proved unable to maintain party discipline down the line. When the militants summoned a congress in the Sahil town of Ksar Hellal on March 2, 1934, representatives from forty-nine Dustur branches, most of them in the Sahil and the Tunis regions, answered their call, while eleven others sent messages of encouragement. They voted to dissolve the executive committee and create a new one, called the political bureau, consisting of Bourguiba, his brother Muhammad, Guiga, Sfar (all Western-trained lawyers) and, as president, the physician Mahmud Matari. When al-Safi, Farhat, and their colleagues declined to cooperate in their own ouster, the split was complete and a Neo-Dustur party existed side by side with the original Dustur.

To capture disgruntled Dusturians and those components of the population in which the older party had shown little interest, the political bureau instructed congress attendees to create Neo-Dustur cells in the cities, including their working-class neighborhoods, and in provincial towns. As small merchants and artisans, modern businessmen, and land owners deserted the Dustur for a movement they deemed more likely to advance their interests, the original party shrank to its core of upper-middle-class urbanites and Zaituna ulama, although many of the younger faculty at the mosque-university, as well as its students, gravitated to the new party. The Neo-Dustur also quickly formed cells in the rural regions that the Dustur had neglected but which, in the depths of the Depression, were ripe for incorporation in the anti-French movement. The cellular structure facilitated communications within the party, making possible the rapid mobilization

Figure 3.2. Leaders of the Neo-Dustur political bureau. The four most prominent driving forces behind the Neo-Dustur from its creation in 1934 until the party's suppression on the eve of World War II were, from left to right, Habib Bourguiba, Mahmud Matari, Bahri Guiga, and Tahar Sfar.

of the masses that party leaders regarded as their most powerful weapon. Each cell constituted a self-contained entity, with specific, but limited, links to other cells and to the party hierarchy. In this way, the likelihood was lessened that the party would collapse should the government take repressive measures against it – a scenario that the Neo-Dustur's intention of using aggressive tactics to achieve the restoration of full Tunisian sovereignty made virtually inevitable.

As opening gambits, party leaders brought the rank and file into the streets with protests calling on Tunisians to defy the protectorate by boycotting French products and refusing to pay taxes. After a summer of demonstrations Peyrouton struck in early September, arresting Bourguiba and other Neo-Dustur leaders as well as prominent figures in the Parti Communiste Tunisien, which had also increased its activities in response to the stagnant economy. The Neo-Dustur survived the attempt to decapitate it, but on each subsequent occasion that the party tried to mount a public campaign, more arrests ensued. Over the first twenty months of its existence, the political bureau was reconstituted four times as one set of leaders after another – forty-six in all – were incarcerated. Assuming near-dictatorial powers, Peyrouton "the Satrap" demanded nothing less than the total capitulation of the Neo-Dustur as his price for freeing the prisoners, who remained in detention when he left in March 1936 to take up the post of resident general in Morocco.

Their release came three months later, following the victory of the left-wing Popular Front coalition in French parliamentary elections. Willing at least to listen to the grievances of the colonized, officials of the ministry of foreign affairs authorized Resident General Armand Guillon (1936–8) to release the Neo-Dusturians and invited Bourguiba to Paris for talks. Quite familiar, and comfortable, with the French left from his years as a student in Paris, Bourguiba saw in the government of Léon Blum genuine prospects for ameliorating the political and economic situations in the protectorate. In making the Neo-Dustur case, he specified as priorities the termination of arrangements advantaging French citizens in Tunisia, such as "official" colonization and the "colonial third," along with the installation of a constitutional government. At the same time, he omitted explicitly calling for independence and endorsed the concept of a gradual political evolution that safeguarded legitimate French interests. The Dustur accused its breakaway militants of selling out to gain their freedom. This charge, in conjunction with the continuing downward spiral of the economy, pushed the Neo-Dustur leaders towards stands more intransigent than they might otherwise have adopted. As it pursued its dialogue with the Neo-Dustur, the Popular Front encountered stiff resistance from *colon* interests and from the French military, which feared that loosening the colonial grip on North Africa as a European war loomed could have only negative consequences. Further talks in early 1937 ended with the nationalists and the government still far apart; before the end of the year, the Front collapsed.

The great benefit to the Neo-Dustur of the Popular Front's fifteen months in power was the party's ability, after Guillon lifted the strictures in place since 1933, to recruit and to function openly without fear of repression. *L'Action* reappeared and party membership soared to some 70,000 organized in more than 450 cells. During 1936 and 1937, party leaders cultivated the Neo-Dustur's image as "the party of the whole nation and the emanation of its desires and its will"[16] by expanding into new regions of the country and by consciously forging ties with youth organizations, cultural societies, sports clubs, and other key interest groups. The Etoile Scout and the Jeunesse Libérale Néo-dusturienne became fixtures at party rallies, with the scouts assuming the role of a paramilitary unit maintaining crowd discipline and accompanying party leaders on their travels outside Tunis. Neo-Dustur influences readily penetrated the modern schools that had produced its leaders, and these institutions, along with the Khalduniyya and the Sadiqi College alumni organization, channeled many young men, and a few women, into the party.

Although the public sphere offered limited opportunities for women, some did participate in Neo-Dustur activities. Chedlia Bouzgarou, whose hometown of Monastir was a hotbed of party activity in the Sahil, coordinated a group of women who joined other protesters in appealing to the bey to intercede with the resident general on behalf of Neo-Dustur prisoners in 1935, and did similar work for subsequent party demonstrations. Another female pioneer, B'chira ben M'rad, created the Association des Femmes Tunisiennes Musulmanes in 1936. In the same year, the Neo-Dustur sponsored the publication, albeit in France, of a women's magazine, *Leila*, which attempted to reconcile traditional and modern views on gender-related issues.[17] Most male Neo-Dustur leaders had no objection to including women in the party and to providing a forum for the discussion of issues particularly relevant to them, but they preferred not to unsettle the social status quo until the battle for national liberation had been won.

The party also made an effort to improve relations between Muslims and Jews, which had deteriorated in the 1930s. The growth of Zionism, and particularly its radical Revisionist manifestation, distressed the minority of Tunisian Muslims familiar with the ideology. But for most Muslims, Jewish commercial and financial dealings, which left many Muslims in their debt, constituted a more immediate irritant, the more so as the economic crisis deepened. After violent clashes between Muslims and Jews in Sfax in the summer of 1932, similar disorders broke out in several towns in the Sahil and in suburban Tunis. The *Action* group denounced Zionism no less vigorously than the Dustur leadership, but the more sophisticated younger men drew the distinction between the religion of Judaism, for which there was a place in the Tunisian nation, and the political concept of Zionism, for which there was not. In 1934, to stress the Tunisian identity of both groups, and their shared grievances with the French, Salah ben Yusuf, a young Neo-Dustur militant destined to play a major role in the party, led a crowd of demonstrators in chanting "the Jews are our brothers."[18] The revival of the Neo-Dustur in 1936 coincided with the eruption of chaos in Palestine, to which its leaders responded with unequivocal condemnations of both Tunisian anti-Semitism and Tunisian Zionism.

Although small in number, Tunisia's artistic community helped to advance Neo-Dustur objectives with its emphasis on dramatic, literary, musical, and visual forms of expression underscoring the country's Arab-Islamic identity and its cultural patrimony that predated, and existed independently of, colonialism. In the first half of the 1930s, al-Tamthil al-ᶜArabi, the troupe whose origins lay in resistance to European control of the Tunisian theatrical repertoire, made a practice of staging plays based on events in Arab history or that explored the impact of foreign influences and the cultural clash that came in their wake. Al-Masrah (The Theatre), a company founded in 1934, promoted the growth of a specifically Tunisian theatre by offering prizes and performance opportunities for works written or translated by Tunisians. Between 1931 and 1936, Muhammad Lahbib, the director of al-Saᶜada, the most overtly politicized company, wrote six plays drawn from Arab historical themes, two of them revolving around Tunisian figures of the classical era. At the suggestion of Mustafa Sfar, the mayor of Tunis and a patron of the arts, the city's several troupes merged in 1936 to form al-Ittihad al-Masrahi (The Theatrical Union). In addition to encouraging Tunisian playwrights, the consolidated company also created a division that specialized in developing and staging works focusing on social issues.

Along with these dramatists, the prose and poetry of two Zaituna-trained writers, Tahar Haddad and Abu'l Qasim al-Shabbi, presented themes that supported the nationalist cause and were incorporated into Neo-Dustur thinking. Haddad's innovative essays have already been noted; al-Shabbi's poetry emphasized the dignity of the common people and the value of tradition. Ironically, both men died before the Neo-Dustur truly came into its own, Haddad in 1935 at the age of thirty-six, al-Shabbi in the previous year at only twenty-five. No writers schooled in the protectorate's modern education system established themselves in the interwar period, although some who later carved niches for themselves on the literary scene – most notably Mahmud al-Mas'adi (best known for his 1955 existentialist drama *al-Sudd*) and ᶜAli al-Duᶜaji (whose short stories were anthologized only after his death in 1949) – were part of a bohemian coterie known as the Jamaᶜa Taht al-Sur (the "Under the Ramparts" Group, from the name of a café they frequented). Its participants also included the singer and actress Fathia Khairi, who performed with a number of theatre companies and sang with the orchestra of the Rashidiyya Institute. Khumais Tarnan, a talented musician and composer, founded the institute in 1934 at the instigation of mayor Sfar and Baron Rudolphe d'Erlanger, the leading European expert on classical Arab music, to preserve and promote Tunisia's

Figure 3.3. Abu'l Qasim al-Shabbi and Khumais Tarnan. The preservation of the traditions of Tunisian culture was an important consideration during the interwar period. Al-Shabbi's poetry and Tarnan's music both contributed to this movement.

Arab-Andalusian musical heritage (*ma'luf*). Tarnan's original compositions and the recordings and concerts of the institute's orchestra ensured that the genre was not totally eclipsed by increasingly popular contemporary Arab and European music. European painters had long flocked to their country, but few Tunisians pursued this largely alien art form. The first artist to distinguish himself was Yahya Turki, whose work began appearing in the late 1920s. He displayed little interest in European trends and most of his paintings depicted scenes of everyday life. Like Lahbib's plays, al-Shabbi's poems, and Tarnan's scores, Turki's canvases evoked respect and appreciation for the same Tunisian heritage that the Neo-Dustur defended. This common objective insured a generally warm relationship between nationalist politicians and the artistic community.

ᶜAbd al-ᶜAziz Thaᶜalbi returned from exile in July 1937, believing that his prestige would suffice to restore the unity of the nationalist movement. With the breach closed the Dustur, under his guidance and adhering to his platform, which now included Tunisian independence, would resume the struggle against the protectorate with renewed vigor. But in Thaᶜalbi's absence, the political culture had changed too drastically for that to happen. The Neo-Dustur leaders welcomed him, but had no intention of ceding their authority to him. Indeed, they used their party's eight-to-one numerical advantage over its rival to disrupt Thaᶜalbi's rallies when he toured the country in August, forcing him into the embarrassing position of requiring a police presence to give his speeches.

When the Popular Front fell in the following month, Bourguiba concluded that the Neo-Dustur had nothing to lose in thwarting Thaᶜalbi's attempt to outflank it by assuming a still more radical stand. He asserted that, having failed to win concessions from the Popular Front, none would be forthcoming from a far less liberal Parisian government that, in any case, was focusing on events in Europe. At the autumn 1937 party congress, he warned of the likely extension to Tunisia of the recent suppression of nationalist activities in Morocco and Algeria, and urged his followers to prepare for a direct confrontation with the French. Bourguiba's assessment of the situation carried the day, but only at considerable cost. Several of the Neo-Dustur's highest-ranking members, including Matari, Sfar, and Guiga, resigned in protest over a course of action they deemed dangerous and counterproductive. Nonetheless, they preferred to retire from politics, at least for the moment, rather than rejoin the Dustur.

Even as the Neo-Dustur began to implement its more aggressive strategy, some of its leaders continued to hope that France would yield before the situation spiraled completely out of control. As Europe moved towards war,

Slimane ben Slimane, a member of the political bureau, took the occasion
of the German annexation of Austria in March 1938 to assure protectorate
officials that Tunisians, despite their legitimate grievances, would remain
loyal to France if France granted them their basic rights. By alienating the
Neo-Dustur, he lamented, France hurt itself as well as the party. In view of
well-known Italian overtures to both the Dustur and the Neo-Dustur, such
a declaration had real value, but it elicited no response and demonstrations
and acts of civil disobedience continued, as did the arrest of militants
and party leaders. More than 10,000 Neo-Dusturians participated in a
demonstration in Tunis on April 9 to demand the release of the prisoners.
When the crowd learned of the arrest of a Sadiqi College instructor who had
delivered a fiery speech on the previous evening, a deadly and destructive
rampage ensued.

The Neo-Dustur's course of action in the months since the end of the
Popular Front had paved the way for such a violent outburst. Nor did
Bourguiba necessarily regret it. Although the party accused the police of
deliberately provoking the crowd, Mahmud Matari, who remained close
to Bourguiba despite their disagreement over tactics, wrote in his memoirs
that Bourguiba told him just before the disturbances that to achieve the
party's objectives "it was necessary for blood to flow." Neo-Dustur militants
among the demonstrators were no doubt on the lookout for situations
they could exploit to keep the political situation at a boil.[19] Beyond the
numerous deaths and injuries (of which the Tunisians and the French
gave widely conflicting estimates), the toll of the rioting was high: the
dissolution of the Neo-Dustur, the imprisonment of more than 700 of
its members, including all its key figures, and the imposition of a state of
siege rendering political activity by Tunisians virtually impossible. In the
government camp, Resident General Guillon also fell victim to the unrest.
Powerful businessmen, whom he had alienated by attacking corruption and
mismanagement in lucrative public works concessions, added their voices
to the chorus faulting him for failing to address the dangers posed by the
Neo-Dustur in a more timely fashion. Before the end of the year, Erik
Labonne (1938–40) replaced him, armed with a mandate to prepare the
protectorate to weather the storm of a European war.

Combining clemency for rank-and-file members of the Neo-Dustur with
a tough stand towards those held responsible for the violence, Labonne
lifted the state of siege and freed numerous prisoners. The ban on the
party continued, however, as did the detention of its top echelon, whose
trials were scheduled to be held in France in the hope of avoiding new
demonstrations in Tunisia. Under Habib Thameur, a relatively minor party

Figure 3.4. Poster commemorating the April 1938 nationalist protests. The most intense anti-French demonstration of the interwar period ended with police firing on the crowds (depicted here) and the arrest of virtually all of the Neo-Dustur's leaders. This poster marked the fiftieth anniversary of the event.

stalwart who assumed control of the political bureau, the debilitated Neo-Dustur could do little more than campaign for the release of the remaining prisoners. As a European war drew closer, the pro-Axis sympathies expressed by Thameur and some of his associates reflected views widely held among their countrymen. Bourguiba and a few other party officials took exception, however, cautioning that an alliance of convenience with Germany and Italy might rid Tunisia of the French but would prove disastrous in the long term.

As the Neo-Dustur clung to a precarious existence, the Dustur lay low, hoping for an opportunity to benefit from the crippling of its rival. Between 1934 and 1938 neither party could completely drive the other from the political arena. From 1938 until the start of World War II, neither could organize serious opposition to French rule. With both parties down, and quite possibly out for the count, their prospects of reforming the protectorate, much less terminating it, appeared remote. This dire reality, after two decades of nationalist activity, invited a fresh initiative from an unexpected quarter.

CHAPTER 4

Redefining the relationship, 1940–1956

THE WAR YEARS

Most Tunisians took satisfaction in France's defeat by Germany in June 1940, but the nationalist parties derived no more substantive dividend from the colonial power's humiliation. Following the Franco-German armistice, the government of Marshal Philippe Pétain sent to Tunis as resident general Admiral Jean Esteva (1940–3), who had no intention of permitting a revival of Tunisian political activity. The arrests of Habib Thameur and Taieb Slim, key figures in the Neo-Dustur political bureau and partisans of collaboration with Germany, weakened the party. As had become customary when the Neo-Dustur operated clandestinely, their replacements had been named in advance, but the available cadre consisted primarily of youthful militants with little experience and little chance of eluding the authorities for very long. Sporadic acts of sabotage and terror carried out during 1941 by the Main Noire, a shadowy underground organization, symbolized the nationalists' despair.

The stimulus for renewed opposition to the protectorate came from an improbable source: the palace, where Moncef Bey (1942–3) acceded to the throne in June. The sixty-one-year-old Moncef had cut his political teeth in the 1922 confrontation between Resident General Saint and his father, Nasir Bey, whose streak of defiance towards the French authorities he shared. Rejecting the role of a figurehead, Moncef served notice on Esteva that he expected his subjects and French citizens to enjoy equal treatment. Accordingly, he ordered the extension of the "colonial third" to Tunisian administrators. Moncef toured the country during 1942, dispensing with protocol and making himself accessible to his people in a way that no previous monarch ever had. Well aware that the anti-Semitic propaganda of the Vichy government had triggered clashes between Tunisian Muslims and Jews prior to his accession, the new ruler made a point of expressing his solicitude for the welfare of his Jewish subjects. In a matter of only a few months, Moncef strode into the political space vacated by the enfeebled parties, supplanting them as the rallying point for the nation and assuming their leaders' mission of articulating grievances to the French. Emboldened by his popularity and success, Moncef called for Esteva's dismissal in October. So straightforward a challenge might have proven his undoing, had not the war impinged directly on Tunisia shortly afterwards, altering the political situation in a way that, initially at least, worked to the bey's advantage.

British and US troops landed in Morocco and Algeria in November, opening a North African campaign whose ultimate objective was the capture of Tunisia and its use as a jumping-off point for an invasion of Sicily. When Vichy commanders negotiated a cease-fire, Germany seized the Vichy-administered area of France and Tunisia. German forces poured into the protectorate, halting the Allied advance along a front through the center of the country. Both the Allies and the Axis vied for Tunisian support, but Moncef judiciously declined to take sides. Nevertheless, Esteva intercepted the bey's letters to the US and British governments containing his pledges of neutrality. With the Germans Moncef maintained a careful and correct relationship that neither endorsed their war aims nor provided them with a justification to unseat him.

Shortly after occupying southern France, Germany remanded Bourguiba and the other Neo-Dusturians imprisoned there to its Italian partners, who hoped that the Tunisians would broadcast anti-French propaganda while "guests" of the Fascist state. Certain that Germany would also free political prisoners in the protectorate in a bid to turn them against France, Esteva himself ordered their release in December. Many of them had advocated an alliance with Germany and viewed the occupation as a prelude to the collapse of French rule. The pro-German Habib Thameur, who resumed his 1938–41 position as head of the political bureau, was quite prepared to work with officials of the Third Reich, despite the reproaches of Bourguiba and others. Ordinary Tunisians, however, increasingly resented German food requisitions and labor mobilization as the military campaign continued into spring 1943. To the exceptional financial levies and other discriminatory practices that befell Tunisian Jews fewer objections were raised, but the bey made no attempt to conceal his displeasure.

The Neo-Dustur recovered some of its past strength, but Moncef held uncontested sway over the political arena. Although unwilling to throw in his lot with Germany, he did use the opportunity offered by the occupation to take a bold political step that his nemesis Esteva would never have allowed, had not the Germans compelled him to do so in the interest of not antagonizing a ruler whom they preferred to have as a friend with reservations than an active enemy. Using this leverage, Moncef appointed the first truly Tunisian government since the beginning of the protectorate. He drew from a broad political spectrum, the most prominent figures in which were M'hammed Chenik (from the pro-Allied wing of the Neo-Dustur), the prime minister; Mahmud Matari (an independent, but still widely seen as aligned with the Neo-Dustur); and Salah Farhat (Dustur).

Even before Moncef took this bold step, a shrill chorus of settlers and officials in Algeria, where the Free French supplanted the Vichy authorities after the landings, had begun to denounce him as a German collaborator. With a powerful Allied offensive in the spring foreshadowing an Axis defeat in Tunisia, *colons* and administrators there made similar accusations. In early May, British, US, and Free French forces bottled up almost a quarter of a million German and Italian soldiers on the Cap Bon peninsula. Several thousand escaped by sea, but most surrendered, ending the North African campaign. After assuming responsibility for the protectorate, the Free French moved quickly, exiling Moncef to Algeria and forcing his abdication in favor of his cousin Amin (1943–57). General Alphonse Juin, the military commander in Tunisia after the liberation, doubted that the bey had compromised himself with the Axis and tried to prevent his ouster. But the French community demanded its pound of flesh, and Juin feared a movement to abolish the monarchy altogether if the vengeful settlers were denied the satisfaction of unseating Moncef. The collaboration charges provided a pretext, but it was the bey's defiance of the French that cost him his throne. Resident General Charles Mast (1943–7) steadfastly refused to countenance any discussion of the return to Tunis of "the sovereign [who] had become, if not the chief, at least the standard-bearer of the nationalists."[1] Yet even in exile, and even as other forces asserted themselves, the former bey continued to influence Tunisian politics.

During his sojourn in Italy, Bourguiba proved of little value to his hosts, since he insisted on a commitment to Tunisian independence as the price for his cooperation. In any case, the impending defeat of the Axis in North Africa put paid to Italian ambitions there. Thus he was repatriated in April 1943. Because the reappearance of the Neo-Dustur had coincided with the German occupation and been directed by Thameur and Slim; because Chenik, a prominent Neo-Dusturian (albeit one known for his Allied sympathies), had participated in Moncef's government of Tunisians; and because the French authorities downplayed Bourguiba's condemnation of collaboration, Mast took a dim view of the Neo-Dustur as the former party chief sought to reaffirm his control over the still outlawed organization.

Figure 4.1. General Charles de Gaulle, Amin Bey, and Resident General Charles Mast, 1943. Installed following the deposition of Moncef Bey, Amin spent his reign navigating between the French authorities and the nationalists. When Tunisia was proclaimed a republic in 1957, he abdicated, ending the Husainid Dynasty that had reigned for more than two and a half centuries.

Juin disparaged Bourguiba as a tool of the Axis, but US diplomats, with whom he had initiated contacts (through his wife and son) while still a Vichy prisoner, provided evidence of his loyalty that shielded him from French reprisals. Other high-ranking party militants, however, fled Tunisia just before or after the liberation, either because they had worked with the Germans or because they doubted that French vengeance would discriminate between divergent strands in the nationalist movement. Mast's desire to restore the prewar status quo justified the latter's concerns. Between May and December, 4,000 Tunisians were interned in prison camps.[2]

This sweep primarily targeted Neo-Dusturians, but also rounded up key members of the "Moncefist Committee" created by the former bey's brother Hassine and others in his entourage soon after the deposition. The committee drew support for the reinstatement of Moncef from the Dustur and the Parti Réformiste (largely spent forces whose fortunes could only improve through association with the popular ruler), as well as from activist students and faculty of the Zaituna mosque-university and members of the Parti Communiste Tunisien, but not from the Neo-Dustur. Bourguiba saw no merit in easing the misfortunes that had befallen the one Tunisian political figure capable of short-circuiting the Neo-Dustur's own renaissance or subordinating its agenda to his own. The resident general's repressive tactics limited the immediate impact of this Moncefist bloc, but its existence worried French officials, who also kept a wary eye on Bourguiba and Salah ben Yusuf, now his key deputy and the party's secretary-general.

As the two men set about rebuilding the shattered Neo-Dustur in 1943 and 1944, they expressed the view that the war would leave France a second-tier power, dependent on Britain and the United States and far less able than in the past to stifle nationalist demands, particularly those formulated by leaders, like Bourguiba, who had developed a relationship with the Allies. They recommended that the party maintain a low profile, refraining from provoking the protectorate authorities, but that it prepare to make political capital of French weaknesses as they revealed themselves. Their vision of self-rule under a Tunisian government in which Neo-Dusturians had prominent roles accorded with the December 1943 remark of Charles de Gaulle, the head of the provisional French government, that "we ought to move towards making the administration of Tunisia a Tunisian administration . . . Direct administration is outmoded."[3] Likewise, it found an echo among members of the Tunisian section of the Grand Council, including Tahar ben ʿAmmar, a founding father of the Dustur who had pursued an independent political course since the late 1920s. Slowly but systematically the party began to recoup its losses, with the resident general estimating its strength at 100,000 in late 1944.[4]

Despite this impressive figure, the Neo-Dustur was operating on shaky ground. It remained proscribed, the intensity of its members' commitments varied and was untested, and it had to reckon with the Moncef loyalists who held the political high ground. Although they refused to put the Neo-Dustur's assets at the disposal of its rivals by taking the party into the coalition supporting the former bey, Bourguiba and ben Yusuf also appreciated the risks of criticizing the movement, much less attempting to shoulder it aside, as long as Moncef remained an icon of Tunisian opposition to

France. They made a public show of deference to the deposed ruler but assiduously avoided acknowledging his authority. In these circumstances, they and other top Neo-Dusturians welcomed the opportunity to work with a diverse group of prominent opponents of French rule to formulate a "Manifesto of the Tunisian Front" in February 1945.

THE NEO-DUSTUR REBORN

The gulf between the manifesto's core demand for self-government and an anodyne reform package Mast introduced in the same month doomed to failure the first overture to the nationalists in almost a decade. The Parti Communiste Tunisien alone endorsed the plan, arguing that only solidarity between France and its dependencies could protect both from the clutches of Britain and the United States in the postwar world, a perspective decidedly at variance with the Neo-Dustur leaders' conception of allegiances. Situating the nationalist movement in the context of the looming East–West struggle created a rift between the communists and the Neo-Dustur that persisted well beyond the colonial period. Employing a tactic from his days as a political journalist, Bourguiba sought to undercut the PCT's appeal by decrying the discrepancy between the communists' imported ideology and traditional Tunisian values.

The attempt to placate the nationalists with insignificant concessions convinced Bourguiba that only a combination of Tunisian opposition and international pressure on France would create a political climate conducive to terminating French rule. He left for Egypt in March 1945 to solicit the help of the recently created League of Arab States. In Cairo he, Thameur, Slim, and other political refugees formed the Bureau d'Information du Néo-Destour. The Tunisians joined forces with Algerian and Moroccan nationalists in 1947 to create the Bureau du Maghreb Arabe and then participated in the Comité de Libération d'Afrique du Nord, launched in 1948 under the chairmanship of the Moroccan resistance leader ᶜAbd al-Krim, a recent escapee from French custody. Despite the efforts of these organizations, the members of the League of Arab States provided little assistance. Influential countries such as Egypt and Iraq had poor relations with Britain and thought better of simultaneously antagonizing France. More to the point, however, problems closer to the Middle East, and particularly the question of Palestine, relegated North African issues to a back burner. Bourguiba shifted his public relations campaign from the Arab world to Europe and North America.

Within Tunisia, French unwillingness to carry out meaningful reforms met with anger and hostility. On top of the rising tensions in the protectorate, virulent clashes between Algerian nationalists and *colons* in Sétif on V-E Day sent shock waves across all French North Africa. A few months later, in a drive to dampen nationalist fervor, the French authorities transferred Moncef to France and briefly detained ben Yusuf, who had assumed the mantle of Neo-Dustur leadership from Bourguiba. Rather than diminishing his impact, putting distance between Moncef and his partisans enhanced his image as a martyr. Representatives of all strands of opposition to the French, meeting in August 1946, categorically rejected Tunisian membership in the recently devised French Union. Instead, they pronounced themselves in favor of the exiled bey's immediate restoration and the acknowledgment of full, unrestricted independence. Ben Yusuf not only gave Neo-Dustur backing to this program, but spoke forcefully on its behalf. That the secretary-general's alignment with his Moncefist rivals represented a tactical move rather than a genuine desire to close ranks became evident with the appointment of a new resident general whose socialist background hinted at a loosening of the French grip.

Shortly after his arrival Jean Mons (1947–50) met with prominent figures from all the nationalist factions to learn their views on a "co-sovereignty" regime: a Tunisian prime minister (under the continuing supervision of the secretary-general) presiding over a mixed cabinet of Tunisian and French ministers, with the former more numerous than before. The resident general's discussions revealed important differences among the parties. Salah Farhat, who again led the Dustur following Tha'albi's death in 1944, dismissed Mons' plan as falling far short of the requirements enunciated the previous summer. Ben Yusuf, on the other hand, showed more interest. While committed to independence, he nonetheless expressed a willingness to proceed in stages and without the restoration of Moncef.

Despite the certainty of ongoing French control under the proposal, many of the 130,000 French settlers, businessmen, and bureaucrats condemned it as inimical to their interests. With the right-wing Rassemblement Français de Tunisie having won 60 percent of the votes in the 1946 constitutional referendum establishing the Fourth French Republic and holding thirty-five of the fifty-four seats on the Grand Council, Mons could not discount its insistence that the French (less than 4 percent of Tunisia's population) would never accept subordination to the Tunisian majority. In a pointed barb drawing a parallel between the attachment of the French to North Africa and the Muslims to the Iberian Peninsula, Antoine Colonna, the founder of the Rassemblement, expressed his contempt for the resident general by suggesting that he would end his administration much as Abu ᶜAbdallah, the last Muslim king of Granada, had ended his reign – weeping like a woman over what he could not defend like a man.[5]

The implementation of the reforms by the appointment of Mustafa Kaak, a lawyer open to cooperating with France, as prime minister and the exclusion from the cabinet of both the Dustur and Neo-Dustur satisfied no one. For the nationalists, it was too little; for the *prépondérants*, even this essentially meaningless nod in the direction of giving Tunisians a voice in the management of the protectorate appeared as the thin edge of a wedge that would sooner or later pry open the door to self-government. Kaak's minimal support evaporated further in August 1947, when police in Sfax fired on workers participating in a nationwide general strike called by the recently established Union Générale des Travailleurs Tunisiens (UGTT), killing twenty-nine and injuring 150.

The unceremonious demise of the Confédération Générale des Travailleurs Tunisiens in 1925 and a failed attempt to revive it in 1936 had left the organization of Tunisian labor in the hands of the French Confédération Générale des Travailleurs (CGT) and its Tunisian affiliate, the Union Départmentale des Syndicats de Tunisie (UDST). Distaste for the communists, who controlled both unions, prompted Farhat Hached, a veteran UDST activist in Sfax, to establish the UGTT in 1946. He and most of the 12,000 workers who followed him into the new union were avowed nationalists. Indeed, some powerful labor leaders, such as Habib ᶜAchour, who succeeded Hached at the head of the Sfax local, already enjoyed some standing in the Neo-Dustur. Nevertheless, the UGTT cultivated a distinctive identity based on the belief that the social and economic liberation of Tunisian workers required the liberation of the Tunisian state from colonialism. The union applauded ben Yusuf's efforts to rebuild the Neo-Dustur and encouraged its members to join the party, giving it a significant labor constituency for the first time in its history. But with the future prospects of the Neo-Dustur still in doubt, and the nationalist movement badly fractured, the audacity of the 1947 general strike propelled the UGTT into the vanguard of the opposition to French rule.

The UGTT did not, however, have a monopoly on the organization of Tunisian labor. A few months after its founding, the UDST separated from the CGT, became the Union des Syndicats des Travailleurs Tunisiens (USTT), and offered workers a communist Franco-Tunisian union, with an ideology built around class struggle, as an alternative to the UGTT. As the two unions vied for the loyalty of Tunisian workers, they created

Figure 4.2. Labor leaders Farhat Hached and M'hammed ᶜAli. The political agenda of the short-lived CGTT, founded by M'hammed ᶜAli in the 1920s, provided a model for Hached when he organized the UGTT and tied it closely to the Neo-Dustur in the years following World War II.

antagonisms analogous to those between the Parti Communiste Tunisien and the Neo-Dustur. Hached and his USTT rivals also competed for legitimization within the global labor movement. The World Federation of Trade Unions (WFTU), an influential umbrella organization, denied the UGTT's application for admission on the grounds that limiting its membership to Tunisians was racist – an assessment revealing the WFTU's failure to appreciate the circumstances of colonialism, and one which Hached refuted vehemently. On the other hand, the USTT gained admission within weeks of its formation. Hached had misgivings about the WFTU's communist leanings, but he put them aside in the belief that international recognition and the contacts attendant on affiliation with the federation were crucial to the UGTT.

Given the WFTU's preference for communist organizations, it promoted either the subordination of the UGTT to the USTT or a merger that dissolved the former into the latter. Hached and his colleagues regarded such outcomes as variations on the theme of "co-sovereignty," which they refused to countenance on either the labor or the political front. Following the Sfax tragedy the USTT chastised UGTT decision-makers for playing into the government's hands to the detriment of all workers. Later in the year Hached broke off contact with the USTT until such time as the WFTU admitted the UGTT. That occurred in 1949, but even then Hached resisted any attempt to bring the two groups together. The ideological gap between them was too wide, and the UGTT simply could not accommodate itself to the USTT's willingness to embrace members of any nationality, which resulted in the organization having a French majority. In any case, the UGTT's numerical edge over its rival negated the need for it to compromise. More anxious to develop national consciousness than class consciousness, the UGTT swelled its ranks with the addition of associations representing not only salaried workers, but teachers, bureaucrats, and other tertiary-sector employees. By the end of the decade its strength had increased to nearly 50,000, while the USTT's numbers remained static. In 1950 the UGTT withdrew from the WFTU and affiliated with the recently created International Confederation of Free Trade Unions (ICFTU), whose anti-communism and Anglo-Saxon leadership were more to Hached's liking.

Resident General Mons also sought to smash the UGTT. He reacted to the 1947 general strike by removing union representatives from national boards, thus greatly impairing the UGTT's ability to influence decisions affecting its members' welfare. Amin Bey flatly rejected Mons' demand that he dissolve the union. To the contrary, he expressed his condolences to the victims and contributed heavily to a fund for their support. He also granted an audience to a UGTT delegation that impressed upon him the plight of ordinary Tunisians, who were seeing postwar inflation and the devaluation of the French (and Tunisian) franc slash their purchasing power as a severe drought caused food shortages throughout the country and famine conditions in some particularly hard-hit areas.[6] Although ben Yusuf and a few other Neo-Dusturians with connections to the royal family had been attempting to draw Amin into their camp for some time, the bey had shown little inclination to challenge the protectorate authorities. Both his indignation with them and his compassion for his subjects caught up in the violence at Sfax appear to have been genuine expressions of his convictions rather than acts calculated to improve his image among those Tunisians who regarded his accession to the throne as an act of usurpation.

Even amid the political and social turmoil of the postwar era, the arts continued to reinforce the nationalist cause through their exaltation of Tunisian identity. The stage had fallen dark during the war but came back to life in 1945, when the Tunis Municipal Council renewed its patronage by sponsoring a Comité de Défense du Théâtre Tunisien. Its ambitious program included subsidizing the translation into Arabic of foreign plays set in Tunisia, the adaptation of European novels about Tunisia for the Arab stage, the presentation of original plays based on Tunisian history, and the establishment of an Ecole d'Art Dramatique, which opened in 1951. Radio broadcasting offered a new medium for disseminating dramatic works and other forms of entertainment, as well as news. Private radio stations dated from the mid-1930s and a government-operated Radio-Tunis went on the air in 1939, but all shut down during the war. When Radio-Tunis obtained a broadcasting monopoly in 1948, 45 percent of its programming was in Arabic.

A new postwar generation of Tunisian painters followed the lead of already established artists in emphasizing traditional Tunisian life and values. Despite sometimes stark differences between their styles and techniques, their desire to develop an authentically Tunisian artistic personality honoring the country's symbols and expressing them in modern forms brought them together in 1948 as the "Ecole de Tunis." Its adherents, almost all of them in their twenties at the time, would exert a powerful influence on Tunisian art for the next several decades.

The death of Moncef Bey in September 1948 altered the balance of political forces in the protectorate. Deprived of its raison d'être, the Moncefist coalition disintegrated. Ben Yusuf had worked hard to position the Neo-Dustur to capitalize on this moment, and when it came none of the party's rivals could prevent it from resuming its former domination of the nationalist movement. His overtures to Amin developed into a sympathetic relationship between the monarch and the Neo-Dustur that enhanced the standing of the party. At the other end of the socioeconomic spectrum, the party's developing relationship with the UGTT gave the Neo-Dustur an entrée to the Tunisian masses, although its continuing illegality made large public gatherings infeasible. Party leaders avoided antagonizing the French authorities, particularly after conveying to Mons their willingness to participate in a government of reform. On two potentially volatile occasions in 1948 – the tenth anniversary of April 9, 1938, and Moncef's death – ben Yusuf and his lieutenants dissuaded their followers from challenging the forces of order.

As he had from his first days in the Neo-Dustur, ben Yusuf insisted that it should represent all Tunisians. Under his tutelage, the party expanded deeper into areas of the country beyond its traditional bases in the Sahil and Tunis, increasing its membership by 1950 to 210,000 in 260 cells.[7] Following Bourguiba's departure, the secretary-general welcomed into the Neo-Dustur many civil servants and bourgeois capitalists who discerned advantages in distancing themselves from a France shaken by its recent history and contemplating changes in the protectorate that boded ill for their prestige and power. As the party emerged in 1948 from its enforced inactivity, it included substantial new infusions of government employees – from clerks and school teachers to *qaids* and *khalifas* – and of entrepreneurs, two groups once scorned by its leaders. Some of the new members even sat on the Grand Council, whose delegates had rarely seen eye to eye with the Neo-Dustur before the war. The educational and financial resources of these new recruits helped them to acquire positions of influence in the party. In the late 1940s, 42 percent of its leaders (at all levels) also held government jobs, as opposed to a mere 6 percent before the war.[8]

As a native of the island of Jerba, whose people customarily migrated to urban centers to engage in retail trade, Salah ben Yusuf moved comfortably among the businessmen who were gaining new importance in the Neo-Dustur. In 1948, he engaged the party, along with the UGTT, in the creation of a business federation, the Union Tunisien de l'Artisanat et du Commerce (UTAC). The UTAC reflected a shift in the sources of Neo-Dustur support in the business community. Many merchants of long standing in the party objected to the term *commerce* (business), preferring what was for most of them the more accurate phrase *petits commerçants* (shopkeepers). As they feared, wealthier and more powerful entrepreneurs dominated the UTAC, and their financial backing as the Neo-Dustur got back on its feet lessened the smaller merchants' influence in the party.

Before the war Neo-Dustur encouragement of efforts to update the Zaituna mosque-university curriculum – a recurrent but largely unachieved theme during much of the 1930s – had gained the approval of many students and progressive faculty members. Ben Yusuf had been a familiar figure at Zaituna, contributing to its politicization and cementing Neo-Dustur links with its student organizations, some of which participated in the demonstrations of April 1938.[9] But with the Neo-Dustur in eclipse thereafter, Zaituna activists had to fend for themselves. When political activity resumed at the mosque-university following the liberation, parochial concerns again mixed with national issues. A 1944 faculty congress conflated a demand for reforms with one for the restoration of Moncef Bey.

Ben Yusuf viewed the revitalization of the party's Zaituna alliance as important, but Bourguiba preferred to concentrate on the more secular components of the party. Although Ahmad ben Salah, a young Neo-Dustur militant, inaugurated a joint Zaituna–Sadiki student commission in 1944 to lobby for improvements at the mosque-university, Moncefism dominated postwar Zaituna activism. At the same time, pan-Arabism and pan-Islam attracted many mosque-university students and faculty, as they did other Moncefists. The formation of the League of Arab States, the crisis in Palestine, and the establishment of Pakistan as a Muslim state all had an impact on Tunisians with a strong sense of Arab and Islamic identity. Nonetheless, two facts became clear very shortly after Moncef's death: Palestine preoccupied the League of Arab States, which never seriously tackled the issue of colonialism in North Africa, despite the work of the émigrés in Cairo; and the Neo-Dustur was the only viable Tunisian political organization in the protectorate. Zaituna activists responded positively to ben Yusuf's appeals to reconnect with the party, in which they soon constituted an Arab- and Islamic-oriented wing that coexisted, sometimes uncomfortably, with the secular, more or less Westernized, nationalists who constituted its majority.

As the chief architect of the Neo-Dustur's reconstruction, and of its connection (or reconnection) with crucial social and economic forces, Secretary General ben Yusuf established the Neo-Dustur as the sole valid interlocutor with France in the protectorate. In the process he garnered sufficient personal prestige and influence to lead the party in a direction of his choosing. His willingness, at the outset of Mons' administration, to accept a gradualist approach towards the determination of Tunisia's political future if that were the price of serving in the government was a tactic born of the circumstances of the moment, for he had always favored immediate and unrestricted independence and did so forcefully after Moncef's death. Ben Yusuf warned the French that time was running out. The protecting power had to demonstrate its commitment to end the protectorate; the reinvigorated and unrivaled Neo-Dustur would no longer tolerate insincere avowals, insignificant concessions, and other delaying tactics.

BRINGING DOWN THE CURTAIN

But, in a sense, time was running out for ben Yusuf as well. Habib Bourguiba had never relinquished the presidency of the Neo-Dustur. From Cairo he closely followed events in Tunisia, not all of which were unfolding to his liking. He questioned some of ben Yusuf's decisions and doubted the wisdom of drawing into the Neo-Dustur some of the groups favored by his deputy. Bourguiba also feared that the secretary-general would provoke a showdown with France that could easily spiral out of control. On a more personal level, his own prolonged absence had detached him from the day-to-day management of party affairs and he bristled at ben Yusuf's growing popularity. The protectorate authorities knew of Bourguiba's concerns and, with an eye towards promoting dissension within the party, Mons conveyed to Bourguiba an assurance that nothing stood in the way of his return to Tunisia.

Realizing that his attempts to marshal international support had reached an impasse, at least for the moment, Bourguiba left Egypt in September 1949. Both he and ben Yusuf understood the resident general's motives and assiduously avoided playing into his hands. Bourguiba toured the country, sometimes in the company of ben Yusuf, drawing reassuringly large crowds everywhere he went. Consummate politician that he was, he quickly sized up the situation in the protectorate. He recognized the assets that the bourgeois elements ben Yusuf had recruited in his absence brought to the party and implicitly acknowledged the secretary-general's prescience in this matter. But the tensions between the two men were real – on the personal level, with regard to tactics, and in terms of their increasingly divergent global orientations (ben Yusuf to the Arab and Islamic worlds, Bourguiba to the West) – and they eyed each other warily.

The failure of the 1947 reforms, the death of Moncef Bey in the following year, and the reemergence of the Neo-Dustur as a force to be reckoned with thereafter all combined to produce a volatile political atmosphere in the protectorate. The 1949 decision of the United Nations to grant independence to Libya a year hence threatened to provide the detonating spark if Tunisians' own more fully articulated nationalist aspirations remained unfulfilled. Just before the end of the year, the French minister of foreign affairs, Robert Schuman, admitted the urgency of devising a policy accommodating both Tunisian and French requirements. His announcement prompted Amin Bey to align himself more publicly with the Neo-Dustur. The monarch undoubtedly hoped for the popularity that his predecessor had accrued by opposing the protectorate and that the Moroccan sultan Muhammad V had also been acquiring by his defiance of the French. Amin also sought to preclude his marginalization by the nationalist leaders, who would inevitably take the lead in any negotiations. The bey's clearest statement of his views came in May 1950, a month after Bourguiba had laid out a detailed Neo-Dustur proposal – the first in a succession of attempts to redefine the Franco-Tunisian relationship that dragged on over the next five years.

The plan emphasized placing meaningful power in Tunisian hands – a government of Tunisians appointed by the bey, the abolition of the contrôleurs civils, the holding of municipal elections, and the creation of a national assembly mandated to write a constitution and to determine a course for Franco-Tunisian relations that respected both Tunisian sovereignty and French interests. Bourguiba called for cooperation and stressed that the Neo-Dustur wished to avert conflict. Tunisia was too weak militarily and too strong strategically to do without the assistance of a great power. To the extent that it will admit the legitimacy of our demands, we want that power to be France, and we are fully prepared to cooperate with it on a footing of equality between our two people.[10]

But he warned that rejecting legitimate Tunisian expectations might make conflict unavoidable. This first official statement of Neo-Dustur policy since Bourguiba had retaken the helm of the party made it clear that the objective of negotiations was independence. Whether this was to be immediate or accomplished incrementally and, if the latter, over how long a period and with what intermediate arrangements, remained contentious issues within the party.

France accepted the Tunisian proposal as a basis for further discussions, although the Rassemblement dismissed it out of hand, insisting on the nonnegotiability of co-sovereignty, which preserved *colon* influence in governing the country. Inasmuch as co-sovereignty was also nonnegotiable from the nationalists' perspective, a diametric opposition developed. In any case, the Tunisians considered only the French government, not the settlers, as a legitimate negotiating partner – a reasonable view but one certain to complicate any conversations. Already having failed to shepherd one reform process to a successful conclusion, Mons resigned in June. Schuman stated the task of his replacement, Louis Périllier (1950–2), with unambiguous clarity: "to lead Tunisia towards independence." But no sooner had the new resident general arrived in Tunis than he began to backpedal, declaring that he hoped to guide Tunisia "by progressive institutional modifications towards internal autonomy."[11]

The resident general's waffling cast doubts on the willingness of the French government to stay its course in the face of pressure from the right, whether in the form of *colons* in the protectorate or parliamentarians and other politicians in France. Neo-Dustur leaders anxiously awaited Périllier's first move. To their satisfaction, M'hamed Chenik became prime minister in a cabinet composed equally of Frenchmen and Tunisians including Salah ben Yusuf (as minister of justice) and several independents sympathetic to the Neo-Dustur. Despite apoplectic recriminations by the Rassemblement, the resignation of almost all the French members of the Grand Council, and charges of collaboration from some nationalist quarters, the ministry unveiled a proposal in February 1951 that envisioned, for the first time in seventy years, a fully Tunisian ministry and, for the first time in sixty-eight, a prime minister free from the control of the secretary general. The Neo-Dustur spurned the plan for offering too little, the settlers for offering too much.

Dustur leaders pointed to the impasse as evidence that in their eagerness to enter the government the Neo-Dusturians had either been duped by the French or had conspired with them to thwart the negotiations. Such criticisms from its all but defunct former rival mattered little to the Neo-Dustur, but it took more seriously those emanating from within. A small leftist contingent attacked the party's growing bourgeois appearance and its friendly relationship with Amin Bey, but it was party members and sympathizers who denounced cooperation with the protectorate authorities as a sellout (associated with the return of Bourguiba) that posed the greatest potential problem. Bourguiba's allies met this challenge by disseminating an adulatory pamphlet entitled *Habib Bourguiba: Pages de son combat*. Omitting all but negative references to party leaders, regardless of their past importance, who had questioned the *za'im* (leader), the publication portrayed Bourguiba as the only suitable leader, spokesman, and policy maker of the Neo-Dustur.[12]

Detractors still unmoved by this rather crude propaganda were brought into line through more forceful methods. Among them were Zaituna students, who had mounted protests against the Chenik ministry from its inception, often turning out thousands of demonstrators. As in the past, political and educational concerns fused together. In 1950 Sawt al-Talib al-Zaituni (The Voice of the Zaituna Student), a committee that had enjoyed the patronage of the Neo-Dustur since its founding three years earlier, published a "Sixteen-Point Charter" designed to raise the mosque-university from the lowly status accorded it under the protectorate and to replace the existing school system with one of Arab-Islamic inspiration that would employ Zaituna graduates. The Chenik government accepted the charter in principle, briefly damping down student hostility. But it lacked the ability to implement the demands, and student needling of the government, and of the Neo-Dustur, continued.

In November, critics of the government, with the Zaituna students in the forefront, held Chenik, his cabinet, and, by extension, the Neo-Dustur, responsible for a police assault on protesters in the town of Enfidaville that left seven people dead and dozens injured. Sawt al-Talib al-Zaituni demanded the convocation of a Neo-Dustur congress to purge leaders who had, in its estimation, turned against the Tunisian people. Bourguiba and the Western-oriented modernists who dominated the political bureau prodded party youth groups to confront the members of Sawt al-Talib al-Zaituni in street clashes – an uncharacteristically reckless response that inevitably inflamed matters. Neo-Dustur officials encouraged students to disavow Sawt al-Talib al-Zaituni and form an independent organization that the party promptly brought under its tutelage. Over the next three years the Neo-Dustur marginalized the opposition at the mosque-university and consolidated its supporters there into the Comité National des Etudiants Zeytouinens. This fracturing of the Zaituna student body reflected the gap between Bourguiba's modernist Francophile wing of the party and its more traditionally oriented components. Ben Yusuf, who had courted the latter in the rebuilding of the party, maintained a low profile through-out this process, but it greatly discomfited him. The taming of its Zaituna adversaries served the immediate needs of the Neo-Dustur, but imbued the students with a reservoir of ill will that guaranteed future problems.

The Chenik government soldiered on, introducing a revised reform pro-gram in October 1951. As usual, a government of Tunisians answering to an elected assembly formed its core, but it left France in control of Tunisia's defenses and diplomatic relations and acknowledged the legitimacy of a number of specific French interests. The Neo-Dustur reacted more pru-dently than it had to the government's first proposal, in part so as not to jeopardize the legalization it had secured in the interim, but also to avoid fostering an image of intransigence and negativism abroad, where its leaders were again soliciting support. When Farhat Hached, whose break with the WFTU had made him a favorite in the non-communist trade union movement, visited the United States in 1951 at the invitation of the American Federation of Labor, Bourguiba accompanied him. The union provided them with a platform for familiarizing the American public with the links between trade unionism and nationalism in colonial societies. Both men emphasized the moderation of the movements they led, their anticommunism, and their willingness to negotiate with France.

The Rassemblement equally reviled Chenik for putting the plan forward and Périllier for allowing him to do so. Repudiating the resident general, the *colons* appealed directly to sympathizers in the French government, insisting on the categorical rejection of any arrangement not embracing the concept of co-sovereignty. Their attitudes were the fruit of seven decades of colo-nialism in the protectorate, but the timing of the Bourguiba–Hached foray to the United States intensified *colon* antipathy and helped their cause in Paris. Since the end of World War II, American businessmen had discov-ered Tunisia. American companies held a majority interest in the Société nord-africaine des pétroles that was prospecting for oil in the protectorate, and US diplomats extolled the profitability of investments in agriculture, irrigation projects, small factories, and tourism. The French settlers – and many of their countrymen across the Mediterranean – distrusted American commercial intentions across North Africa and looked askance at Tunisians who promoted ties between the two countries.

The French government's response to the Chenik proposal came in December and revealed the effectiveness of the Rassemblement's campaign. It affirmed that the settlers' participation in fulfilling the mission of the protectorate, and particularly in developing the economy, made their exclusion from Tunisian political institutions unthinkable. In positing this principle as the basis for future discussions, Paris scrapped the concept of internal autonomy, much less independence – a reversal that it underscored by recalling the resident general ostensibly dispatched to lead Tunisia to independence. Jean de Hautecloque (1952–3), a Quai d'Orsay official better known for his links to conservative French political circles than for his diplomatic skills, replaced Périllier.[13] A firestorm roared through Tunisia. In a rare show of unanimity indicative of the magnitude of resentment, the Dustur and the USTT joined the Neo-Dustur and the UGTT in a three-day general strike. Bourguiba and Chenik each concluded that further negotiations were futile, and each changed course as the new year began. Echoing the rhetoric he had employed in 1937 to harden the stance of the Neo-Dustur, Bourguiba urged his followers to prepare for "combat on a grand scale. A revolt is going to develop and blood is going to flow."[14] France, he warned, risked losing everything. Chenik expressed his frustration by adopting a strategy Bourguiba had been urging on him for some time. He sent two of his ministers, Salah ben Yusuf and Muhammed Badra, to Paris to lodge a complaint with the United Nations that France was in violation of its treaties with Tunisia.

Hautecloque lost no time in doing what he had been sent to do, but he plunged the protectorate into turmoil in the process. The arrest of most of the Neo-Dusturian leadership incited riots that took the lives of several dozen participants, policemen, and soldiers. In retaliation for particularly fierce opposition in the Cap Bon area (where many residents possessed weapons abandoned by retreating German troops a decade earlier), Foreign Legionnaires conducted a brutal search-and-destroy operation to root out nationalists. They killed and captured some militants, but also caused the death or injury of scores of innocent persons and the extensive destruction of homes, fields, and other property. The sweep hardened opposition to the French throughout the country.

Since taking office Hautecloque had pressured the bey to dismiss Chenik. The seventy-three-year-old Amin held his ground as long as he dared, but the arrest of Chenik and all but one of the Tunisians in his cabinet, along with thousands of Neo-Dusturians and UGTT members, frightened him,

Figure 4.3. Place des Martyrs, Sousse. The statue memorializes nine demonstrators killed in January 1952 while protesting the refusal of France to grant autonomy to Tunisia.

as did reports of the Moroccan resident general's recent abusive treatment of Sultan Muhammad V. With no reason to believe that Hautecloque would not follow suit, and isolated from potential supporters, the bey yielded, naming another septuagenarian and former *qaid* who was sure to toe Hautecloque's line, Salaheddin Baccouche, as prime minister in March. Anxious for himself, his family, and his dynasty, the elderly ruler saw no other option, but his collapse angered some Neo-Dustur leaders. In an ironic bid to lend credibility to his government, Baccouche named Hedi Nouira, who sat on the Neo-Dustur political bureau and, remarkably, remained at liberty, to a cabinet position. When Nouira refused to accept a portfolio, he too was jailed.

Falling back on the Neo-Dustur's proven method of survival, middle-level cadres managed the party while key leaders were in detention or overseas (ben Yusuf and Badra had fled Paris for Cairo one step ahead of the French police). But it was Farhat Hached who emerged as the de facto leader of the nationalist movement after the 1952 arrests. In the crucible of French repression, the already numerous linkages between party and union, reflected in their extensively overlapping constituencies, evolved into an almost total identification between the two as the union subordinated its social and economic agenda to political action. The networks and skills of UGTT organizers enabled them easily to mobilize their 56,000 members for anti-French demonstrations, thus ensuring that the voice of the Neo-Dustur continued to be heard in the streets. Despite his followers' defiance of the French, Hached's high international profile endowed him with a measure of immunity from official retribution. He forcefully argued the nationalist position on a broadly representative commission convened by Amin Bey to evaluate Hautecloque's version of governmental reform. Its firm rejection of the plan did not, however, prevent the resident general from bullying the bey into approving some of its provisions, including the holding of municipal council elections predicated on a fifty–fifty split of seats between Tunisian and French representatives – a formula anathema to the Neo-Dustur. The party's successful boycott of the balloting rendered it meaningless.

As the committee disbanded in September, Hached issued a bleak assessment of the political situation, concluding that "when all negotiation becomes impossible, people will have recourse to arms."[15] Less than two months later, he was dead, assassinated by the Main Rouge, a *colon* terrorist organization that viewed his international linkages not as a shield against harm but as an incentive for it. Whatever satisfaction Hautecloque derived from the murder (in which the UGTT, the Neo-Dustur, and even some of the resident general's colleagues thought him complicit) quickly evaporated, as many Tunisians acted on Hached's estimate of the situation. Gangs of *fellagha* (literally, bandits), often consisting of unemployed workers led by men with experience in the UGTT, began to prowl southern and western Tunisia. They attacked French farms and police stations and sabotaged lines of communication, motivated by poverty and frustration as much as by political conviction, although they were too valuable a resource to remain outside the nationalist orbit for very long. The fear they sowed in the French community heightened tensions and invited reprisals by the army, the police, and the Main Rouge. Hautecloque's approach revealed not only the limits of repression, but also its risk of international censure. A bloc of Afro-Asian states in the United Nations proposed that the organization facilitate Franco-Tunisian negotiations, but France staunchly opposed the internationalization of what it insisted was an internal matter. But for how long its iron fist policy could withstand outside scrutiny remained to be seen.

Hautecloque departed, to the jeers of the Tunisians and the consternation of the settlers, in autumn 1953. His manifest failure to impose order compelled France to reopen negotiations, although Pierre Voizard (1953–4),

Hautecloque's successor, intended to keep the Neo-Dustur out of the process. The bey, whose confidence Voizard gained by showing him the respect that Hautecloque never had, recommended Muhammad Salah Mzali, a lawyer and a veteran of several governments, including Chenik's, and a man with strong ties to palace circles but few to the population at large, to the resident general as someone who could help him "disentangle this whole thing."[16] Mzali and Voizard drew up a plan of reforms that Amin approved along with his appointment of Mzali as prime minister in March 1954. While this scheme strengthened the powers of the prime minister, it also included a national assembly with equal French representation in budgetary deliberations and endorsed settler participation in the municipal councils. Its preservation of co-sovereignty guaranteed Tunisian opposition, which increased when Voizard sent Bourguiba to a French prison, physically detaching him from the country as he had earlier detached him from its political arena. In the end, the plan proved too little, too late and, most of all, too out of sync with nationalist requirements.

Mzali resigned after only three months in office, the reforms stillborn and the country in chaos. To demonstrate that France could not finesse them with impunity, the Neo-Dustur and the UGTT had responded to Voizard's exclusionary strategy by strengthening their links with the *fellagha*. Party and union men helped in their training, usually in Libya, where they acquired modern weapons. By mid-1954, they numbered several thousand and had evolved from rural bandits into competent guerrillas, touted as a patriotic army of liberation by the nationalist leadership, but rarely truly controlled by it. *Fellagha* operations tied down tens of thousands of French troops and threatened to turn Tunisia into another Indochina. Convinced that a continuation of the deadlock entailed unacceptable risks, the French prime minister, Pierre Mendès-France, determined to take previously unacceptable steps to break it. Assured by a confidant who had recently met with the Neo-Dustur chief that "a policy can be directed against Bourguiba . . . or it can be formulated with Bourguiba . . . It is inconceivable without Bourguiba,"[17] Mendès-France quietly initiated talks with him.

With more fanfare, he and Pierre Boyer de la Tour, his choice as resident general (1954–5), informed Amin Bey at a July audience that France now recognized Tunisian internal autonomy. They encouraged the ruler to appoint a government reflecting a range of Tunisian political views to manage the transition, in the hope – however far-fetched – that the inclusion of men outside the Neo-Dustur would minimize adverse settler reaction. Almost half of Prime Minister Tahar ben ʿAmmar's cabinet were Neo-Dusturians, as were two of the three delegates it selected to hammer out the precise terms of the new arrangement. As a sine qua non for proceeding, however, the French demanded the curbing of the *fellagha*. In an unprecedented display of cooperation expedited through the "back channel" contacts with Bourguiba, the Neo-Dustur, the Tunisian government, and the French civil and military authorities drew up a plan to disarm and amnesty the guerrillas. The party and the UGTT used all their influence to win over the *fellagha* who, with few exceptions, surrendered their weapons in an orderly procedure in early December.

The official negotiations moved forward slowly, and not without opposition. Correctly viewing the successful conclusion of the talks as the end of their way of life, the *colons* kept up an unrelenting attack on all those, Tunisian or French, who favored them. More ominously, not all Neo-Dustur leaders endorsed the dialogue, which brought the long simmering feud between Bourguiba and ben Yusuf into the limelight. The latter most often attacked the willingness of Bourguiba and his allies on the political bureau to discuss an agreement offering less than full independence, but the divergent worldviews of the two men ensured a tension that went well beyond tactical disagreements. Ben Yusuf had gravitated more and more into the pan-Arab camp just as his rival was laying the groundwork for the preservation of a strong, if decidedly altered, relationship between Tunisia and France. Bourguiba's role in the negotiations shifted from behind the scenes to center stage when Edgar Faure, the new French prime minister, solicited his active participation as the negotiations threatened to bog down.

Agreement on the terms of an internal autonomy convention came in late April 1955. By its provisions, France retained control of Tunisia's foreign relations and defense (in accordance with the Bardo Treaty), but it abrogated the clauses of the La Marsa Treaty that successive residents general had interpreted as empowering them to rule the country. The accord allowed the French of Tunisia to retain their metropolitan citizenship and guaranteed their rights to own property, pursue cultural, religious, economic, professional, and social activities, and have recourse, for a five-year period, to their own courts. On the other hand they lost their political rights except at the municipal council level, where demographic formulas for French representation assured them of as many as three-sevenths of the total seats in cities with large *colon* populations. Other facets of the convention ensured the continuation of close economic ties, arranged for the transfer of police powers from French to Tunisian hands after two years, and gave the French language a privileged status, particularly in education. In May, between 15,000 and 20,000 settlers demonstrated against the

Figure 4.4. The return to Tunis of Habib Bourguiba, June 1, 1955. Bourguiba met with a
tumultuous reception in Tunis following his release from prison and his successful
negotiation of an accord with the French government granting Tunisia internal autonomy.

agreement in Tunis, but their hopes that the French parliament would reject
it were dashed in July.[18] Thereafter, most turned their attention to salvaging
what they could, although diehards unwilling to accept the failure of the
Rassemblement joined Présence Française, a still more radical paramilitary group determined to perpetuate French control by whatever means
necessary.

Ben ᶜAmmar formed a majority Neo-Dustur government at the end of
the summer, but Bourguiba, who had returned to a tumultuous reception
in June, declined a portfolio. Instead, he rallied support for the accord,
stressing that internal autonomy represented an interim status towards
independence and not – despite Mendès-France's view – an end in itself.[19]
Bourguiba explained his acceptance of this incomplete arrangement by
arguing that the French defeat in Indochina, the outbreak of revolution in
Algeria, and the strength of opposition to decolonization prevented France
from placing any greater concession on the table. Political realism required
adopting a step-by-step approach, taking what was on offer and building
on it to secure a more advantageous agreement when better circumstances
arose. Ben Yusuf reentered the country in September, also to an enthusiastic welcome, and immediately took the offensive against what he labeled
as "a step backward."[20] At first, Bourguiba and ben Yusuf occasionally
appeared together, but their personal, political, and ideological differences
made reconciliation impossible. In October, the political bureau ousted the
secretary-general from the party.

The expulsion intensified ben Yusuf's campaign, which especially drew
support from disenchanted Neo-Dusturians and several of the national
organizations he had helped to form after the war. Although Ahmad ben
Salah, who succeeded Hached at the helm of the UGTT, kept most of his
powerful forces in the Bourguibist camp, many members of the UTAC and
the Union Générale des Agriculteurs Tunisiens (UGAT) gravitated to the
Yusufist ranks. So did Zaituna students and the remnants of the Dustur, two
other groups with scores to settle with the Neo-Dustur. Ben Yusuf assailed
the convention, the economy (which was faltering under the Neo-Dustur
minister of national economy, Muhammad Masmoudi), and the entire ben
ᶜAmmar government (which was falling short of many Tunisians' naively
high expectations). In encounters reminiscent of ᶜAbd al-ᶜAziz Thaᶜalbi's
1937 appearances, Neo-Dustur militants disrupted ben Yusuf's speeches and
roughed up his sympathizers. Bourguiba's embrace of liberal values did not
extend to the tolerance of contrary views.

The confrontation climaxed at a party congress in November 1955. Ben
Yusuf's attempts to block it or to organize a boycott failed. With Bourguiba
and his allies providing the orchestration, congress delegates endorsed the
accords, along with all other decisions of the political bureau since the party's
last general meeting in early 1952. The congress also adopted a UGTT report
outlining a progressive social and economic agenda implicitly rejecting ben
Yusuf's preference that the party focus on pan-Arab issues. Despite this
setback, ben Yusuf and his followers – 20,000 of whom came into the streets

of Tunis to protest against the congress[21] – carried on. Some organized rival party cells; others turned to violence against the mainstream Neo-Dustur that extended to a recrudescence of *fellagha* bands. With the country on the verge of civil war, ben Yusuf fled to Cairo in January, but continued to berate his former comrades until his assassination by an unknown assailant in 1961.

Just as the Franco-Tunisian talks wound down in 1955, France began discussions with Morocco that produced a nationalist government and restored the pro-nationalist Sultan Muhammad V, deposed two years before. Eager to shift resources from Morocco, whose independence now seemed inevitable, to Algeria, whose rebellion it had to crush, France terminated its protectorate over Morocco in early March. Bourguiba lost no time in demanding similar treatment for Tunisia, and France assented on March 20. Nonetheless, pro-Yusufist *fellagha* fought on in the south and west. It was no coincidence that the areas where the Yusufist threat lingered longest were the most economically depressed of the country. The unsettled conditions at the moment of independence highlighted serious problems facing the state's leaders: the need to close political fissures, the need to promote social and economic development, and the need to lessen the disparities between coastal areas and the interior. In tackling the first two they met with varying degrees of success; the third proved impervious to their decidedly less resolute efforts.

CHAPTER 5

The independent state sets its course, 1956–1969

STATE IN THE SERVICE OF THE PARTY, PARTY IN THE SERVICE OF THE PRESIDENT

The magnitude of the support for ben Yusuf appalled Bourguiba. Basking in the titles *al-za'im* (the leader) and *al-mujahid al-akbar* (the supreme combatant), he had persuaded himself that his combination of charisma and dedication to the nationalist struggle ensured him the gratitude and loyalty of all Tunisians. The rebellion that had, at its height in late 1955, threatened to plunge the country into civil war still cast a pall over the celebrations marking the end of the protectorate in March 1956. It provided Bourguiba with a sobering reminder that the Tunisian public knew that others, whose thinking differed from his, had also played important roles in the acquisition of independence. The presidency of the Neo-Dustur did not translate into the unswerving allegiance of the masses, particularly if the party suffered from internal fragmentation.

Bourguiba had masterfully employed the rhetoric of nationalism to mobilize hundreds of thousands of ordinary Tunisians behind the readily comprehensible demand to end French rule, but with independence fiery anti-colonial speeches lost most of their currency. To move from that achievement to the construction of a viable, prosperous, and modern state required convincing those same Tunisians of the merits of social and economic ideas that had taken a back seat during the campaign against the protectorate regime – ideas whose value they did not always find inherently obvious and that rarely enjoyed the breadth of support national liberation had. Ensuring their widespread acceptance required a lengthy process of education. As that went forward, Bourguiba prepared to advance his post-independence agenda and to guard against future challenges by securing a role in the new government and strengthening his position within the Neo-Dustur. With a self-confidence that frequently slipped into arrogance, Bourguiba cast himself in the roles of patriarch, teacher, and disciplinarian, making it clear that he, the founding father of modern Tunisia, knew better than anyone else what its people, his children, required.

Scheduled prior to the French decision to end the protectorate, elections for the assembly charged with writing a constitution took place as planned on March 25, less than a week after independence. In a secret meeting with the bey in January, Bourguiba had threatened to publicize Amin's sympathy for the Yusufists unless he enacted an electoral law by which voters cast ballots for a list of candidates drawn up by the party, with the list receiving a majority in a district winning its seat. This guaranteed that Neo-Dustur candidates chosen by the political bureau would control the constituent assembly, but flew in the face of recurrent nationalist demands for a popularly elected assembly, since voters had to accept or reject in its entirety a list formulated by party officials. Both the surreptitious manner in which Bourguiba negotiated this arrangement and its substance distressed many high-ranking Neo-Dusturians who preferred a more democratic approach accommodating a wider range of views and offering an opportunity for party dissidents like ben Yusuf to engage their rivals peacefully within the political arena rather than violently outside it.

The Neo-Dustur list, which included candidates selected in consultation with the UGTT and other national organizations controlled by the political bureau, won all ninety-eight seats in the assembly, although abstention rates of 71 percent in Jerba and 41 percent in Tunis demonstrated that ben Yusuf continued to command a substantial following.[1] Replacing ben ʿAmmar as prime minister following the elections, Bourguiba saw to the quelling of the Yusufist uprising, but he had no remedy for the sullen opposition of those who had refused to lend legitimacy to the voting by their participation. Because the Tunisian army consisted of only a few thousand men, many of them former guerrillas lacking adequate training, ending the rebellion required the assistance of the former colonizer. With some reluctance, the French army and police cooperated with the Bourguiba government, as they had with ben ʿAmmar's, and by June 1956 the last of the *fellagha* were killed or captured. A "High Court," created specifically for the purpose, tried them and other partisans of ben Yusuf accused of criminal activity. Bourguiba justified this exceptional measure on the rather dubious grounds that ben Yusuf's tenure as justice minister had given him extensive contacts with judges that might color their assessment of his followers. The court also punished Tunisians who had profited from collaboration with the French. In 1957, laws of "ill gotten gains" and "national indignity" set in motion a succession of show trials that lasted until 1959, ruining the reputations and careers of prominent figures such as Tahar ben ʿAmmar,

Figure 5.1. Salah ben Yusuf. The differences between ben Yusuf and Bourguiba came to a head in the months immediately preceding independence. When it beame clear that ben Yusuf would not prevail, he fled to Cairo, where he was assassinated in 1961.

Salah al-Din Baccouche, and Muhammad Mzali, but also of scores of lesser functionaries.

The formation of the "High Court" was but one of several steps taken by Bourguiba to shape the political system so as to maximize his powers. Ignoring the objections of liberal deputies, he encouraged the assembly to focus exclusively on devising a constitution and used the bey's legislative power to relegate it to a largely consultative role. The assembly did, however, vote in July 1957 to abolish the office of bey, create a republic, and vest Amin's legislative and executive powers in the president, a title it bestowed on Bourguiba, making him the head of state as well as the head of the government. The promulgation of the constitution came only in June 1959. By then, Bourguiba had concentrated virtually all the state's power in his hands, creating a "presidential monarchy" legitimized by the fundamental law. The Neo-Dustur swept parliamentary elections held later in the year, with list voting giving the party all the seats in the toothless National Assembly. Bourguiba won massive public support in an unopposed bid for a five-year term as president, a scenario repeated in 1964 and again in 1969.

As he was consolidating his control of the government, Bourguiba was also asserting his primacy in the Neo-Dustur. He had never relinquished its presidency and by the end of the 1950s he stood at the apex of a system weaving together the institutions of the party, the state, and the national organizations. In 1957 the Neo-Dustur boasted of an astonishing 600,000 members – almost twice as many as it claimed at the time of the party congress only two years before. While certainly exaggerated, the figure nevertheless reflects a surge in party membership as Tunisians who had previously stood aloof rushed to affiliate with the winners of the long battle for independence. For the first time in its history, public attachment to the party entailed no risk. On the contrary, the absence of ties created potential problems, since the post-independence Neo-Dustur operated a patronage network providing sinecures for its stalwarts. Party membership was *de rigeur* for government jobs; a record as a militant was frequently the key qualification for the more important posts. Following the artificial spike in 1956 and 1957, the introduction of a distinction between militants and adherents leveled off the number of activists at around 350,000, with the number of cells dropping from 1,830 to 1,000.[2] At the command echelon, the political bureau, now restyled as the central committee, grew from fifteen to fifty members during the first few years of independence. While still an elite component of the party, it no longer wielded the power of its smaller, closely knit predecessors. Its influence diminished further with the establishment in 1964 of a fifteen-member political bureau, handpicked by the president to make policy and set the party's course. Except for Bourguiba, these bodies included none of the first-generation leaders of the party, all of whom had come into conflict with him, often amid accusations of betrayal or abandonment in moments of crisis. Not all the men climbing the Neo-Dustur's leadership ladder unquestioningly toed the party line on all matters, but few of them had the backing to challenge Bourguiba and the loyal coterie surrounding him.

Ahmad ben Salah did. The UGTT illustrated a dilemma confronting the Neo-Dustur after 1956. Universal concurrence on the need for independence, despite tactical disagreements about how to achieve it, had unified the various constituencies within the party, but once that goal had been attained, greatly divergent views about the nature of the independent state came to the surface. Particularly acute philosophical differences between the union and the party meant that tightening Neo-Dustur control over the UGTT assumed an extremely high priority following independence. Bourguiba believed that the socialist programs ben Salah had called for at the 1955 party congress would jeopardize crucial Western support for his government and had no intention of implementing them, even after they received the endorsement of a majority of the union's 150,000 workers at its 1956 congress. Privately encouraged by Bourguiba, Habib ᶜAchour, an aide to Hached in the earliest days of the UGTT and a Neo-Dusturian even before that, challenged ben Salah by enticing a third of the UGTT's membership into a rival organization that demanded his removal as a condition for reuniting the labor movement. When Bourguiba publicly threw his weight behind ᶜAchour, the UGTT administration fell into line and appointed a new secretary-general, Ahmad Tlili, who also served on the Neo-Dustur political bureau. Ben Salah resigned, and for the next fifteen years the union disappeared from the political stage except as an appendage of the party. Symbolizing this demise, UGTT members of the constituent assembly secured no more than a passing mention of social guarantees in the final draft of the constitution, which did not even sanction workers' right to strike.

Ben Salah fared better personally than did the UGTT institutionally. Less than five years after being discredited, Bourguiba rehabilitated him, added him to the Neo-Dustur political bureau, and appointed him minister of national planning, charging him with the supervision of a major overhaul of the economy. Many came to regard him as Bourguiba's choice for his successor. On the political bureau, ben Salah replaced Muhammad Masmoudi, a rival whom Bourguiba believed had intrigued to bring about his downfall. As minister of information, Masmoudi oversaw *L'Action* (the renamed *L'Action Tunisienne*, which had resumed publication in 1955). After several years during which the paper had made scathing comments on the 1956 electoral law, the work of the constituent assembly, and the "High Court" trials, as well as on the direction of the country's foreign policy, Bourguiba expelled Masmoudi from the party. Like ben Salah, he subsequently regained a position of prominence, ironically when ben Salah's fortunes again took a turn for the worse late in the 1960s. Banishing his critics from the inner circles of the state and the party only to summon them back, appropriately chastened after a period of powerlessness – a severe deprivation for members of the Tunisian political elite, most of whom had dedicated their adult lives to the quest for power – remained a favorite technique of Bourguiba, whose intolerance for opposition showed no signs of abating after 1956.

THE TRANSFORMATION OF THE SOCIAL ENVIRONMENT

In spring and summer 1956 Bourguiba took advantage of the national enthusiasm for independence, his own generally positive image and high public profile, and the considerable power he was already amassing to impose state control over certain aspects of religion. To do so reflected a very significant contrast between the views of Bourguiba and those of ben Yusuf on the important issue of the role of Islam in the state. The choice of these reforms and the speed with which they proceeded revealed Bourguiba's eagerness to assert the domination of his interpretations, not those of his rival, over the Tunisian body politic. The Habus Council, which managed land set aside for the support of mosques, Qur'anic schools, and other Islamic institutions, came under fire first. The government confiscated the property of the administration, which was tainted by its willingness to provide land for colonization during the protectorate, thus bringing the religious, educational, and charitable institutions that were beneficiaries of the agency's funds under state control. A year after dismantling the "public" *habus* system, the government ordered the distribution of "private" *habus* lands (whose usufruct accrued to the heirs of the founder, who had ceded ownership rights by creating the endowment) among the heirs as private property.

The state judicial system absorbed the two sharia courts (one for adherents of the Maliki rite, the other for Hanafi Muslims) in August 1956, clearing the way for the introduction of a Personal Status Code altering certain practices sanctioned by Islamic law but regarded by progressives as prejudicial to women. The code strengthened the nuclear family and fostered a more equitable relationship between the genders. Women won new rights, including those of divorce and the approval of arranged marriages, and expanded existing entitlements in questions of child custody and inheritance. At the same time, the code explicitly placed obligations on women, such as contributing to the maintenance of the household if their means allowed. Other provisions outlawed polygyny, ended the male right of repudiation, and set minimum ages for marriages.

The most innovative legal reform in the Muslim world since the abolition of the sharia in Turkey in the 1920s, the Personal Status Code clearly revealed the social trajectory envisioned by the country's leader. He took

Figure 5.2. Postage stamp publicizing the Personal Status Code, 1958. The Code introduced dramatic changes in the law, banning polygyny, setting minimum ages for marriage, and enabling women to initiate divorce proceedings. It represented the most revolutionary such legislation in the Muslim world since the reforms of Mustafa Kemal Ataturk in the Turkey of the 1920s.

pains, however, to portray himself not as sweeping aside Islam, as had Ataturk, but rather as reinterpreting it through *ijtihad*, or independent reasoning – a process esteemed by the nineteenth- and twentieth-century Islamic reformers as well as by Bourguiba, for whom the rationalism instilled by his French education ranked among the most noble of human qualities. Addressing an audience of Europeans and Tunisians not long after the enactment of the code, the prime minister observed that Tunisia's deeply rooted Arab and Islamic traditions in no way lessened its desire

to live in close communion with the modern world . . . [and] to open windows on other cultures, particularly Western culture, in order to come to grips with reality. In this way, our country can remain faithful to its cultural past while forging the instruments required for its future.[3]

By appointing a moderately forward-looking figure as rector of the Zaituna mosque-university, reorganizing the sharia courts and reassigning or retiring some of their judges, and by offering blandishments of various kinds to other prominent members of the religious establishment, the government succeeded in muting opposition to the code. Many less well-placed ulama cast aspersions on both the senior officials' timidity and Bourguiba's temerity, but they knew they were powerless to stop him. Ben Yusuf thundered that Bourguiba had taken it upon himself to "prohibit what God has authorized and authorize what God has prohibited"[4] – an inversion of a traditional obligation of the just Muslim ruler – but he spoke from Cairo and could not affect developments in Tunis.

For the male Neo-Dusturians who engineered the Personal Status Code – not until 1955 did women enter the inner circle of the party, and then only a few – the full emancipation of Tunisia required the elimination of antiquated social practices, in gender relations no less than in labor relations. This attitude, rather than a more feminist one, gave rise to the code, as it did to a campaign to discourage all forms of traditional dress, but particularly veiling. Bourguiba believed that old-fashioned clothing encouraged old-fashioned modes of thinking and acting; those who chose to wear it were, at least subconsciously, expressing their rejection of the modern world. In speech after speech during the first years after independence, he condemned the veil as an "odious rag" that demeaned women, had no practical value, and was not obligatory in order to conform to Islamic standards of modesty. Always appearing in public in a coat and tie – another point of divergence from ben Yusuf – the Neo-Dustur leader made similar arguments concerning traditional male garments. Despite his strong personal convictions,

Bourguiba well understood the tenacity with which many Tunisians clung to customs they had followed since childhood and, except for banning the veil in classrooms, he refused to proscribe traditional clothing.

To educate Tunisian women about the Personal Status Code, encourage them to venture beyond habitual limits, and offer them opportunities to improve their day-to-day lives, a number of women related to Neo-Dustur leaders formed the Union Nationale des Femmes Tunisiennes (UNFT) in 1956. The party had some ties to the Union Musulmane des Femmes de Tunisie, an organization founded in 1936 on the Salafiyya reform model, but had generally shown little interest in supporting such associations. In the 1930s most were too conservative for Neo-Dustur tastes; in the postwar years, the most active groups were communist fronts. Beginning in the early 1950s, with more women taking more active roles in the nationalist campaign than ever before, they began creating networks of assistance for families whose men were in prison or had joined the *fellagha*. Some women also joined the guerrilla bands, while others provided information, served as scouts, or transported small arms, since French soldiers and policemen were unlikely to stop and search them. In 1955 a congress of three hundred women demanded civil and political equality with men, enfranchisement, the right to stand for elected office, and greater attention to female education, but the ben ʿAmmar government set the women's agenda aside while it focused on bringing the protectorate to an end. The Neo-Dustur, on the other hand, responded with the Personal Status Code and the UNFT. By 1960 the latter had almost 14,000 members in 115 branches.[5] In addition to promoting the Personal Status Code, particularly in rural areas where women and men alike had reservations about the reforms, the UNFT concentrated its initial efforts on urging women to exercise their right to vote, granted in 1957, on sponsoring literacy classes for the 96 percent of the female population who could not read or write, and on developing health programs, some of them devoted to family planning. In the decade between 1956 and 1965 women's literacy rose and their fertility fell, both quite dramatically. While by no means solely responsible for such reversals, UNFT members unquestionably contributed to them as the organization's educational work benefited tens of thousands of women in the early years of independence.

Hundreds of thousands of their daughters profited from party and government campaigns in favor of formal schooling for young women. Because a modern education had played so formative a role in the life of most of independent Tunisia's leaders,[6] they recognized the importance of expanding the state education system, aligning it with contemporary national needs, and drawing more students into it. In the past few girls had attended school, but Neo-Dustur officials knew that providing girls with a modern education would influence the social values they would impart to their families when they became wives and mothers. In the mid-1950s few women worked except in their homes and fields, but efficient economic development necessitated an increase in the number of women in the workforce and the opening of new sectors to their employment, thereby creating additional impulses to educate more females. The last decade of the protectorate had seen significant growth in the primary school population – a doubling for boys, a quadrupling for girls – but in 1956 still only 13 percent of primary-school-aged girls attended classes regularly.[7] The comparable figure for boys (33 percent) reveals that educational deficiencies, while most acute among women, were by no means gender-specific. Past the primary level, enrollments declined precipitately for both.

Starting in 1958, with the objective of providing a primary education for all children within a decade while also improving secondary schools, the government began dedicating approximately one-fifth of its budget to the construction of new schools, the training of additional teachers, and the revamping of the curriculum. One crucial early decision determined the language of public instruction. Despite the status of Arabic as the official national language, government and party leaders recognized the importance of French as a bridge to the world beyond Tunisia and an essential tool for economic development. In any case, the country's reliance on a cadre of foreign instructors to supplement the 6,000 Tunisian teachers available at independence, and the disinclination to recruit educators from Arab countries with quite divergent political outlooks, made some instruction in French inevitable. Satisfied with the resulting bilingual system, the government made a commitment to eventual Arabization but took no significant steps in that direction. In primary schools the first two years were taught in Arabic, the remainder in French or a combination of the two languages. French was the norm at the secondary level, although the use of Arabic gradually became more common in subjects such as history, geography, and philosophy. This bilingual structure, along with the paring down of religious instruction in the curriculum, left Zaituna graduates, many of whom traditionally pursued teaching careers, with few prospects in the post-independence education system.

A second important decision concerned the method of promoting education. To fill the schools, government and party leaders preferred to utilize their considerable powers of persuasion rather than to make education compulsory. Enrollments at the primary level climbed steadily, eventually peaking (in the 1980s) at around 85 percent of the boys and 70 percent of the girls aged between six and eleven. A similar trend occurred in the secondary schools, except that attendance never exceeded 40 percent of the twelve- to seventeen-year-old population and only about a third of all students were women.[8] The ambitious goal of universal education was achieved only after the passage of a 1991 law making school attendance mandatory for all children between the ages of six and sixteen.

The social revolution set in motion during the first several years of independence brought Tunisia into the international spotlight. Devised by high-level Neo-Dustur and government officials, and imposed from above by a regime enjoying broad support but hardly respectful of democratic conventions, the reforms embodied the agenda of a leader confident that he knew (better than they) what his countrymen needed and determined to build a "modern" society respected by the global community. At a time when colonial mentalities about the Afro-Asian masses' need for enlightened (Westernized) guidance remained prevalent, neither the arrogance of the reformer nor his sometimes heavy-handed methods drew criticism from abroad. Instead, the Bourguiba government won praise for its assault on "outmoded traditions" and its expansion of education and enhancement of the status of women. These social policies, coupled with Bourguiba's unflinching Cold War alignment with the West, helped to secure the economic assistance of the United States, which touted Tunisia as a model for other developing countries, comparing it particularly favorably with Arab states that had sacrificed social progress to revolutionary politics. By the 1960s, with decolonization in full stride across Africa, independent Tunisia's social programs had taken root and were bearing fruit. Some emerging leaders in former French colonies had personally known Bourguiba in their student days in France; others, from all over the continent, knew and respected his reputation as a nationalist and an advocate of social change. The Tunisian example influenced many of them as they set their countries' postindependence courses.

Respect in the international arena meant little to resolute opponents at home, especially within the religious establishment. The many Zaituna students, faculty, and alumni who had broken with the mainstream Neo-Dustur leadership either in the last years of the independence struggle or in the midst of the Yusufist challenge resented the placement of the mosque-university under the supervision of the ministry of education in 1956, regarding the step as a prelude to more stringent official control over religious matters. The subsequent state domination of Islamic educational, legal, and other institutions once within the purview of Zaituna ulama bore out their concerns. But it was Bourguiba's public disparagement of the Muslim fast during the month of Ramadan that caused their indignation to boil over.

In a 1960 speech the president asserted that Tunisia's involvement in a jihad against underdevelopment absolved its citizens from fasting, just as warriors in a jihad in defense of Islam were exempted. To sanction this interpretation as a product of *ijtihad* (as he had justified controversial provisions of the Personal Status Code), Bourguiba demanded a fatwa of endorsement from the mufti of Tunis. When his statement failed to offer unequivocal support, he lost his job. Even among the party faithful, however, few Tunisians heeded their leader's advice. In the following year, as he prepared to renew the campaign, rioting erupted in Kairouan. A Yusufist stronghold since well before independence, this venerable religious center had discovered that the price of its defiance of Bourguiba and his allies was its exclusion from the projects that were improving the quality of life elsewhere in the country. Its influential ulama openly denigrated Bourguiba's views of Islam and despised his efforts to cast himself as a religious authority. A government decision to reassign a popular and outspoken imam sparked a day of street battles between demonstrators and the police in the most serious and bloodiest challenge to the political establishment since the crushing of the Yusufist *fellagha*.

Bourguiba subsequently smeared the religious leaders with allegations that their loss of economic power with the confiscation of *habus* lands, rather than spiritual concerns, lay behind their discontent and the encouragement they had given to the protesters. He made a point of once again urging Tunisians to ignore the fast, but then let the matter drop. Regardless of the extent to which new schools and new legal codes were transforming their society, the vast majority of Tunisians had no intention of breaking with the fundamental religious practices that defined them as Muslims. The assault on Islamic institutions and practices between 1956 and 1961 confirmed the ulama in their abhorrence of the Neo-Dustur and its secular leader, but they knew they were powerless to defy them. As if to underscore that reality, when the University of Tunis opened later in 1961, it absorbed the Zaituna mosque-university as a faculty of theology, clearly subordinating it to the state and its graduates to their countrymen with a Western education. Since both Bourguiba and the ulama understood that the state had the power to hold the religious establishment in check, there was, for the moment, no merit in either continuing to antagonize the other.

THE LINGERING SHADOW OF FRANCE

Bourguiba's permission for the Algerian Front de Libération Nationale (FLN) to establish camps inside Tunisia – a decision designed in part to outflank ben Yusuf, who had maintained close relations with the FLN since its inception – strained independent Tunisia's rapport with France, leading to the suspension of promised economic assistance between 1957 and 1963. Only the infusion of substantial aid from the United States prevented the withholding of French funds from crippling the reforms already under way. Tunisians enthusiastically backed the Algerian revolution, and the government of the newly independent state could hardly fail to help its neighbor attain its own independence. Although Bourguiba attempted to balance Tunisian support for the Algerian military campaign with steps promoting a peaceful settlement, a combination of French intransigence and virulent opposition to compromise among vocal Arab nationalist proponents of the FLN, led by the Egyptian president, Jamal ʿAbd al-Nasser, undermined that approach. Because of his distaste for Nasser's pan-Arab rhetoric (which had made Cairo a comfortable political environment for ben Yusuf since 1956) and for the Egyptian leader's domination of the League of Arab States, Bourguiba endeavored to distance his country from the turbulent politics of the Arab east. Tunisia did not join the League until 1958, and its decision to do so then stemmed less from a reorientation of interests than from the need to avoid isolation as its relationship with France deteriorated.

   In February of that year, French aircraft attacked Sakiet Sidi Youssef, a village on the Algerian border, causing scores of civilian deaths. Bourguiba responded with a revival of anti-colonial rhetoric, mobilizing public opinion behind a demand for the withdrawal of most of the several thousand French troops still garrisoned in Tunisia and the restriction of the remainder to a few posts in the Sahara and the massive naval installation at Bizerte. The formation of a provisional Algerian government in Tunis later in the year provided an additional irritant to France, but it was an incident at the Bizerte base that provoked an armed confrontation in July 1961. To pressure France into acceding to his demand to evacuate the base, Bourguiba urged party militants to form a "people's army" to join soldiers and policemen in blockading the French positions scattered throughout the vicinity of Bizerte. In several days of clashes for which they were woefully ill prepared, thousands of these volunteers were killed or wounded as French troops seized key parts of the city and the surrounding region. Tunisia appealed to the United Nations, which ordered France to pull its forces back to the naval base and urged negotiations to resolve the dispute. After delaying

"I DON'T LIKE TO BE RUSHED."

Figure 5.3. American cartoonist Bill Mauldin on the Bizerte crisis. Mauldin had been with US forces in Tunisia during World War II and retained an interest in the country afterwards, drawing several editorial cartoons on the situation there in the early 1960s.

serious discussions on the status of the base until the Algerian war ended
in summer 1962, France then agreed to hand it over in the following year.
Despite his responsibility for the heavy loss of life at Bizerte, Bourguiba's
firm grip on party and state minimized any serious internal backlash. The
recklessness of the venture did, however, shock Western friends of Tunisia,
although their concerns abated as it became clear that the incident did not
signal a Cold War realignment. If, however, Bourguiba had entertained
expectations that the restoration of the Bizerte base to Tunisian sovereignty
might cause him to be lionized outside the country in the way that the
expulsion of the British from Suez had enhanced Nasser's regional prestige,
he was mistaken.

The last French soldiers left Tunisia on October 15, 1963, although several
thousand French settlers still refused to join the exodus that had followed
independence. Between 1955 and 1959, 170,000 Europeans – roughly two-
thirds of the total – left the country. Among them, in the first eighteen
months alone, were 8,000 French functionaries. Tunisian lycée and university graduates filled some of the higher-level posts that they vacated, but
party loyalists filled many more, despite their frequent lack of appropriate skills. The rolls of Muslim public employees rose from 12,000 prior to
independence to 80,000 five years later. Reduced, like the French, to the
category of resident aliens, a third of the 67,000 Italians in Tunisia in 1956
left before the end of the decade.[9] Some settlers left because they could
not, or did not wish to, cope with the adjustments necessitated by independence. For others, the businesses in which they worked closed down or
government restrictions made it difficult for them to earn a living.

Nor were foreigners the only emigrants from Tunisia during these years.
The creation of Israel in 1948, at a time of uncertainty about the future
of their own homeland, prompted almost 15 percent of the Jewish population of roughly 85,000 to leave in the four succeeding years. In the year of
Tunisian independence, 6,500 departed, leaving the new state with some
58,000 Jewish citizens.[10] The number of emigrants declined significantly
over the next several years, as none of the misfortunes feared at the end
of the protectorate befell the community. To the contrary, a prominent
Jewish lawyer served in the first administration and Jewish members of the
liberal professions held other state offices, the new government made no
attempt to block Tunisian Jews from emigrating to Israel, and, although
not publicly known at the time, Bourguiba maintained discreet contacts
with officials of the World Jewish Congress, with whom he discussed matters of common interest and to whom he revealed, as early as 1957, his
view that the Arab states needed to reconcile the justice of the Palestinians'

cause with the acceptance of the existence of Israel.[11] Eight years later he made a public proposal that the newly created Palestine Liberation Organization accept the 1947 UN partition of Palestine as a point of departure for negotiations with Israel. In response, Nasser orchestrated a barrage of ridicule and hostility so scathing that Tunisia severed diplomatic relations with Egypt in 1966. But the outbreak of war in the following year between Israel and its Arab neighbors revealed that few Tunisians shared their president's view on the emotionally charged issue of Palestine. Anti-Zionist demonstrations erupted throughout the country, some of them provoking assaults on members of the Jewish community or damage to synagogues and other Jewish-owned property. Despite Bourguiba's denunciation of these incidents, a sustained wave of Jewish emigration following the war rapidly reduced the community to less than half its 1956 size.

FROM LIBERAL ECONOMY TO "NEO-DUSTUR SOCIALISM"

The outflow of Europeans in the first few years of independence created many economic difficulties for the new government but also provided it with some opportunities. On the one hand, the country lacked the resources adequately to offset the loss of large numbers of health care professionals, lawyers, engineers, civil servants, entrepreneurs, middle-level managers, skilled workers, and, perhaps most critically of all, commercial farmers, whose share of output was greatly disproportionate to their numbers or the extent of their property because they used machinery and modern techniques on particularly rich parcels of land. Their departure had an extremely negative impact on agricultural productivity. In other sectors of the economy, few Tunisians were in a position to fill the vacuum created by the massive flight of capital, while those who were hesitated to act. Government attempts to draw local investors into the management of the public utilities that it had nationalized in 1956 failed, leaving the state to operate those services itself, less by choice than by necessity. In a more positive vein, Europeans' decisions to leave made jobs available to Tunisians (albeit primarily to those with an education who lived in urban areas) and the government's seizure of land abandoned by settlers returning to France and Italy brought under its control thousands of hectares of valuable rural real estate.

Responsibility for managing the economy fell to Hedi Nouira, the director of the Central Bank of Tunisia from its inception in 1958 until 1970. A member of the Neo-Dustur political bureau, Nouira's personal friendship with Bourguiba, a contemporary and fellow native of the Sahil town of

Monastir, gave him influence and latitude. Like his chief, Nouira believed that preserving the liberal economy of the protectorate era held the key to creating prosperity while keeping Tunisia on an even economic keel during its transition to independence. In accordance with this thinking, the state provided land for peasant farmers who had little or none, but did so without infringing on private ownership rights. Instead, it distributed farmland abandoned by former *colons*, property recovered from the Habus Council, and estates that it purchased from willing European sellers still resident in the country. The new owners were urged to form cooperatives that enabled them, while retaining their individual titles, to secure advantageous credit terms and gain access to farm machinery. Along with evidence of social progress and political reliability, this course of economic moderation brought some $50 million in US aid to Tunisia in the first five years of its independence.[12] Disappointingly, however, neither foreign nor domestic investment came close to attaining their desired levels.

As population growth, which had not yet begun to respond to government efforts to curb it, outstripped the growth of the economy, the latter stalled, causing discomfort for some Tunisians and serious hardship for many more. Coping with this situation required state and party leaders to move beyond the previously dominant ideology of nationalism, with its scant attention to economic issues, while attempting to prevent the multiplicity of classes and interest groups that had united in the independence struggle from turning against one another. They did so by focusing attention on a systematic battle against underdevelopment. As early as 1958, a rather ineffectual National Planning Council linked representatives of the major national organizations – the UGTT, the UNAT (Union Nationale des Agriculteurs Tunisiens, which had supplanted the Yusufist UGAT after 1955), and the UTIC (Union Tunisien des Industriels et Commerçants, the name adopted by the UTAC after independence) – with appropriate government officials. The Neo-Dustur congress of the following year issued a call for the creation of a national plan to address the problems of the economy, but in the months following the bombing of Sakiet Sidi Youssef the campaign to restrict France's military presence in Tunisia took precedence over all others. Early in 1961 Bourguiba confirmed rumors of an impending significant decision on the economic front by naming Ahmad ben Salah to head a newly formed ministry of planning, thus bestowing on him the influence over the national economy that he had unsuccessfully sought in 1956. As the president made it clear that ben Salah now enjoyed his total confidence, both men began to speak not only of planning, but also of "Neo-Dustur socialism."

The renaming of the Neo-Dustur as the Parti Socialiste Dusturien (Dustur Socialist Party – PSD) at the party congress that took place in "liberated" Bizerte in 1964 conveyed the official embrace of this ideology. Other decisions taken at the congress restructured the party and reformulated its relationship with the national organizations and the government, all with the aim of reviving its pre-independence place at the vanguard of the nation rather than allowing it to slip into a bureaucratic torpor, as some of its leaders feared was happening. The PSD tightened its control over the national organizations, seen now less as partners of the party calling its attention to the interests of their members than as subordinate agencies expected only to endorse and promote its views. The party insisted that members of the national organizations also join the PSD as individuals (instead of automatically acquiring membership through affiliation with the organizations, as had been the case in the past). This measure eliminated the possibility of an organization pressuring the party by threatening to sever its connection and withdraw its members. The party congresses of 1955 and 1959 had sidestepped the issue of the relationship between party and state, but the 1964 session explicitly tied them together, with the party acting as the agent of impulsion, the state the agent of execution. Regional and local branches of the party had paralleled the structure of the government since 1958, but now regional governors simultaneously represented both the state and the PSD. Moreover, substantial numbers of well-educated technocrats began to replace unskilled party loyalists in key executive positions in both government and PSD agencies, especially those engaged with the economy and planning. Officially the only party in the country after the Parti Communiste Tunisien was banned in 1963 following its implication in an antigovernment conspiracy, the Parti Socialiste Dusturien emerged from the 1964 congress with a tighter grip on the state and its citizens than ever before, while Bourguiba left the gathering with the party equally well in hand.

In the three years between ben Salah's appointment as minister of planning and the Bizerte congress, "Neo-Dustur socialism" had taken shape. The first Ten-Year Plan (1962–71) envisaged an annual growth rate of 6 percent that would increase self-sufficiency, raise living standards, and begin to achieve an equitable distribution of income. Limited structural reforms anticipated state intervention in critical, but previously neglected, sectors of the economy, such as industry; bringing foreign-owned enterprises under Tunisian control (the last stage of decolonization); and the establishment of a network of agricultural cooperatives. Carrying out so ambitious an agenda demanded greater investment in the economy than had previously

Figure 5.4. President Habib Bourguiba at his desk, ca. 1965. As prime minister, president, and party leader, Bourguiba charted the political, economic, and social course of independent Tunisia. His bold approach won him the friendship of many Afro-Asian leaders, but also of prominent political figures in the West.

materialized. From the early 1960s to the end of the decade, the proportion of gross domestic product (GDP) represented by investment climbed from 10 percent to 23 percent, but reliance on external loans and grants for more than a third of the financing of development projects during those same years created great difficulties. Although some established aid donors' unhappiness with the turn to socialism prevented foreign aid from attaining what ministry of planning officials regarded as optimal levels, public and private inputs from abroad reached $31 per capita in 1969, a figure higher than almost anywhere in the world. Because most funds came in the form of loans, they contributed to a quadrupling of government debt between 1960 and 1972, producing a ratio of debt to GDP also higher than almost anywhere in the world.[13]

THE INDUSTRIAL SECTOR

Industrialization projects designed primarily to lessen reliance on imports also served other economic and political purposes. Food processing plants and textile factories in less developed parts of the country – the center, south, and west – not only provided consumers with import substitutions, they also balanced economic growth by extending modern industries beyond the capital, where they had been concentrated in the colonial period, and shored up regions whose economic plight had helped to propel them into the Yusufist camp at the end of the protectorate. Some small and medium-scale endeavors of this type met with success; many others did not. Low wages and high unemployment limited the demand for their products, the capital imports that they required compounded balance of payment problems, and they did not create enough jobs to stimulate the economy.

In terms of heavy industrial projects, the two most successful ventures involved subsoil resources. The relatively high cost of mining Tunisian phosphate prevented the raw mineral from competing with deposits elsewhere in the world, but government construction of plants to manufacture phosphate by-products revived the mines, which had been in a slump since before World War II. International contracts for the purchase of fertilizers and phosphoric acid generated substantial income, but their contribution to export earnings paled in comparison with revenue produced by the sale of petroleum. Beginning with the 1964 discovery by an Italian company of commercial quantities of oil at al-Borma, joint ventures between the government and foreign concessionaires brought a number of fields in the Saharan region into production. After a decade of steadily increasing exports that ended with the jump in crude oil prices following the 1973 Arab–Israeli war, petroleum became the most valuable of the country's export commodities in 1974. The construction of a refinery at Bizerte soon after the initial discoveries made possible the processing of modest amounts of crude oil that lessened reliance on imported petroleum and its derivatives, but because of the high international earning power of crude, more was usually exported than was retained for the domestic market.

Many other large, capital-intensive, showpiece projects failed to meet planners' expectations because of their high construction costs, inefficient management, often owing to the monopoly, or near monopoly, that they enjoyed, and the paucity of downstream industries requiring their output. Industrialization made both the coastal cities and the regional centers magnets for rural residents hoping to find jobs and improve the quality of their lives. Although the factories fostered an image of dynamic development, they simply could not absorb more than a modest fraction of these migrants, most of whom swelled the ranks of the urban unemployed. Those who did find jobs faced a steadily rising cost of living throughout the 1960s with only a single, and modest, adjustment in the minimum wage. The inability of the once powerful but now completely emasculated UGTT to defend workers' interests lost the union what little influence it retained and its leaders the respect of the rank and file.

THE AGRICULTURAL SECTOR

When the Ten-Year Plan took effect, the agricultural sector accounted for approximately a quarter of GDP, half of all exports, and half the workforce. Planning Ministry officials believed that they could rationalize agricultural production through a centrally controlled system of state cooperative farms. The rural bourgeoisie, many of whom had long-standing ties to the Neo-Dustur, took a dim view of this threat to their ownership rights, but in the first years of the cooperative experiment their land remained undisturbed. In 1964 strong anti-French sentiments in the aftermath of the Bizerte crisis enabled the government to confiscate real estate still held by Europeans. This decision brought the state some half million hectares of the country's best crop land, but it also led to the termination of French economic assistance and set in motion the departure of most of the remaining foreign population, which soon plummeted to around 7,000. The seized property became the core of the cooperative system, to which were added the amalgamated holdings of many peasant farmers. By 1968 the cooperatives included more than a third of all rural land and a quarter of the rural population (750,000 people).[14] Although wealthy landowners did not see their property swept into the cooperatives, many of them began to diversify their investments as a hedge against the possibility of more aggressive property acquisitions by the state in the future, putting money into the public works and other construction projects that blossomed after the initiation of the plan.

The planners' high expectations for the farms – that they would finance the development of other economic sectors by producing surpluses for export or would ensure artificially low prices for basic commodities in urban markets, and that they would arrest the flight of the rural population to the cities and, increasingly, overseas by offering it gainful employment – did not materialize for many reasons. Peasant cultivators forced into the cooperatives resented the loss of their land, had little regard for the farms' managers, who were frequently technocrats with no practical knowledge of rural society, and rarely viewed the arrangement as improving their lives. Because the government purchased their produce at low prices, their earnings, which in 1968 amounted to only a third of what the plan had projected, often represented a decline in their real income. Lengthy gestation periods involved in converting land customarily planted with cereals to the production of more profitable export-oriented crops such as olives and citrus fruits had a negative impact on production in the short term. These factors, compounded by weather conditions that caused a succession of ruinous harvests between 1964 and 1968, resulted in an overall drop in agricultural production in the 1960s. At the end of the decade only 15 percent of the more than 250 cooperatives were operating at a profit.[15]

Believing that only drastic action could save his agricultural policy, at the start of 1969 ben Salah announced his intention to bring all remaining farmland into the cooperative system. The proposal unleashed a furious reaction. Thousands of large landowners used their considerable influence at the highest levels of the PSD to protest against the application of the principles of Neo-Dustur socialism to their property. Despite the formidable power of his opponents, as well as strong warnings from a growing number of prominent figures within the party, ben Salah determinedly pressed ahead, even devising a plan to bring local government officials under the control of his ministry in a bid to bypass the PSD. Outraged by ben Salah's defiance and his imprudent alienation of important components of the party with his overly zealous promotion of the cooperatives, Bourguiba turned on his protégé. Ben Salah forfeited his ministerial portfolio and, for a second time, his place in the political bureau. More ominously, he stood accused by the president of deliberately misleading him about the implementation and objectives of agricultural policy. After Bourguiba's about-face, other critics of ben Salah voiced concerns they had feared to articulate while he remained in favor. Some objected to his economics, others saw dangerous precedents in his sweeping powers, and still others simply envied his proximity to Bourguiba. Rumors of widespread corruption in the ministry of planning abounded. Charged with treason, ben Salah was tried, convicted, and imprisoned. He escaped from custody in 1973 and fled abroad, where he remained until after Bourguiba's death.

As the government distanced itself from the disgraced former minister, it also renounced his plan to eliminate private agricultural property. Farmers already in the cooperative system were permitted to withdraw, which they did in droves, effectively reducing it to the property of the former *colons*. Direct government investment in that land gave way after 1969 to the provision of credits and subsidies – to all intents and purposes the privatization of the remaining cooperatives. In these circumstances, the former *coopérants*, bereft of property or capital, had no options beyond taking jobs on the estates of large landowners or going to the cities in search of work in the emerging industrial sector. Those who made the former choice soon fell into debt to their employers; those who made the latter rarely found the opportunities they sought. In a reprise of the 1930s, the shattered agricultural economy drove the desperate rural population into the already overcrowded urban *bidonvilles*.

TOURISM

Under the Ten-Year Plan, more consistent growth occurred in the service sector of the economy than in either agriculture or industry. Few elements of the tertiary sector performed as impressively as the burgeoning business of tourism. Over the long term, the Société des Hôtels Tunisiens Touristiques (SHTT) may well have compiled the most successful record of all of the approximately 160 state-run enterprises created in the 1960s. Between 1965 and 1967 alone, investments in SHTT projects more than doubled, from 6.5 million dinars (the unit of currency that replaced the franc in 1958 and whose value stood at roughly US$2) to 13.8 million, and the pace of growth quickened further in the years that followed.[16] The SHTT selected pristine Mediterranean beaches on the island of Jerba and along the east coast, in the Sousse–Monastir area and around Hammamet, at the base of the Cap Bon peninsula, as locations for the construction of its first luxury hotels. Before the end of the decade, the company was building properties in less developed areas of the country, on the north coast at Tabarka and in southern oases such as Tozeur and Gafsa. Planners correctly calculated that European tourists would flock to high-quality resorts whose profitability would stimulate significant private investment in tourism. The construction of hotels and the establishment of companies to manage them did attract considerable capital from abroad, as well as from rural landowners who worried throughout the 1960s about ben Salah's ultimate plans for the agricultural sector.

In working to attract European visitors to Tunisia, the SHTT and its private-sector competitors were not embarking on a novel endeavor, but rather reviving a dormant business that had begun even before the French

Figure 5.5. The beach at Monastir, ca. 1985. Tourism became a major industry in Tunisia following independence. Although many visitors came primarily to enjoy the country's superb beaches, historic and cultural sites often formed a part of their itineraries as well.

protectorate. Unlike the European middle- and working-class population that the industry targeted with elaborate advertising campaigns in the 1960s, however, the earliest foreign sightseers in Tunisia were upper-class men and women who alone enjoyed the wealth and leisure time that nineteenth-century travel required. Indeed, until tourism dried up amid the international crises of the late 1930s, above-average incomes characterized almost all visitors to the country. Its winter climate attracted those in search of a more exotic locale than the French or Italian Riviera or of a variation on the theme of the better-known winter season in Algiers. Tunisia offered early generations of travelers opportunities to engage in pursuits particularly appealing to their class and background. Two Britons who traveled in the protectorate in 1883 and again in 1885 urged prospective visitors not to venture into the interior without a gun – not for reasons of security, but because of the superb hunting. The countryside "abounds in game . . . The gazelle as well as the wild boar haunts the plains; [and] the panther and the hyena are as yet far from exterminated"[17] – although, thanks in no small part to European sportsmen, they soon vanished. The classical education of many of these wealthy travelers piqued their interest in the sites of antiquity scattered across Tunisia and prompted them to explore the ruins with an almost scholarly thoroughness, occasionally referring to the works of Latin authors or, more rarely, medieval Arab writers to enhance their understanding of what they were seeing. In 1902 the ultimate symbol of inclusion in the most fashionable European tourist itineraries of the day – a branch office of Thomas Cook and Sons – opened in Tunis. No longer could new arrivals in the capital feel, as did an 1882 visitor, that they had "got beyond the reach of Mr. Cook and his 'personally-conducted' flock."[18]

What few of these visitors came expressly to do, even as late as the 1930s, was sunbathe, swim, or engage in other water sports, but these were precisely the preferred activities of the "recreational" tourists of the 1960s. With memories of the colonial era receding into the past, most of them knew very little about Tunisia, its history, or its culture, leading them to fall back on stereotypes of the country and its residents. The holiday packages that brought most of this new wave of tourists to the country usually included a foray into a medina and a tour of an archeological site, but the exceedingly unfamiliar atmosphere of the former, the sublime monuments of the latter, and the aggressive sellers of cheap, pseudo-artisanal souvenirs at both more likely contributed to reinforcing stereotypes than to refuting them. Many tourists' hedonistic pursuit of personal pleasure, boisterous behavior, and ideas of acceptable public contact between the sexes or appropriate attire on the streets so contrasted with Tunisian standards that they offended their hosts without intending to, or even knowing that they did so. But the goal of tourism was not to promote cross-cultural understanding, which, in any event, was probably no more remote in 1970 than in 1900, but to earn foreign currency, and this it did extremely well. From the middle of the 1960s until the escalation of oil prices after 1973, tourism produced more such revenue – often as much as one-fifth of the annual total – than any other source.

Set against the substantial economic benefits of tourism were a variety of costs and risks, most of them more problematic than visitors' limited understanding of the country. The industry was extremely vulnerable to factors over which Tunisians exercised no control. Economic conditions in their own countries or political instability anywhere in North Africa or the Middle East constrained Europeans' travel and vacation plans, as revealed by the June 1967 Arab–Israeli war. The threat of fighting, and then its outbreak, slowed the flow of tourists to a trickle, confronting the hotels with their first major crisis. The government acted promptly to reverse the trend. Bourguiba offered public assurances to prospective European visitors of their security and although tourism revenues did decline in 1967, they rebounded strongly in the following year. On the other hand, Tunisian officials made the decisions regarding the location of the new hotels, and their initial concentration along the Mediterranean aggravated the disparate pace of development between the coastal zones and the interior.

The jobs offered at the new hotels, and the many others that they spawned in supporting businesses and industries, provided much needed relief at a time when the unemployment rate regularly hovered around 15 percent. But most work in the hotels consisted of low-wage menial labor (as maids, porters, waiters, janitors, gardeners, and the like) that replicated colonial conditions of Tunisian subservience to Europeans. In the SHTT properties, Tunisians did fill the more remunerative and responsible administrative and managerial positions, but at the many privately owned hotels operated by multinational corporations, foreigners generally performed those functions. In areas targeted for the most intensive development, hotels and other tourist facilities added to the woes of the already beleaguered agricultural sector by taking thousands of hectares of farmland out of production and creating demands for water that drove its price beyond the means of local farmers working irrigated plots. Economic planners, investors, and government officials alike paid scant attention to ecological issues in the early years of the tourist boom or, if they did, dismissed them as insignificant when compared with the profits the industry generated. The magnitude of new construction and the influx of huge numbers of visitors to the new centers of tourism did, however, pose threats, even if not always immediately apparent ones, to fragile environmental conditions in both coastal and desert regions.

In early 1968, the growth rate of the overall economy stood at 3.3 percent a year, an impressive figure for a developing country, but only about half the rate anticipated. Well before the Ten-Year Plan had run its course as the blueprint for the economy, it had become clear that the original estimate of growth, like many of its other targets and policies, had been unrealistically ambitious or far out of alignment with existing economic and social realities. Critics skewered the ministry of planning for these technical miscalculations. They trod on far more sensitive ground when they questioned the extensive powers wielded by ben Salah, the fervent support he enjoyed for many years from Bourguiba, or the president's rush to discredit him as his plans came undone. On a scale not seen since ben Yusuf's challenge at the 1955 congress, party dissenters, most of them in early middle age – the generation that entered politics in the waning years of the protectorate – were voicing doubts about the political acuity and judgment of "the supreme combatant" and his narrow circle of advisors. The failure of the Ten-Year Plan to attain so many of its goals made a reexamination of national economic policy inevitable and a reorientation all but certain. Under the circumstances, such a reappraisal could hardly avoid grappling with discontent over the allocation and exercise of political power.

CHAPTER 6

Regime entrenchment and the intensification of opposition, 1969–1987

REPAIRING THE DAMAGE OF THE SOCIALIST EXPERIMENT

In the aftermath of the experiment in economic planning, the Parti Social-iste Dusturien found itself at a fork in the political road. Since indepen-dence a small coterie of party leaders had determined state policy and then imposed it through the agency of interlocking party and state organ-isms. The paternalistic conviction that the party–state president and, by extension, his inner circle inherently understood Tunisians' needs and aspi-rations, rendered the reverse flow of information irrelevant, or at least of negligible interest to its recipients. Redefining the relationship between the party and the national organizations following the 1964 congress was merely a variation on this theme. Any semblance of dialogue between party and people disappeared, as the PSD's obdurate support for the cooperatives in the face of mounting popular opposition illustrated. The party's claim to embody the collective will of the Tunisian people had served it well against the protectorate and in the consolidation of the independent state, but rang hollow by the late 1960s as broad resentment of economic policies opened a gulf between state and society. At the same time, the crystallization in the PSD's upper echelons of an opposition bold enough to challenge the authority and the methods of the increasingly isolated leadership revealed similar fissures within the party elite.

As in the past, the highly centralized, authoritarian power structure of the party could readily stifle internal critics. The choice confronting party leaders at this critical juncture lay between resorting to this technique at a time when discontent in the party paralleled widespread restlessness in the society at large or, as their critics urged, adopting more open procedures, widening the circle of key decision-makers, and limiting personal power with institutional constraints, all with an eye towards giving voice to a more diverse array of views that would enable the party to establish strong con-nections with as much of the population as possible. Dissidents argued that resistance to change would cause the party to atrophy, while its entrenched leaders feared that acceptance of these demands would ultimately lead to their replacement, the diminution of their power, or their relegation to symbolic roles.

In 1970 the most influential spokesperson for the liberal viewpoint within the PSD was Ahmad Mestiri. Few contemporaries of the forty-five-year-old Mestiri could match either his party credentials or, as the son-in-law of M'hamed Chenik, his family connections. Appointed to the Neo-Dustur political bureau in 1957, he also sat in the National Assembly from its inception; headed the ministries of justice (1956–8) and of finance and commerce (1959), and served abroad in ambassadorial posts in Moscow, Cairo, and Algiers (1960–6). Returning to Tunisia for the first time since the introduction of Neo-Dustur socialism, he became minister of national defense. Mestiri had no use for ben Salah's economics, which he publicly condemned as ruinous. Convinced that ben Salah remained in power only because of the personal favor of a president on whom there were no checks, his criticisms soon extended to Bourguiba as well. Finding himself in an untenable position, Mestiri resigned in 1968.

When ben Salah's own dismissal appeared to bear out Mestiri's misgivings, Bourguiba invited him to reenter the political fold, naming him minister of the interior in 1970. He and other party liberals drew up reforms to democratize the transaction of party business and restrict the exercise of arbitrary power, presenting them at the 1971 PSD congress, a gathering marked, in a manner unthinkable at any of the previous seven, by expressions of considerable doubt about the president. These stemmed primarily from his relationship with ben Salah, but also derived from the sixty-eight-year-old leader's increasing medical problems. Bourguiba's poor health had necessitated lengthy treatment abroad in recent years and had contributed to his decision to step down as prime minister in favor of PSD secretary-general Badi Ladgham in 1969. Critics argued that prolonged absences affected the president's grasp of important matters of state and subtly suggested that his health might render him unfit to fulfill the duties of his office. In this climate, congress delegates ignored Bourguiba's wishes by electing liberal candidates to the central committee that selected the political bureau and by endorsing a presidential succession process that prevented the chief executive from naming his successor.

The opposition had won a tactical victory, but the party apparatus provided no mechanisms for enforcing it. Shortly after the congress ended, Bourguiba ordered the expulsion of Mestiri and other outspoken critics. With their voices silenced inside the party, their ideas were ignored and their reforms evaded. The men who for more than thirty-five years had presided over the PSD, and before it the Neo-Dustur, had no intention of delivering the party into their hands. Three years later, when the PSD congress next convened, a much healthier and more aggressive Bourguiba asserted his control over the party, crushing any lingering tendencies towards the democratization of its inner workings. Delegates to the 1974 congress discarded the practice of the central committee electing the political bureau in favor of the appointment of that body by the party president, a position they offered to Bourguiba as a lifetime appointment. In the same year the National Assembly, composed exclusively of PSD members, bestowed on him the title "president [of the republic] for life." The most powerful figures in the party and the state never doubted which fork of the political road they would follow. Their decision not only to continue along the path of authoritarianism, but to reinforce their powers, to control opinion rather than to mobilize it, slammed the door on the expression of opposing political viewpoints. Symbolic of the prevailing climate for much of the decade was the 1976 amendment of Article 4 of the constitution, altering the motto of the republic from "liberty, order, and justice" to "order, liberty, and justice."

Reform-minded party members who had avoided the 1971 purge wisely lowered their profile thereafter. Many who had been swept up in it joined Mestiri in promoting concepts of political participation and transparency among the Tunisian people, but in the face of PSD absolutism they encountered little success beyond a small circle of intellectuals. Ben Salah's efforts to maintain a support base were even less effective. His Mouvement de l'Unité Populaire (MUP – Movement of Popular Unity), organized after his escape to France in 1973, espoused his socialist principles but consisted almost exclusively of fellow exiles. One other group that coalesced around this time deserves mention. Zaituna mosque-university students founded the Association pour la Sauvegarde du Coran (Association for the Preservation of the Qur'an) in 1970 to express their anguish over the diminishing Muslim identity of Tunisia and the parallel deterioration of moral standards, both of which they attributed to government policies of secularization and Westernization. Framing its message primarily in cultural and religious terms, the association urged Tunisians to place Islam at the center of their personal lives as the essential first step towards overcoming these ills. In contrast with their previous attitude towards the religious establishment, national political leaders made no attempt to interfere with the association, probably in the hope of lessening tensions with the religious authorities at a time when the party was dealing with intense criticisms from its own liberal wing, but perhaps also with the thought that the association might provide a useful counterweight to secular opponents of the regime.

With the same enthusiasm that it employed in resisting political change, the PSD engineered an extraordinary overhaul of the national economy following the dismissal of ben Salah. Supervising the recovery from the damage inflicted by the previous decade's often poorly designed socialist policies fell to Hedi Nouira, Bourguiba's designee as prime minister in 1970. An economic liberal skeptical of ben Salah from the outset, Nouira held decidedly illiberal political views that accorded with the impulse, prevailing at the highest levels of the party, to quash dissent. Private capital dedicated to industrial expansion, much of it inevitably coming from abroad, formed a crucial component in Nouira's economic salvage operation. To reassure investors apprehensive about the state's recent economic past, the government devised attractive concession packages that targeted foreign entrepreneurs willing to develop export-oriented industries providing desperately needed jobs but not offering competition for Tunisian products. During the first planning cycle under Nouira's direction (1973–7), more than 500 foreign-owned factories opened. As the maintenance of a centralized planning process suggested, however, the state did not abandon all economic activity to the private sector nor, except for a few disastrous ventures – most notably the cooperatives – did it withdraw its participation from existing public-sector undertakings. Nearly a hundred new state companies, most of them heavy industries turning out primary products, emerged in the 1970s. The percentage of government spending on the public sector more than doubled between 1972 and 1984, while the state's share of total capital investment never fell below 50 percent.[1]

Increased industrialization created thousands of new jobs, most requiring minimal skills, paying low wages, and presenting limited opportunities for advancement or the acquisition of technical expertise. Yet it did not appreciably lower unemployment nor did it generate substantial export revenue. Throughout the 1970s, the official national unemployment rate fluctuated between 13 and 16 percent, but reached markedly higher proportions in the cities and among the young. By the middle of the decade, the continuing flight from the countryside had brought the urban and rural populations into balance for the first time ever, a process that contributed significantly to urban unemployment. Young men between the ages of fifteen and twenty-five suffered a rate of joblessness approaching 50 percent and accounted for almost three-quarters of those without work.[2] The birth of some two million Tunisians between 1956 and 1976 simply outstripped, by far, the government's ability to generate jobs.

Figure 6.1. "I was born in Tunisia." The sign in the rear window of this vehicle makes this statement in French and Arabic. Renault was one of many European businesses to set up manufacturing plants in Tunisia during the 1970s and 1980s.

Two other factors provide further explanations of the new industries' negligible impact on unemployment. In the 1970s, women went to work outside their homes or fields in much larger numbers than previously, often holding jobs once reserved for men. In 1975, women comprised slightly more than a quarter of the economically active population, over a third of them employed in the industrial sector.[3] This situation reflected the evolving status of women since independence, the economic straits of many Tunisian families, and the greater willingness of foreign entrepreneurs (in comparison with their Tunisian counterparts) to hire women, albeit usually at lower wages than men. This augmentation of the workforce meant that reducing overall unemployment figures necessitated creating new jobs at a more feverish pitch than planners had foreseen or could accomplish. The second explanatory factor lay in the government's persistent unwillingness to come to grips with the problem of regional imbalances. During Nouira's first five-year plan, it made no greater effort than its predecessors to disperse the new industries beyond the coast, and particularly the Tunis area. As a result, the relief that they provided had no impact on the south, center, or west, traditionally the regions with the most severe levels of unemployment. Many of the plants built by private investors manufactured either textiles or clothing. Because government dispensations and low wages held down their production costs, these goods initially found profitable markets across the Mediterranean. In 1977, however, the European Economic Community (EEC) imposed high tariffs on products of this kind in order to protect its own industries from being swamped in a flood of inexpensive imports. The impact on Tunisia was so devastating that many factories closed in the final year of the five-year plan, contributing to its falling short of the 10 percent expansion originally envisioned for the industrial sector. Even so, at the conclusion of the plan, the industrial sector accounted for almost 20 percent of all employment (nearly a quarter of a million jobs) and manufactured products comprised more than a third of all exports.[4]

EEC import restrictions also hurt Tunisian agriculture. Following the collapse of the cooperatives, large landowners relentlessly squeezed out smaller farmers, mechanized their own operations more thoroughly, and concentrated on raising crops for lucrative markets abroad rather than domestic consumption. Diverse government assistance programs, not the least of which entailed the construction of several dams under consideration since the colonial period, benefited those in a position to pursue large-scale farming. But the need to import significant quantities of basic foodstuffs counterbalanced the profits derived from agricultural exports. Although the rate of growth of the agricultural sector doubled between 1969 and 1977 (from a starting point driven down by the miscalculations of the ben Salah era), farm exports during those years rarely covered even half the cost of imported food. Tunisia's most valuable agricultural commodities, olive oil and citrus fruits, replicated those of Greece, Spain, and Portugal. To strengthen the economies of those countries as a prelude to their admission to the EEC, the Community raised barriers against competitive agricultural products in 1977, effectively sealing off the European market to Tunisian growers.

The Nouira government stabilized the economy, set aside the unworkable and damaging strategies of the socialist era, restored the trust of investors, and plotted a recovery course that, while imperfect, nevertheless achieved a growth rate of 5.6 percent a year between 1973 and 1977. Such a turnaround could not have occurred as rapidly as it did without the impressive capacity of tourism to earn foreign revenue, the confidence of international creditors, and fortuitous financial underpinning from two local sources of unanticipated magnitude. Tunisia's ability to contract substantial foreign loans facilitated the execution of Nouira's initial plan, but the worldwide hike in crude oil prices as it went into effect proved even more beneficial. Government coffers soon bulged with petrodollars, for although oil exports held steady throughout the decade, their value increased tenfold. By the final year of the plan, income from the sale of oil made up one-sixth of the government's revenue. It used this windfall to finance its own investments in the industrial and service sectors, fund capitalist agricultural ventures, offset the concessions tendered to entice foreign investment, subsidize the prices of essential commodities, utilities, and housing to curb unrest among the poorest (and frequently unemployed) segments of the population, improve the overall quality of life by expanding and accelerating the delivery of educational and social services, and maintain the balance of trade at an acceptable, although still negative, level.

Remittances from overseas workers constituted the other unforeseen source of wealth in the 1970s. Limited labor migration to France predated independence and after 1956 some Tunisians also found their way to Italy, Germany, and other European countries, but what money they sent back had little impact on the national economy. Most held unskilled jobs in factories, construction, or public works, often of sorts disdained by local workers. The oil boom of the 1970s created large demands for labor in the sparsely populated Arab oil-producing states. Unemployed, underemployed, and employed but underpaid Tunisians had only to cross the border into Libya to benefit from this situation, and tens of thousands of them, mostly from depressed and neglected areas of the country, did so. Because secondary schools and universities were producing more graduates than the economy could absorb, the profile of Tunisians seeking economic opportunity abroad assumed greater diversity and sophistication during the 1970s. In addition to laborers, teachers, clerks, technicians, and semi-skilled workers dispersed throughout the Arab world, but particularly the Arabian Peninsula, and Europe. By the end of the decade, remittances from the more than quarter of a million Tunisians working outside their country constituted almost a quarter of the gross domestic product.[5] The increase in labor migration brought large sums of money into the country at an extremely opportune moment, but its usefulness as a safety valve transcended its monetary importance. In addition to curbing domestic unemployment and the anger and malaise that accompanied it, emigration prevented already overcrowded urban slums from deteriorating still further.

For the most part, the 1973–7 Five-Year Plan expanded the economy through circumstantial, as opposed to structural, modifications. A handful of Tunisians able to make substantial investments, enter into partnerships with foreign entrepreneurs, or provide the intermediary services required by outsiders doing business in the country turned huge profits in the booming economy. Many of these wealthy capitalists owed their prosperity to the ownership of rural property and all enjoyed considerable influence in the PSD. Wage earners did not fare so well. Although average income climbed steadily, the percentage of national revenue allotted to salaries dropped. Moreover, the high production cost of local goods and the expense of now readily available imports drove consumer prices upward twice as rapidly as salaries. Disparities between rich and poor were hardly unknown, but the mechanisms of the liberal economy dramatically deepened the gulf between classes. During the 1970s, the expenditures of the wealthiest 20 percent of the population exceeded those of all other Tunisians combined, while the poorest 20 percent accounted for only 5 percent of spending.[6]

So acute a compromise of workers' interests aroused the UGTT from years of lethargic subordination to the party. In the transition from the socialist to the liberal economy, a succession of wildcat strikes revealed the PSD's inability to keep the union under its thumb. This renewal of activism coincided with the return of Habib ᶜAchour as UGTT secretary-general, a post he had held from 1963 until 1965, when his attempts to assert the union's independence led to his dismissal from the PSD. Reinstated in 1971, his resumption of the leadership of the union and appointment to the powerful party political bureau reflected his quarter-century-long affiliation with both. But ᶜAchour faced a virtually impossible task: to foster an autonomous union effectively addressing issues critical to the welfare of the working class while ensuring that labor unrest did not thwart the attainment of overall PSD goals, from whose formulation, however, the UGTT remained excluded. In 1973, the government introduced an institutionalized bargaining system that provided a mechanism for it, the union, and employers to discuss wages, working conditions, and other relevant questions, but at the same time it outlawed work stoppages. With no other weapon at their disposal, union members did not hesitate to strike in defiance of the ban, but the authorities' resort to the police and the army to break the strikes left no question in their minds regarding the government's position on their demands. ᶜAchour genuinely sympathized with the workers, and under his direction the UGTT became the sole national entity potent enough to confront the PSD.

The inauguration of Nouira's second five-year plan in 1977 brought the tension between the UGTT and the government to a head. Believing that ongoing labor unrest jeopardized support from the international lending agencies upon which the new plan relied more heavily than its predecessors, PSD leaders pressured ᶜAchour to bring the union into line. As an inducement they proposed to raise the minimum wage and promised additional increases linked to inflation over the course of the plan. Despite UGTT acceptance of this "social contract," the government failed to address workers' grievances and the strikes continued. ᶜAchour resigned from the political bureau in disgust at the end of the year and the union scheduled a general strike – the first it had called since independence – for January 26, 1978. Like its forerunners in the waning days of the protectorate, this general strike had strong political overtones, since UGTT leaders coupled demands for political pluralism with others of a more purely economic nature. In cities throughout the country, the protest ended in violent clashes as demonstrators vented their frustration by attacking the symbols of the regime, including its policemen and soldiers. The number of fatalities reported ranged from forty-seven to more than four times that number; hundreds more, including ᶜAchour, received prison sentences for their involvement. The PSD promptly installed a more malleable UGTT executive committee, but its obvious subservience prevented it from bringing the outraged rank and file under control. Even though few Tunisians had ever doubted either the government's capacity or willingness to quash serious opposition, its actions on "Black Thursday" revealed an unexpectedly ruthless dimension that many found frightening and repellant.

Political liberals seized the opportunity presented by apprehension over the government's behavior to acquaint more Tunisians with their own thinking. Since leaving the PSD, Mestiri and his associates had campaigned for a more open society, played an instrumental role in creating the Ligue Tunisienne des Droits de l'Homme (LTDH – Tunisian League of Human Rights), the first such body in the Arab world, in 1977, and consistently supported workers' demands for a more equitable society. In June 1978 Mestiri announced the formation of the Mouvement des Démocrates Sociales (MDS – Movement of Social Democrats). The government denied an MDS request for recognition as a political party, but the organization quickly became a rallying point for leftist dissidents, while its French and Arabic newspapers served as forums for outlining their criticisms.

At about the same time an opposition political movement centered on religious conviction surfaced for the first time in almost twenty years. The growing influence of the UGTT disconcerted leaders of the Association pour la Sauvegarde du Coran and similar Islamic groups. Fearful that abandoning the political arena to the union and the emerging secular organizations would greatly impair their ability to deliver their message to the public, they formed the Harakat al-Ittijah al-Islami, known in French as the Mouvement de la Tendance Islamique (MTI – Islamic Tendency Movement). Inspired by the example of the Islamic Revolution in Iran (although not entirely wedded to its ideology) and led by Rashid Ghannushi, a former secondary school teacher, and ᶜAbd al-Fattah Mourou, a graduate of both Sadiqi College and the faculty of theology (the former Zaituna mosque-university), the MTI reiterated the earlier Islamic organizations' calls for individuals to embrace the moral and ethical values of the religion in their personal lives, but went on to demand that the government reverse its ruinous economic policies and craft a more representative political structure. It gained a following in several, often overlapping, quarters: among poor and disadvantaged Tunisians victimized by a freewheeling economy that reduced a third of the population to poverty by the end of the decade, among young persons who had no respect for the PSD as the party that had won independence (for most, before they were born) but rather regarded it as an anachronism with little to offer them, and among many older middle-class men and women who turned to their Islamic heritage when both socialism and capitalism failed to fulfill the expectations of prosperity and security they had raised.[7]

Despite mounting pressures to reform a system described by a Western social scientist as a mixture of a "Smithian way of getting rich with a Hobbesian way of governing,"[8] the high command of the PSD made only insignificant concessions. For the 1979 National Assembly elections, the party presented lists with twice as many candidates as seats, but all had to be party members in good standing. Critics refused to participate in the election or spoiled their ballots, pointing out that so ineffectual a modification demonstrated how thoroughly the party had lost touch with much of the population, replacing concern for it with contempt. On January 26, 1980, the second anniversary of "Black Thursday," a band of guerrillas seized police and military installations in the southern phosphate mining center of Gafsa, hoping to spark a general uprising. A steady decline in phosphate prices had stalled the region's already depressed economy, creating exceptionally high unemployment and exceptionally bitter resentment. At least thirty-seven people (the official estimate), but quite probably many more, died in the battle to regain control of the city. Tunisia accused Muammar Qadhafi, with whom Bourguiba had conducted a running feud since rejecting Libyan overtures to unify the two countries in 1974, of training and equipping the attackers. Foreign complicity aside, the Tunisian authorities could not wash their hands of responsibility for the atmosphere that had spawned the raid. The admiration expressed by a senior commander of the mission for Salah ben Yusuf implicitly indicted the government for not having redressed the grievances that had propelled so many southerners and other aggrieved citizens into the Yusufist ranks twenty-five years earlier. As the new decade began, the malaise that had gripped the least privileged segments of Tunisian society was spreading. "Black Thursday" and the sortie at Gafsa laid bare the fragility of the regime, making it impossible to put off major political and economic reforms any longer. When the powerful and well-connected Nouira, identified so closely with the formulation of the policies of the 1970s, suffered an incapacitating stroke a few months after the Gafsa raid, many in the upper echelons of the PSD must have breathed a sigh of relief.

<h2>SPIRALING OUT OF CONTROL</h2>

The Tunisian constitution provided for the prime minister to succeed the president in the event of the latter's death or incapacitation. With Bourguiba continuing to experience recurrent health problems, this proviso significantly enhanced the prestige and power of the head of government. Inasmuch as Bourguiba effectively controlled the appointment of the prime minister, policies emanating from his office bore the imprimatur of the chief executive. Following Nouira's stroke, Muhammad Mzali, a politician with a history of allegiance to the party chief, became prime minister and PSD secretary-general. The president set him a difficult task: to shore up what had once been a monolithic political and economic system but was now so fissured by particularistic interests as to verge on disintegration, and to do so while retaining maximum control at the party core, where it had always resided. Rather reminiscent of the opening gambits of reform-minded residents general in the colonial era, Mzali inaugurated his administration by releasing Habib ᶜAchour and other labor activists imprisoned after "Black Thursday." He then filled several cabinet positions with individuals not affiliated with the party and induced Mestiri to return, with his MDS colleagues, to the PSD fold as a loyal opposition movement.

These gestures smacked of the Bourguibist device of marginalizing, then reinstating, senior party members who had crossed him. More innovative, and potentially more significant, was the pursuit of political pluralism. Scheduling new elections for 1981, the government invited political organizations to present lists of candidates, provided only that they did not draw support from outside the country, did not advocate class struggle or sectarianism, and agreed to avoid criticisms of the "president for life." Mzali pledged to grant official recognition as political parties to those receiving at least 5 percent of the vote. In a show of harmony intended to underscore the evolving political atmosphere, the PSD and the UGTT combined forces to offer a "National Front" list. None of the fledgling groups had the resources to mount an effective campaign and all fell short of the threshold, barely capturing 5 percent of the vote between them. Despite the electoral results, the government initiated a multiparty system of sorts in 1982 by legalizing the Parti Communiste Tunisien (which had only about 2,000 members) on the grounds that, unlike the other political organizations, the PCT had been functioning in 1963 when the ban on opposition activities took effect. Bourguiba made it clear that he regarded such reforms as, at best, necessary evils, grousing that "I gave them pluralism . . . They will not be able to say they had to wait for the death of that fascist Bourguiba."[9]

A particularly disturbing feature for the secular PSD leadership in the run-up to the 1981 elections was the strong popular enthusiasm for the MTI, the only political group other than the communists that did not trace its roots to the PSD. Intent on laying the groundwork for an Islamic government, Ghannushi tested the limits of the regime's tolerance, often using mosques as the venues for his condemnation of twenty-five years of Neo-Dustur and PSD policies that had removed virtually any trace of an Islamic dimension from Tunisian public life. The arrest of Ghannushi, Mourou, and scores of MTI adherents on charges of defaming the "president for life" threw the movement into disarray shortly before the elections. Nevertheless, in the voting, candidates linked to the MTI fared as well as, and often better than, their secular counterparts. Most of the latter viewed as cynical and opportunistic subsequent proposals by the Islamists that they forge a common front, convinced that the MTI wanted primarily to take advantage of the networks and organizational structures they had painstakingly built. The specter of an alliance, however unlikely, between the MTI and one or another of the secular opposition parties alarmed the government enough for Mzali to attempt to forestall it in 1983 by recognizing as political parties the MDS and the Parti d'Unité Populaire (PUP – Popular Unity Party), a group that had broken away from ben Salah's MUP. Citing the prohibition against sectarian parties, the prime minister rejected repeated MTI demands for the same status.

In less than three years Mzali had undercut PSD opponents' criticism of the party's monopolization of the political arena, although the pluralism that emerged had limits and had not yet weathered a genuine electoral contest. He had also succeeded in playing important components of the opposition off against one another. He had not, however, managed to unite all the influential figures of the party behind him, and pockets of disapproval formed within its inner circle. Censure came from old-guard PSD conservatives, but also from high-ranking younger party members to whose political ambitions the prime minister represented an obstacle. By virtue of his post, he, and none of them, would accede to the presidency; unless he fell from power before Bourguiba's demise, others had no hope of attaining the country's highest office. Moreover, pluralism potentially jeopardized the party's guaranteed access to powerful government offices. Some of the bitter debates that developed within the PSD over the wisdom of Mzali's policies reflected genuine substantive misgivings, but others served as ploys to maneuver their proponents into advantageous positions on the matter of presidential succession. In addition to these open confrontations, the prime minister's enemies also conducted a campaign of innuendo to discredit him with the president. An adept politician, Mzali retained Bourguiba's confidence and shouldered aside his challengers. In the process, however, he alienated men and women who, in less combative circumstances, might have helped advance the reforms.

Political infighting left Mzali vulnerable when economic circumstances produced a situation of crisis proportions. The first plan formulated under his direction (1982–6) centered on investments in industries outside the petrochemical sector, with the objectives of reducing unemployment, bolstering exports, and cutting imports. Until substantial progress towards achieving those goals materialized, however, the preservation of stability necessitated the maintenance of state subsidies on basic commodities, despite the budgetary strain they created. When Nouira inaugurated the first post-socialist five-year plan in 1973, the government expended some ten million dinars a year on subsidies; a decade later, the annual burden approached eighty million dinars.[10] Serious problems arose in the very early stages of the implementation of the 1982–6 plan, as the income that financed the subsidies, especially revenue from the sale of crude oil, unexpectedly leveled off and unfavorable weather conditions resulted in several exceptionally poor harvests. To cope with the deepening budget deficit, the government imposed austerity measures that reduced its own spending, restricted imports, and, with considerable trepidation, marginally reduced some subsidies. Its increased borrowing abroad reflected the priority assigned to ensuring political calm, even at the expense of sound economics.

Late in 1983 the International Monetary Fund (IMF) and the World Bank demanded the lifting of subsidies on bread and semolina, the basic ingredient of couscous, the staple of the national diet, as a requisite for their continuing support. The doubling of the price of these commodities triggered two weeks of anti-government demonstrations throughout the country in

January 1984. On one occasion, protesters went so far as to stone a vehicle in which Bourguiba was riding – a gesture once unimaginable and indicative of the depth of frustration and rage among the poorest and most afflicted Tunisians. As on "Black Thursday," the police and the army restored order, but only at the cost of thousands of civilian casualties. Mzali's political foes within the PSD condemned both the cancellation of the subsidies and the method of quelling the ensuing disorders, but the recently legalized political parties, still uncertain of their limits, refrained from actively fanning the unrest.

In order to distance himself from the public outrage and to polish his somewhat tarnished image, Bourguiba restored the subsidies, allowing Tunisians to believe that the prime minister had acted without his authorization. Yet he did not dismiss Mzali, preferring that his current protégé, now instilled with a heightened appreciation of the reality that supreme power resided with the president, not the prime minister, remain in office. Ironically, Bourguiba suffered a severe heart attack a few months later, enabling the chastened Mzali to strengthen his position. Aware that future economic adjustments were imperative, but would meet as hostile a reception as had the termination of the subsidies, he took steps to minimize the effectiveness of the opposition. Among other measures, he recalled General Zine al-ᶜAbidine ben ᶜAli from an ambassadorial appointment in Europe to resume his position as Director General of National Security, a post in which he had achieved prominence with his forceful suppression of the 1978 disturbances. Precisely because of that record, the UGTT questioned ben ᶜAli's reappointment. In retaliation, the government brushed the union aside in favor of a rival body, the Union Nationale Tunisienne du Travail (UNTT – Tunisian National Labor Union), whose members had separated from the UGTT in the previous year because they objected to its militant and confrontational approach to the government. The split only intensified ᶜAchour's rhetoric, and the outspoken UGTT secretary-general was imprisoned for a second time in 1985.

By closely monitoring the political parties' leaders and their newspapers, ben ᶜAli and Mzali (who was minister of the interior as well as prime minister) ensured that they did not challenge the government. It was, however, the MTI that came under the most intense scrutiny. Accusing the organization of masterminding the 1984 riots, the government arrested scores of its sympathizers. Although MTI leaders, in contrast with their secular counterparts, had encouraged their followers to participate in the protests, the authorities could produce no evidence that they had engineered them. The Islamists jailed in January, along with Ghannushi and Mourou, both of whom had been in detention since 1981, were released a few months later, but the government persisted in its refusal to permit the MTI to organize as a political party. What many Tunisians perceived as government persecution added to the movement's stature, enhancing its standing as an independent organization committed to championing equitable and culturally appropriate solutions to the country's problems.

The traumatic events of January 1984 constituted but a prelude to a period of economic calamity brought on by an unforeseeable confluence of circumstances that took a particularly harsh toll on the most highly profitable facets of the economy. A fall in crude oil prices on the international market translated into a staggering reduction of the revenue generated by petroleum exports – for years the lifeblood of the economy – from 778 million dinars in 1984 to 322 million in 1986. The return to Tunisia of tens of thousands of workers from Libya and elsewhere as a result of the recession in the petroleum industry posed a double liability, depriving the national economy of their remittances even as it aggravated already high levels of unemployment. During the same two-year period, a sustained drought cut the cereal harvest by half.[11] The Tunisian decision, taken reluctantly and at the urging of the United States, to allow the Palestine Liberation Organization to establish its headquarters in Tunis following the 1982 Israeli invasion of Lebanon put the tourism industry at risk by identifying the country with the Palestine–Israel conflict, a drawback it had avoided in the past. A spate of terrorist attacks around the Mediterranean basin and in Europe after 1982, the 1985 Israeli bombing of a Palestinian compound in the Tunis suburb of Hammam Lif that killed sixty-eight Palestinians and Tunisians and injured over a hundred, and air raids by the United States on Libyan targets in 1986 further stifled tourism, with consequences that rippled through the economy. With oil revenues in precipitate decline and other sources of income also falling off significantly, the government could no longer sustain its previous spending levels. Investments and the jobs they produced dried up, the balance-of-payments deficit increased, foreign reserves dissipated, international borrowing rose, and the annual growth rate of the economy over the span of the 1982–6 planning cycle plummeted to 2.9 percent, the lowest level since independence. As the ill-fated plan stumbled towards its conclusion, the external debt reached approximately $5 billion, or nearly 60 percent of gross national product (GNP), while its servicing consumed slightly more than a quarter of the government's receipts.[12]

All Tunisians felt the pinch of the deteriorating economic situation, but it naturally afflicted the poor most severely. Although the MTI drew support from a wide cross-section of the population, many of its more impoverished constituents experienced acute misery and often suffered the indignity of lacking the resources needed to provide, even minimally, for their families – a state of affairs utterly antithetical to the concepts of community, justice, and human dignity that the Islamist movement advocated as the philosophical underpinning of national life. Consequently, the MTI vigorously and persistently inveighed against the government. Some of its proposals focused on correcting fundamental deficiencies in PSD economic policies and had no direct links with religion or culture. Rather than building an economy dependent on international tourism and manufacturing "things we don't need with cheap labor for the West,"[13] MTI leaders advocated achieving greater autarky by increasing food production through the modernization of agriculture and by developing industries that met the needs of the domestic market. Other recommendations for dealing with the economic crisis derived more explicitly from Islamic contexts, often reflecting long-established views on gender roles. In 1985, the movement sought a national referendum on the Personal Status Code, contending that its facilitation of women's entry into the public sphere encouraged them to take jobs once reserved for men, the traditional breadwinners. By so doing, women aggravated the problem of (male) unemployment, but also undermined what the Islamists regarded as a basic societal and familial precept dictating distinctly different male and female responsibilities. In related issues that went beyond economic concerns, the MTI also promoted the limitation of contacts between the sexes and the revival of traditional forms of dress as a manifestation of the rejection of foreign influence. The PSD, the opposition parties, and women's advocacy groups all came to the defense of the code, thwarting any immediate prospect of its abolition, which the MTI continued to favor.

Consistently denied legitimization as a political party, and thus officially excluded from the dialogue set in motion by Mzali, the MTI risked less in attacking the government than did the MDS or the PUP, whose primarily middle-class adherents were, in any case, better equipped to survive the economic shocks the nation was undergoing. But, in reality, the very concept of pluralism was foundering. Convinced that the prevailing political and economic climate militated against free elections that might empower opponents of the government, all the parties except the PSD boycotted the balloting for municipal councils in 1985, thereby rendering Mzali's political opening meaningless. Not even the collapse of the multiparty experiment assuaged the staunchest party conservatives, however, for they deeply distrusted the instincts and ambitions of the man who stood first in line to replace the president. As Bourguiba resumed a more active political role after recovering from his heart attack, influential associates who had his ear sowed seeds of doubt about the judgment, competence, and loyalty not only of his prime minister, but of other prominent members of the party's inner circle, including his wife, Wassila ben ᶜAmmar, and his son, Habib Jr.

Intent on clinging to the power he had wielded for half a century, in 1986 the aging leader moved against those whom he believed threatened his authority. Mestiri, who had epitomized the liberal opposition since its inception, was arrested in April while leading a demonstration protesting the government's failure to condemn an attack by the United States on the Libyan cities of Tripoli and Benghazi. At the same time, Bourguiba appointed several hardnosed party conservatives to important ministerial positions, relieved Mzali of responsibility for the interior ministry, naming ben ᶜAli to that post, and severed his ties with both his wife and son. When the axe inevitably fell on Mzali in July, he fled the country in fear of additional reprisals which did, in fact, follow, in the form of trials *in absentia* that imposed prison sentences for financial and political improprieties alleged to have occurred during his ministry.

The most urgent task facing Rashid Sfar, the president's choice to replace Mzali, was to put an end to the economic slide. As the 1982–6 planning cycle had drawn to a close, the IMF and the World Bank had begun to warn Tunisian officials that the country risked losing its access to credit unless it carried out a structural overhaul of the economy that reduced the deficit and relieved the mounting pressure exerted by external debts. Mzali's last budget, for 1986, trimmed government expenditures by 15 percent from the previous fiscal year and included deep cuts in basic food subsidies,[14] but the structural adjustment program envisioned by the international agencies entailed policy revisions reaching to the very roots of the economy. Their agenda included trade liberalization and the devaluation of the dinar to facilitate integration with the global economy, extensive privatization and deregulation to enhance the influence of the market, the stimulation of sound investments to reduce unemployment, and the reduction of public expenditures, particularly by the elimination of subsidies. The 1987–91 plan drawn up by Sfar's economic advisors spelled out the detailed implementation of this sweeping program, for which the IMF and the World Bank made available some $800 million.[15]

Whatever the economic merits of the structural adjustment program, the likelihood of its success hinged on the PSD's ability to persuade the Tunisian people, at a time of considerable economic and political uncertainty, of its necessity and to rally them behind the belt-tightening it required – a

challenge of significant proportions. Although the party counted more than
4,400 cells and a million members (15 percent of the total population),[16]
its militant fervor had evaporated since independence, few of its members
accorded it more than *pro forma* allegiance, and its leaders had come to
rely more on repression than on mobilization to achieve their objectives.
Obsessed with the retention of power and convinced, in no small part
because of the innuendoes circulated by Mzali's conservative opponents in
the party, that political enemies abounded, Bourguiba adamantly refused
to relinquish control over the party or the state, even though recurrent
bouts of physical, and occasionally mental, infirmity prevented him from
playing an effective public leadership role. Anxious to avoid the upheavals
that had accompanied the 1983 price hikes, the government attempted to
disguise the withdrawal of the subsidy on bread by reducing the weight of
a standard loaf rather than raising its price, but it could not conceal, nor
even appreciably soften, the hardships attendant, at least in the short term,
on structural adjustment. In addition to their distress over the economic
consequences of the program, its critics also expressed disgust at the surrender of sovereignty embodied in allowing the IMF and the World Bank to
formulate national economic and fiscal policy. Sfar made it clear from the
outset, however, that his government would not tolerate challenges to its
authority. In so uninviting a climate, the opposition parties again refused to
participate in elections, this time for the National Assembly, in November
1986.

After a spate of demonstrations in the following year, the authorities
arrested Ghannushi and other prominent MTI figures, charging them with
fomenting a plot to overthrow the government and create an Islamic state.
Consistently denied recognition as a legitimate political organization in an
allegedly pluralist system, the MTI appeared to be charting a collision course
with the government as it sought to position itself to seize power. Bourguiba
and his closest associates thoroughly despised the Muslim activists, deeming
their aspiration to center public life on Islam as the antithesis of the modern, Western-oriented, secular outlook that the party and state had assiduously promoted. Conversely, MTI members believed that their movement's
exclusion from the political process represented only the most recent manifestation of a systematic campaign, dating from before independence, to
push Tunisian Islam to the sidelines. In their view, the rejection of Islamic
values in favor of imported ideologies, all of which had failed to create a
just society, had been a grave error. Restoring hope to the Tunisian people
required a state committed to encouraging and assisting them to cultivate
their deep, but long neglected, Islamic roots.

Acting under presidential orders, ben ᶜAli turned the extensive resources of the interior ministry towards crushing the movement. The ensuing spiral of violence came to a head in August 1987, when bombs exploded at tourist hotels in Sousse and Monastir. Because Bourguiba and other prominent PSD officials hailed from Monastir and retained close ties with the city, but also because the incidents occurred on the eve of the national holiday marking the president's birthday, they conveyed a sense of personal vendetta. Moreover, an outrage of this kind in cities that had grown into beach resorts popular with international visitors, weakened the government by guaranteeing an economically destructive decline in the vital tourism industry. At the same time it enabled its perpetrators forcefully to convey their discomfort with the offensive behavior of many Western visitors. The blasts, for which the MTI denied responsibility, created a highly charged atmosphere at the trials that convened a few weeks later for the Islamists arrested earlier in the year. Those proceedings imposed the death penalty on several key leaders, including Ghannushi, and lengthy prison terms on scores of lesser party militants.

Bourguiba applauded the sentences, but ben ᶜAli, a police and security specialist, won the president over to his and other ministers' rationale that capital punishment risked endowing the prisoners with an aura of martyrdom, thereby fueling an already blazing fire. Bourguiba expressed his respect for ben ᶜAli's judgment by promoting him to the office of prime minister in October 1987, but then reverted to his insistence on the execution of the Islamist leaders. The elderly chief executive's physical deterioration and erratic behavior convinced ben ᶜAli that he no longer had the capacity to govern and he requested that a team of physicians assess the state of the president's health. They reached the same judgment and, in accordance with the provisions of the constitution, declared him unfit to remain in office. Zine al-ᶜAbidine ben ᶜAli assumed the presidency on November 7, 1987; Habib Bourguiba retired to Monastir where he died thirteen years later, aged ninety-seven.

As head of state, head of government, and head of the sole effective political party (the post of PSD secretary-general having been held by the prime minister since Nouira's time), and as the man who had engineered a peaceful transition sparing the country further stress, ben ᶜAli had enormous powers concentrated in his hands, but he also benefited from vast reservoirs of goodwill that were deepened still more by his apparent willingness to reach out to all segments of the population and by the fact that few Tunisians mourned the end of Bourguiba's sixty years of public life. Even the former president's strongest supporters had recognized, although hardly any had publicly acknowledged, the signs of physical and mental deterioration that had in recent years rendered him dangerous to allies and enemies alike and a liability to the nation. To put in order the political, economic, and social disarray of the house he had inherited, ben ʿAli required all the advantages he had in his possession.

THE ARTS AND LITERATURE IN BOURGUIBA'S TUNISIA

The thirty-one years during which Habib Bourguiba presided over Tunisia witnessed the development of a rich, diverse, and expressive national culture frequently contrasting with the repressive political environment and the debilitating fluctuations of the economy. After World War II, the well-known history of collaboration between the Neo-Dustur leadership and the theatrical community in the 1930s hindered a genuine revival of the theatre until 1954, when the Tunis municipal council created al-Firqa al-Baladiyya (The Tunis Municipal Theatre Company). With independence, the ministry of cultural affairs assumed financial sponsorship of the troupe, providing it with a sizeable annual subsidy that enabled the talented young actor ʿAli ben ʿAyad, who served as its director from 1963 to 1972, to mold al-Firqa al-Baladiyya into the most professional and successful company in the country, and to win international acclaim in tours throughout the Arab world and in Europe. After its leader's sudden death, the company faltered and, although it continued to mount successful seasons, later under the name Masrah al-Madina (The City Theatre), it rarely recaptured the dynamism of the ben ʿAyad era.

Government support for the Tunis company reflected a policy enunciated in 1962 by Bourguiba, whose elder brother Muhammad had directed and acted in a number of troupes in the 1930s. The president characterized stage productions not merely as entertainment, but as vehicles for popular education and the nurturing of national pride. Thereafter, the ministry of cultural affairs took a number of measures to fulfill his vision. It created two agencies, the Service du Théâtre to promote the work of existing companies and foster the creation of new ones and the Commission Nationale d'Orientation Théâtrale to review material and prevent the staging of "inappropriate" productions. The ministry also organized annual theatrical festivals showcasing Tunisian amateur and professional companies, to which it later added two additional celebrations, the Festival du Théâtre Maghrébin for North African amateur companies and the Festival du Théâtre Arabe for professional troupes from throughout the Arab world. The generally high quality of these events attracted an international audience and enhanced the reputation of Tunisian theatre within the country and abroad. Finally, in an effort to overcome the elitist aura of the theatre, the ministry offered extensive subsidies to local and regional companies in the early 1970s. Occasionally, however, this program backfired. The highly successful troupe created in Gafsa, for example, tailored its productions to the city's largely working-class population, staging satires of contemporary political and social issues in the regional idiom and accent – a provocative artistic philosophy that fueled the discontent spreading, particularly in the south, as the economy deteriorated.

In 1974 Fadhel Jaibi, an actor and director who had supervised the regional theatre movement, became the head of the Centre d'Art Dramatique in Tunis, a school established by the French in 1951 to provide training in the management of theatrical enterprises. Jaibi reoriented the center's curriculum, introducing courses in performance, direction, and technical aspects of the theatre that, for the first time, made it possible for Tunisians to receive professional training in these areas in their own country. Along with several of his colleagues at the Centre d'Art Dramatique, the pioneering Jaibi opened Tunisia's first private commercial theatre, the Théâtre Nouveau, in 1975. Drawing heavily on the talents of the center's faculty and students, who acted in, but also frequently wrote or adapted, productions addressing controversial social and political issues, the Théâtre Nouveau gained rapid recognition as the preeminent company in the country. In the face of better organized and more vocal political opposition after Muhammad Mzali became prime minister in 1980, the government was loathe to abandon the theatrical milieu to potential critics. In 1983, the ministry of cultural affairs launched the Théâtre National Tunisien, although its endeavor bore fruit only several years later, when Muhammad Driss, a playwright, director, and principal in the Théâtre Nouveau, accepted the position of director. Driss saw to the expansion of the national company and its acquisition of suitable facilities. He also used his standing in the theatrical community to forge productive contacts between his company, the Théâtre Nouveau, and the many private theatres springing up around the country.

Among the innovations of the Théâtre Nouveau were two experiments in filming stage productions for release as motion pictures, but Jaibi and his collaborators lacked training in cinematic techniques. As a result, their work had little impact on a relatively sophisticated industry in which film production by Tunisians dated back to the 1920s. Albert Samama, a Tunisian Jew known professionally as Chikly, made the first Tunisian short film, *Zohra*, in 1922, and the first feature, *La Fille de Carthage | ʿAyyil al-ghazwa*, two years later. Both exemplified the "mysterious Orient" genre popularized by Paramount Pictures' 1921 hit, *The Sheik*. ᶜAbd al-ᶜAziz Hassine, an actor, directed a second feature, *Targui*, in 1935, but for the next three decades no other Tunisians followed the trail blazed by these pioneers. During the 1920s and 1930s, however, the mild, sunny climate – not unlike that of southern California – attracted Western filmmakers, mostly European, but including the American actor and director Rex Ingram, who shot *The Arab* in Tunisia in 1924.[17]

Following independence a state corporation, the Société Anonyme Tunisienne de Production et d'Expansion Cinématographique (SATPEC; Tunisian Company for Film Production and Expansion), assumed responsibility for regulating the importation, distribution, and exhibition of the foreign motion pictures that were, and have remained, the most popular and most readily available fare in the nation's theatres. The output of the Tunisian industry has averaged only two feature films a year since SATPEC built a studio in the Tunis suburb of Gammarth in 1966 in furtherance of an additional mandate to promote the development of cinematic production. In the same year, the ministry of cultural affairs organized the first Journées Cinématographiques de Carthage (Carthage Film Festival), which awarded the Tanit D'Or prize to the best entry in a competition among Arab and African films. The biennial festival immediately became a landmark event in non-Western film circles. Its inaugural session, however, included no Tunisian contender for the Tanit d'Or. The first Tunisian feature film since the 1930s, *al-Fajr/L'Aube* directed by Omar Khlifi, a self-taught amateur filmmaker, appeared in 1966, but too late for consideration. A patriotic film about three youths who die in the independence struggle, it formed the first episode in a trilogy including *al-Mutamarrid/Le Rebelle* (1968) and *al-Fallaqa/Les Fellagas* (1970), each recounting historical instances of Tunisian resistance to outside control. A fourth film, *al-Surakh/Hurlements* (1972), focused on the constraints imposed on women by traditional Arab society. Other amateur filmmakers emerged in the late 1960s and 1970s, but few made more than a single successful feature or had any significant impact on cinematic thinking in Tunisia. Ridha Behi's *Shams al-dhiba/Soleil des Hyènes* (1977) forcefully condemned the destructive effects of the international tourism that had by then become an essential element in the Tunisian economy. Although the controversial feature, which Behi chose to shoot in Morocco, enjoyed critical praise in Europe, SATPEC's refusal to distribute it nullified the impact of the movie in Tunisia itself.

A quartet of young men and two young women, all of whom had studied at prestigious French (or in one instance, Belgian) film schools and refined their professional skills in Europe before returning to Tunisia, mostly in the late 1960s, greatly influenced the country's nascent film industry. Historical topics figured in the filmography of Brahim Babaï and ᶜAbd al-Latif ben ᶜAmmar, as they had in that of Klifi, but they and their colleagues Sadoq ben ᶜAicha and Naceur Ktari devoted greater attention to the malaise gripping Tunisia as ben Salah's socialist experiment collapsed and the freewheeling economy of the 1970s began to take its toll on the lower and middle classes. Ben ᶜAicha's *Mukhtar* (1968) examined the disillusion and frustration of young Tunisians; Babai's *Wa ghadan?/Et Demain?* (1972) told the by then tragically familiar story of a young man's journey from a drought-stricken village to Tunis in search of work; and ben ᶜAmmar's *ᶜAziza* (1980) won the Tanit d'Or for its exploration of the debilitating problems of urban life. The conflict between Tunisian and European cultures – readily comprehended by filmmakers with a foot in both camps – lay at the core of ben ᶜAmmar's *Hikaya basita kahadhihi/Une Si Simple Histoire* (1970), while Ktari's *al-Sufara'/Les Ambassadeurs* (1975), the first Tunisian film awarded the Tanit d'Or, in 1976, described the difficulties faced by Tunisian labor emigrants to France. Similar social concerns characterized the work of Tunisia's first female directors. Selma Baccar's *Fatma 75* (1978) sketched a series of cinematic portraits of Tunisian women from the Carthaginian era to the twentieth century. In *al-Sama/La Trace*, the story of a young village woman from the south, Neija ben Mabrouk wove together issues relating to gender, poverty, and emigration. Ben Mabrouk completed its filming in 1982, but a dispute with SATPEC, the producer, delayed its release until 1988.

SATPEC's involvement in the production of some of Tunisia's better films in the 1970s, but also in numerous and often not very successful co-productions with European directors, gave it a mixed record. In 1981, the Mzali government withdrew SATPEC's import and distribution monopoly, at the same time levying a 6 percent tax on box office receipts to finance a fund promoting independent cinematic ventures. Among the new companies benefiting from this initiative was Cinétéléfilms, which rapidly assumed pride of place among production companies. Its owner, Ahmad ᶜAttia, used his considerable knowledge of Tunisia's film industry, in which he had worked since finishing his directorial studies in Rome in 1970, to identify promising young directors whom he encouraged to craft semi-autobiographical movies. His first protégé, Nouri Bouzid, boldly confronted questions of sexuality and homosexuality, subjects rarely approached in previous motion pictures made in the Arab world, in *Rih al-sadd/L'Homme de Cendres* (1986). Despite, or perhaps because of, its controversial nature, *Rih al-sadd* received the Tanit d'Or at the 1986 Carthage Film Festival, the third Tunisian feature to achieve that accolade. ᶜAttia also encouraged Férid Boughedir, an established film critic and historian, to explore this genre after he had completed three highly acclaimed documentaries on African and Arab cinema: *Caméra d'Afrique* (1983), *Cinéma de Carthage* (1984), and *Caméra Arabe* (1987). With social and economic problems persisting in the 1980s, many directors making their feature film debuts in those years continued to be drawn to themes reflecting the national malaise. *Zill al-ard/L'Ombre de la Terre* (1982) by Taieb Louhichi, for example, tells the tale of an isolated rural community devastated by natural disaster and the intrusion of modernity. More successful at the box office than any of the weighty films of social commentary, however, was *Farda wa liqat ukhtaha/Deux Larrons en Folie*, a 1980 comedy directed by ᶜAli Mansour, although even it centered on the theme of migration from the countryside to Tunis.

Like others who made their mark in the film industry (including ben ᶜAicha, Behi, and Baccar), Mansour had begun his career in the television section of Radiodiffusion Télévision Tunisienne (RTT), which started transmitting limited programming to northern Tunisia in 1966 and by 1971 reached the entire country. As in the case of the theatre, government officials hoped to exploit television as an educational and civic tool – an experimental broadcast aired the 1964 party congress in Bizerte at which the Neo-Dustur redesigned itself as the Parti Socialiste Dusturien – in addition to its role as an entertainment medium. In a speech inaugurating the station, Bourguiba urged every family to buy a television set. To make such a purchase possible for average Tunisians, the government drove down the price by importing thousands, although it also adopted the practice of charging a small annual licensing fee, as it did for radios, which remained in effect until 1980.

In keeping with the government's aspirations, news reports, religious presentations, documentaries, instructional programs, and cultural performances initially dominated the airwaves. But a limited capacity for original production created a difficulty as the broadcast day gradually lengthened from its original three hours. Even after a decade of operation, the RTT relied on foreign sources (both Western and Arab) for more than half its televised material. The ease, at least in densely populated northern Tunisia, of receiving broadcasts from France and Italy increased pressure on the RTT to fall into line with Western programming. As it did so, however, the MTI and other conservatives expressed distaste at the content of much of the imported programming, which they also attacked as an example of the country's abandonment of its indigenous heritage.

Although a similar shift occurred in the field of painting in the 1960s and 1970s, it did not elicit the same criticisms because conservative Muslims disliked the figural representations common in the art of the "Ecole de Tunis." Independence lessened the urgency for Tunisian painters to establish a visual record of the country's heritage, which many of them had come to regard as a patriotic obligation, and also facilitated their access to the global artistic community. A wave of experimentation with new, primarily abstract, forms of expression followed. By encouraging Tunisian painters to broaden their horizons, Hedi Turki and Hatim al-Mekki, successful artists who had traveled widely in Europe and North America, helped to endow Tunisian art with a cosmopolitan aura it had not previously known. Of the two Turki was the more self-conscious, disdaining what he viewed as his contemporaries' provincialism, while al-Mekki's eclecticism and curiosity ruled out any prospect of limiting himself to a single genre.

Many younger artists influenced by Turki and al-Mekki embraced the new forms without reservation; others took advantage of the progressive creative climate to try their hand at media previously little known in Tunisia, including engraving and printmaking. The most successful newcomers in the first generation after independence, however, were artists who found ways to distinguish their work by infusing it with indigenous cultural features. Najib Belkhodja and Nja Mahdaoui established reputations in the 1960s by utilizing Arabic calligraphy to design abstract paintings in which the significance of the text was entirely subordinated to the visual impact of the work, occasionally going so far as to employ brush strokes that resembled Arabic letters, but were not. An older and already established painter, ᶜAli Bellagha, affected a similar blend by combining cubist techniques and traditional Arabic geometric patterns. A few artists doggedly resisted the prevailing trends and continued to produce ingenuous depictions of traditional life. Largely ignored in the enthusiasm for innovation marking the first two post-independence decades, the canvases of ᶜAli Guermassi and other adherents of a naïve school of painting came back into vogue in the 1980s, their wistful commemoration of a Tunisia few of its citizens had ever personally experienced acting as a soothing balm to men and women frazzled by the volatile nature of the times in which they lived.

The social and economic transformations that flowed from political independence provided an abundance of multifaceted themes and evocative settings for the generation of poets, short-story writers, novelists, and essayists whose careers more or less coincided with the era of Bourguiba's presidency. But two of the country's most promising literary figures, Hachemi Baccouche and Albert Memmi, viewed the termination of the protectorate as an event likely to circumscribe their artistic license, and both moved permanently to France, Memmi in 1956, Baccouche in the following year. The first novel of the French-educated, bourgeois Baccouche, *Ma foi demeure* (1958), explored the complexities of a mixed Franco-Tunisian marriage that served as a metaphor for the many cross-cultural linkages of the colonial period that the author doubted would survive the triumph of nationalism. Memmi, also the recipient of a French education that included a degree from the University of Paris, came not from the urban middle class but from the Tunisian Jewish community. Prior to independence, he published two largely autobiographical novels, *Le Statue de sel* (1953) and *Agar* (1955), that examined the impact of colonialism on an individual doubly marginalized, first as a Tunisian, then as a Jew. A cogent treatise on oppression, *Portrait du colonisé précédé du portrait du colonisateur* (1957), established Memmi's reputation as a social analyst and was followed by other essays on identity (particularly Jewish identity), dependency, and racism. In subsequent works of fiction, Memmi, like Baccouche, availed himself of Tunisian themes and milieus, but the self-imposed exile of both men for more than half their lives calls into question their categorization as "Tunisian."

Although some authors publishing in Tunisia after 1956 used French, most preferred Arabic, a language in which they enjoyed greater facility and which made their work accessible to the widest local audience. The literary review *al-Fikr*, begun in 1955 by the same Muhammad Mzali who later became prime minister, provided an invaluable outlet for aspiring writers over the next three decades. Among the writers first published in *al-Fikr* was Bashir Khurayyif, a transitional figure in the shift from the nationalist and patriotic topics that had dominated earlier fiction towards themes derived more directly from contemporary Tunisian society. Often hailed as the first modern Tunisian novelist, Khurayyif built his fiction around straightforward descriptions of Tunisian life. *Iflas aw Hubbuka darbani* (1959) depicted the lives of the country's youth as modernist pressures reshaped their environment, while *al-Daghal fi ʿarajiniha* (1969) focused on the particularly trying economic and social conditions of the underdeveloped south.

Following independence women began to publish in much larger numbers than previously. In the late 1960s, no doubt influenced by trends in Europe and North America, a wave of feminist writing took place. Short stories by Hind ʿAzzuz, collected as *Fiʾl-Darb al-tawil* (1969), explored the circumstances of middle-class women and addressed such sensitive topics as birth control and abortion; Laila ben Mami's novel *Sawmaʿa tahtariq* (1968) portrayed the lives of women who had achieved high levels of sexual freedom; and a collection of poetry by Zubaydah Bashir, *Hanin* (1968), embodied her disillusion and rebelliousness over the social constraints imposed on women. Prominent male authors joined these female pioneers in employing their literary talents to draw public attention to the problems facing Tunisian women. Two novels set against the background of rural decay, the collapse of the cooperative movement, and increasing migration to the cities, ʿAbd al-Qadir ben al-Shaykh's *Wa nasibi min al-ufuq* (1970) and ʿUmar ben Salim's *Waha bi-la zill* (1979), presented perceptive vignettes of women's fears and concerns as they made the case for emancipation and the easing of traditional restrictions. While not specifically focused on women, their evolving status is a recurrent theme in a trilogy of historical novels by Muhammad Salah al-Jabiri – *Yawm min ayyam Zamra* (1968), set in the late colonial period, *al-Bahr yanshur al-wahahu* (1975), recounting the political and social challenges of a newly independent state, and *Laylat al-sanawat al-ʿashr* (1982), exploring many of the issues that gave rise to the 1978 "Black Thursday" riots.

Bourguiba's early insistence on the importance of education found an echo in numerous essays and fictional works. Among the most popular of the latter was *al-Munbatt* (1967), a semi-autobiographical novel by ʿAbd al-Majid ʿAtiyah about the efforts of a government clerk to improve his lot. But as political and economic difficulties multiplied in the 1970s and 1980s, many of the country's leading writers found themselves more frequently at odds with the authorities than enthusiastic about their programs. Such men and women turned their imaginative powers to producing works whose criticism of the Parti Socialiste Dusturien and the government had considerable power, despite being camouflaged within a fictional context. *Fi Bayt al-ʿankabut* (1976), Muhammad al-Hadi ben Salih's first novel, took as its theme the exploitation of the masses. In a second book, *al-Haraka wa intikas al-shams* (1981), ben Salih followed the lead of other literary figures, including the poet and critic Salah Garmadi and the playwright and essayist Samir al-ʿAyyadi, as he struggled to comprehend and articulate the obligations of intellectuals in the midst of social and political unrest. As the Bourguibist regime began to crumble, ʿUmar ben Salim produced two more novels that addressed contemporary issues. *Daʾirat al-ikhtinaq* (1982) concerned the beleaguered union movement and *Abu Jahl al-Dahhas* (1984) tackled questions of emigration, racism, and nationalism. At the same time, ʿArusiyah Naluti, who had won considerable popularity when some of her short stories were read on the radio, published *Maratij* (1985), a novel that examined the emotions of Tunisian students in France as their country was buffeted by the political turmoil of the late Bourguiba years. When Prime Minister ben ᶜAli eased out the ailing president two years later, the literary community could take satisfaction in the part it had played in the downfall of the regime and, like other Tunisians, look forward to better days ahead.

CHAPTER 7

Constancy and innovation in the "new" Tunisia, 1987–2003

SETTING THE NEW REGIME IN PLACE

Zine al-ᶜAbidine ben ᶜAli's deft removal of Bourguiba produced a public reaction well described by using an analogy to the world of sports. Just as knowledgeable spectators respond to the retirement of once-great athletes who have extended their playing days well past their prime, have lost the gift for making the big play, and have become a liability rather than an asset to their teams and a source of embarrassment, perhaps not to themselves, but certainly to aficionados of the game who remember their peak performances, Bourguiba's departure evoked a deep sense of relief among his countrymen. Ben ᶜAli promptly stepped into Bourguiba's role not only as head of state, but also as head of the PSD, suggesting that whatever transformations might flow from the "Historic Change," they would not include a disentangling of the thoroughly interwoven lines between the state and the party. To symbolize the advent of a new leadership, however, the PSD was renamed the Rassemblement Constitutionnel Démocratique (RCD – Democratic Constitutional Rally). The retention of the reference to the constitution tied the party to its predecessors, but the remainder of the title anticipated a broader and more egalitarian institution than the Dustur, Neo-Dustur, or Socialist Dustur had ever managed to become.

Nevertheless, the first RCD congress, in 1988, invested ben ᶜAli with complete control of the party and, by extension, the state. The political bureau shrank from twenty-two members to seven, all of them avowed supporters of the new president, and Hedi Baccouche, a party veteran who had assisted ben ᶜAli in easing Bourguiba out, became vice-president of the RCD and prime minister. Staunch Bourguiba loyalists soon found themselves marginalized in both the party and the government. A few of the former president's close associates whose venality was common knowledge were arrested, but the absence of any more stringent measures contributed to keeping the transition on an even keel. Conversely, ben ᶜAli freed thousands of political prisoners, including Ghannushi and other MTI detainees, and encouraged opponents of Bourguiba who had gone into exile to return to Tunisia, assuring them that his government intended to foster a plural political environment capable of accommodating the RCD and its rivals, both secular and religious. Prominent among the returnees was Ahmed ben Salah, the minister of planning who had come into conflict with Bourguiba in 1969.

The "Historic Change" of 1987 enabled intellectuals who had fled Tunisia in search of a less restrictive environment and young men and women who had remained abroad at the conclusion of their higher education or professional training programs to consider returning to their homeland. Some did, but others, including exiles who had successfully established reputations in international circles – among them the authors Tahar Bekri, ᶜAbd al-Wahhab Meddeb, and Mustapha Tlili – did not. The early poetry and prose of Bekri, who left Tunisia after serving time in jail as a result of his political activities while a student in the 1970s, often reflected the emotional pain of displacement. Bekri regarded his decision to stay in France after 1987 as artistic rather than political, and Tunisian cultural and historical influences continued to inform his writing. Unlike many other exiles, he continued to publish in Arabic as well as in French, which made his work accessible to readers on both sides of the Mediterranean. His contemporary Meddeb published only in French, but his novels *Talismano* (1979) and *Fantasia* (1989), *Le Tombeau d'Ibn Arabi* (1988), a collection of poetry, and the essay *Suhrawardi Shihab al-Din Yahya. Récits de l'exil occidental* (1993) all reveal his deep knowledge of classical Arab–Islamic civilization, which has assured him an audience among Tunisian, as well as other Arab, intellectuals. The eldest of this trio, Tlili completed a philosophy degree at the Sorbonne, worked for over a decade at the United Nations, and then took up residence in France in 1980. His novels condemned corruption among the elite, but until the appearance of *La Montagne du lion* (1988), which was set in Tunisia, none had any relationship to his North African heritage. Like Hachemi Baccouche and Albert Memmi in an earlier generation, the mentality, themes, and impact of writers in more or less permanent exile all set them apart from their colleagues working in Tunisia itself.

By and large, novelists and poets popular in the 1970s and 1980s continued to dominate the literary scene during ben ᶜAli's presidency. Muhammad al-Hadi ben Salih's novel describing the 1978 riots, *Sifr al-nuqla wa'l-tasawwur* (1988), embodied criticisms of the previous regime, but when the political atmosphere under ben ᶜAli failed to change in the ways that he and other writers had hoped it would, they lost no time in articulating their dissatisfaction with the new government. Ben Salih reopened the issue of the role of the intellectual in *Min haqqihi an yahlum* (1991), sadly concluding that neither he nor most of his colleagues had lived up to their obligations. Frustration with the absence of meaningful change permeated ʿUmar ben Salim's novel, *al-Asad wa 'l-timthal* (1989), in which animal characters illustrated the course of modern Tunisian history. *Wa kana ʿurs al-hazima* (1991), a novel by the feminist Hayat ben al-Shaykh, revisited the still pertinent issues of corruption and the abuse of power. In *Feux d'oiseau* (1989), a poetess and one of the minority of Tunisian authors regularly publishing in French, Amina Saʿid, sought to bring individual and collective memories to light as a means of understanding the impact of the past on the present – a theme that had attracted the attention of the poet and literary critic Muhammad ʿAziza (writing under the pseudonym Chems Nadir) a decade earlier and that underpinned two collections of his verse, *Silence des semaphores* (1978) and *L'Astrolabe de la mer* (1980).

Like most writers and other intellectuals, the new president had little sympathy for the vision of the Islamist movement, but he believed that it constituted a greater potential threat outside the political tent than within it. To demonstrate his willingness to deal seriously with the MTI, ben ʿAli accommodated some of its more symbolic demands, publicly affirming Islam as the state religion, authorizing Tunisian radio and television stations to broadcast the call to prayer, and legalizing an MTI student organization that mobilized post-secondary students. In addition, the president made a highly publicized pilgrimage to Mecca. In autumn 1988 the MTI was invited to send a representative to join government officials, leaders of civil society, the heads of the secular political parties, and other prominent national figures in deliberations to formulate a statement of political philosophy and objectives on which all could agree in advance of the first elections of the post-Bourguiba era, scheduled for early in the following year.

Ben ʿAli unveiled the National Pact on the first anniversary of his accession to the presidency. It acknowledged the centrality of the Arab and Islamic heritages of Tunisia that many citizens believed that the Bourguiba government had deliberately disparaged, calling for closer ties between Tunisia and the rest of the Arab world, and particularly the other countries of the Maghrib. The document made reference to the importance in nineteenth- and twentieth-century Tunisia of the movements of Islamic reform and modernism, but also expressed an appreciation of the Personal Status Code, which it insisted should remain unassailable. In becoming a signatory to the National Pact and thus agreeing to this assessment, the MTI made a major concession. The government also offered a significant

Figure 7.1. Zine al-ʿAbidine ben ʿAli. As prime minister in 1987, ben ʿAli invoked constitutional provisions on presidential incapacity to remove the ailing Habib Bourguiba from office and replace him as chief executive, a post which he has held since that date.

concession – not specifically to the Islamists, but to the entire spectrum of the opposition – by accepting the pact's proposal to remedy the political shortcomings of the past through pluralism, respect for human rights, and explicit guarantees of basic freedoms.

The National Pact appeared to offer the MTI its first opportunity to enter the political arena. In order to conform to electoral laws prohibiting religious terminology in the names of political parties, the organization became the Hizb al-Nahda (Renaissance Party) and applied for political party status. Despite the rhetoric of the pact, suspicions that the Islamists' ultimate goal remained the dismantling of the secular state led the government to temporize. Desperate for a mechanism to pressure the authorities without provoking a self-destructive backlash, Ghannushi launched a drive to recruit new members for al-Nahda within the UGTT, hoping eventually to barter Islamist influence in the union for official recognition as a party. But the government, intent on rebuilding (and controlling) the UGTT following its near collapse in the last years of Bourguiba's presidency, thwarted al-Nahda at every turn. When campaigning for the April 1989 legislative contests began, the party remained ineligible to offer lists of candidates. Determined not to accept their exclusion from the electoral process, Ghannushi and other members of al-Nahda stood for National Assembly seats on an independent list in twenty-two of the country's twenty-five electoral districts. They accused the government of impeding the emergence of genuine democracy in Tunisia by excluding Islamist groups from its conceptualization of pluralism and reminded voters that pressure brought to bear by the Islamists earlier in the decade deserved much of the credit for precipitating political reform, however incomplete it might have proven. Occasionally they explicitly asserted that without the Islamist movement, Bourguiba would have remained in power.

Tunisia's political evolution, or lack thereof, from 1989 until the early years of the new millennium is clearly discernible in the three national elections held during that period. Of the five secular opposition parties that competed in the 1989 contest, only Mestiri's MDS had an organization capable of mounting a viable nationwide challenge to the RCD (and the independents). Neither the Parti d'Unité Populaire nor three new parties legalized in 1988 – the Union Démocratique Unioniste (UDU – Democratic Unionist Union), the Parti Social du Progrès (PSP – Social Progress Party), and the Rassemblement Socialiste Progressiste (RSP – Progressive Socialist Rally) – managed to field candidates in more than a quarter of the districts. The RCD won a landslide victory, winning almost 80 percent of the popular vote and sweeping all of the parliamentary seats. Slightly

more than 15 percent of the overall vote went to the al-Nahda "independents," although in some districts in the south and in the Tunis suburbs
where they enjoyed particularly strong backing, they obtained more than
30 percent of the ballots. Together, the secular opposition parties garnered
a mere 5 percent of the vote. Only the MDS surpassed the 1 percent mark,
an anemic showing attributable to widespread defections from the party
to the RCD following Bourguiba's removal from office. In the presidential race, ben ᶜAli ran unopposed and secured 99 percent of the vote. The
1989 elections created a foundation for the new government in a manner
reminiscent of the first post-independence elections in 1956. On both occasions, a serious regime competitor – the Yusufists in 1956, the Islamists in
1989 – appeared to lack adequate popular support to claim a role in shaping
Tunisia's political future, but only because on both occasions the dominant
party had tilted the playing field to its own advantage.[1]

Nevertheless, the elections established the Islamists as a political factor
of greater significance than the secular parties and second in importance
only to the RCD. When al-Nahda's leaders used the results to press their
case for recognition as a party, their demand was again denied. A disgusted
Ghannushi abandoned Tunisia for exile in France (as did an equally disenchanted Ahmed ben Salah). The management of al-Nahda's day-to-day
business fell to its secretary-general, ᶜAbd al-Fattah Mourou, who, unlike
Ghannushi, claimed not to have lost faith in the democratic process as a
means of achieving the organization's goals. But Ghannushi, who retained
his position as spiritual and political mentor of al-Nahda, threw down the
gauntlet to the political establishment: "Until now," he warned ominously,
"we sought only a shop and we did not get it. Now it's the whole souk (mar-
ketplace) we want."[2] Militant Islamists were no longer content to secure
seats in a multiparty parliament – even if such a body were to come into existence, which they now had reason to doubt – but rather sought to dominate
the political realm. Comments such as these enabled ben ᶜAli to cast himself
as the defender of a progressive, secular republic under threat from religious
chauvinism and to meld his vision of constrained political pluralism with
a modified version of his predecessor's authoritarianism. Filling such a role
brought him the support of the many Tunisians who wanted an Islamist
government no more than they had wanted the autocracy of Bourguiba.
It also assured him of the sympathy of Tunisia's Western allies, who had
viewed the political resurgence of Islam since the Iranian Revolution with
a jaundiced eye.

Neither economic nor foreign policy received much attention in the
first year of the ben ᶜAli presidency, but after the RCD's commanding

victory in the 1989 elections, the government intensified the application of the structural adjustment plan devised at the end of the Bourguiba era. The deleterious impact on middle- and working-class Tunisians of the IMF's prescription for resuscitating the Tunisian economy continued to provoke angry reactions from an already aggrieved al-Nahda and milder criticisms from within the tattered and demoralized ranks of the secular opposition. When Baccouche, fearing a repetition of the 1978 and 1984 riots, urged restraint on the economic front, ben ᶜAli removed the cautious prime minister, replacing him in late 1989 with Hamid Karoui, a veteran of several of Bourguiba's cabinets. By the time the 1987–91 plan had run its course, the economic slide had been arrested and a healthy annual growth rate achieved.

The government also devoted considerable attention to an initiative combining economic and foreign policy while advancing an important objective of the National Pact. The growing movement within the European Communities (EC) towards greater integration and the eventual creation of a single continental market compelled Tunisia and its neighbors in the Maghrib to explore cooperative arrangements making it possible to better cope with the challenges and seize upon the potential opportunities presented by the evolving economic situation across the Mediterranean. In February 1989, Tunisia, Libya, Algeria, Morocco, and Mauritania established the Union du Maghreb Arabe (UMA – Arab Maghrib Union) not only with an eye to the situation in Europe, but also to foster partnerships among states that had much in common but that had, since gaining independence in the 1950s and 1960s, as often been at odds with or ignored each other as they had worked together. The union raised the level of regional cooperation, particularly in the cultural, educational, and scientific fields, but its members proved unable to lay aside political differences concerning the fate of the former Spanish Sahara. Algerian support for the Polisario Front, an indigenous liberation movement that opposed Moroccan efforts to absorb the territory it had occupied since 1976, split the organization. Since the approval of UMA business required the consent of all five states, significant initiatives ground to a halt in 1995.

In the Arab world beyond North Africa, the Tunisian government devoted more effort than in the past to cultivating strong relationships, particularly targeting the Arabian Peninsula oil states, whose investment petrodollars it hoped to attract for development projects in the country. Nevertheless, in the wake of the Iraqi invasion of Kuwait in summer 1990 – an event that affected Tunisia more profoundly than any other that had occurred in the Arab East since 1956 – ben ᶜAli refused to support Saudi

Arabia's appeal for the creation of a multinational military force including European and US troops. Tunisia did not sanction Iraq's seizure of the emirate, but did insist that intra-Arab problems required intra-Arab solutions, a stance applauded by its own citizens across the political spectrum but viewed dimly by traditionally friendly powers such as the United States and France, to say nothing of the irritation of Saudi Arabia and Kuwait. During the autumn, Ben ʿAli sent a ministerial-level delegation to Iraq in an unsuccessful attempt to stimulate negotiations between the opposing factions. Similarly, Rashid Ghannushi, now residing in Algeria, joined two other prominent Islamist leaders, the Algerian ʿAbbas Madani and the Sudanese Hassan Turabi, in an equally futile effort to open a dialogue between Baghdad and Riyadh that would avert the stationing of non-Muslim soldiers in Saudi Arabia. On the domestic front, the UGTT, along with several opposition parties, set up a National Committee to Resist Aggression against the Arab World and to Support Iraq, and the first legal public demonstrations since the "Historic Change" coincided with the arrival of Western troops in the Arabian Peninsula. The outbreak of the Gulf War in January 1991 generated new large-scale protests that the government monitored closely in order to prevent its opponents from taking control of them and using them to push it towards a more pro-Iraqi position than it wished to adopt.

For a time, at least, Tunisia paid dearly for its policies during the crisis in the Gulf. With Westerners hesitant to travel to the Arab world, and especially to a country that had opposed the United States-led coalition, 600,000 fewer European tourists visited Tunisia in 1991 than in the previous year, a drop of 36 percent. An almost equal increase in the number of tourists arriving from other Maghrib countries partially compensated for the decline in Europeans, although the North Africans spent considerably less during their stays. Tourism statistics for 1992 closely matched those of the prewar years – more than three million visitors annually (more than half of them from Europe) pumping almost a billion dollars into the economy – and thereafter the industry experienced steady growth for the remainder of the decade, attracting five million visitors annually at the turn of the century.[3] The United States retaliated against Tunisia by slashing its economic assistance from roughly $30 million in 1990 to $8 million in 1991 and a mere $1 million in 1992 and by terminating military aid altogether. In 1993, however, disbursements climbed back to their earlier levels. Donations from the Gulf states, which plummeted from $100 million in 1990 to less than $3 million in 1991, were resumed more slowly, with Kuwait refusing even to restore diplomatic relations with Tunisia until 1994.[4]

BRINGING THE OPPOSITION TO HEEL

The Gulf conflict led directly to a split within al-Nahda. Most of its members lined up behind Ghannushi, whose move into the Iraqi camp as Western troops poured into the region put him at odds with official Tunisian policy. On the other hand, Mourou, who had studied in Saudi Arabia and maintained numerous links to that country, endorsed its appeal for international military assistance, with the result that his influence in the organization dwindled virtually to nil. With its radical wing in control, the Islamist movement turned against the government with a ferocity not seen since the last days of the Bourguiba regime. Late in 1990 a number of militants were arrested on charges of planning terrorist attacks that included a plot to assassinate ben ʿAli. In February 1991 a deadly act of arson at an RCD office in the Tunis neighborhood of Bab Souika caused a wave of public revulsion at the extremists' resort to the kind of indiscriminate violence that placed innocent persons at risk. Judging that the situation verged on spiraling out of control, ben ʿAli directed his security forces to undertake a severe crackdown on al-Nahda and its sympathizers.

Events unfolding at more or less the same time in neighboring Algeria deeply disturbed many Tunisians and inevitably influenced their assessment of matters in their own country. Local elections in June 1990 gave the Front Islamique du Salut (FIS – Islamic Salvation Front), an Islamist party, control of numerous municipal councils across the country. A combination of its own program of political and social reform and widespread disillusion with the Front de Libération Nationale (FLN – National Liberation Front) that had ruled the country since its independence in 1962 positioned the FIS as a strong contender in legislative elections in December 1991. The Islamists' enormous success in the first of two rounds of voting set in motion a catastrophic chain of events: army officers forced the president to resign, took control of the government, cancelled the elections, and soon faced a vicious civil war as the Islamists attempted to gain by force of arms the victory snatched from them at the ballot boxes. Ghannushi, who had developed close ties with the Algerian Islamists, later ruefully observed that the course of events in Algeria did the Tunisian movement "a great disservice" in that it

gave our adversaries the opportunity to appear threatened. It created the impression that the West needed them to face the danger . . . spreading from Algeria towards Europe.[5]

Indeed, as millions of Tunisian citizens looked across their western border in horror, they endorsed, or at least did not openly oppose, harsh measures designed to rein in al-Nahda, lest its clash with the government unleash a nightmare scenario replicating the Algerian tragedy.

Although similar campaigns directed against opponents of the regime – particularly religiously inspired opponents – had often ignored the constraints of the law in Bourguiba's Tunisia, ben ʿAli had made choices early in his presidency that appeared to disavow such cavalier behavior. Citing the need for national reconciliation, he expressed the belief that adherence to the principles of the Universal Declaration of Human Rights constituted the surest means of achieving that end. In his first government, the president entrusted the ministry of health to Saʿad al-Din Zmerli, a medical doctor who had founded the Ligue Tunisienne des Droits de l'Homme (LTDH – Tunisian League of Human Rights). Since 1977 the League had boldly tracked, publicized, and condemned disparities between the law and its application in the government's dealings with its critics, especially trade unionists, students, and Islamists. Whether sincerity or expediency initially motivated ben ʿAli, the violence that erupted after the 1989 elections and the subsequent descent of Algeria into chaos convinced him of the need, and the public support, for aggressive countermeasures. The League did its best to monitor the activities of both the security forces and the Islamists, but in the overheated atmosphere abuses inevitably occurred. In 1992, 279 members of al-Nahda stood trial on a variety of charges, the most serious of which alleged involvement in the preparation of a coup d'état paving the way for the creation of an Islamic state. The movement's most prominent figures (including Ghannushi, who was tried *in absentia*) received sentences of life imprisonment. Defense lawyers leveled accusations of widespread human rights violations, including the use of torture, against the security forces, while also claiming that legal irregularities tainted the trials themselves. Efforts by the League to investigate these allegations completed its transformation, under way since the 1989 elections, into an adversary of the government.

Few Tunisians outside the Islamist camp joined the LTDH in expressing reservations about the state's dealings with al-Nahda. In exchange for protection from the "green threat" of Islamic radicalism, the majority of secular Tunisians turned a blind eye to excesses committed by the authorities. Leaders of the opposition political parties contented themselves with the collapse of so formidable a rival as al-Nahda and, anxious to shield their own organizations from a similar fate, suppressed whatever misgivings they may have harbored. Further encouraging their "go along to get along" attitude was the knowledge that, even after years of recruiting and organizing, no opposition party – nor any combination of them – could survive a head-on confrontation with the government or hope to prevail in an electoral challenge against the RCD, now estimated at 1.6 million strong.[6] As a result, they raised no objections to a law passed in anticipation of parliamentary elections in 1994 that guaranteed opposition parties crossing a relatively low threshold of votes a proportional share of nineteen set-aside seats in the National Assembly. In this way, ben ʿAli cultivated the appearance of pluralism without providing the concept with substance. The system pitted the opposition parties against each other, rather than against the RCD, for a prize of dubious worth: their meager 12 percent of the seats in the legislature assured them of a presence, but denied them the opportunity to have any impact. In the presidential election, not even the pretense of pluralism was advanced. The government rejected the candidacy of Moncef Marzouki, a leading figure in the LTDH and the only person who came forward to challenge the incumbent. Ben ʿAli ran unopposed for a second term.

Despite having experienced major upheavals since the 1989 elections – Ahmed Mestiri left public life in 1990 and a dissident faction withdrew from the party in 1992 when its new secretary general, Muhammad Mouada, applauded some of ben ʿAli's policies – the MDS fared better than its competitors in the 1994 elections, winning ten of the opposition seats. (That it did so on the basis of 31,000 votes, or barely 1 percent of the total number cast,[7] however, reveals the anemic nature of even the oldest and best organized opposition party.) The PUP took two seats, the UDU three, and the Mouvement de la Rénovation (the former Parti Communiste Tunisien) the remaining four. Only the left-wing RSP adopted an aggressively critical stance towards government policies, but it failed, by a considerable margin, to cross the threshold set for representation in the parliament. Pointing to its proven ability to provide security and asserting that economic liberalism was translating into personal prosperity and national development, the RCD captured more than 90 percent of the total vote in every district in the country.

Such lopsided results were in keeping with the pattern of all previous elections. In 1994, as in 1989, even with alternatives available to the voters, the RCD dominated the political arena no less formidably than had its Neo-Dustur and PSD forerunners in a classically single-party setting. Opposition politicians accused the RCD of various improprieties in both elections but, except for the "independents" in 1989, their parties remained so ineffectual, even after years of legal operation, that manipulating vote counts and intimidating the electorate, both of which undoubtedly occurred to some degree, were unnecessary, and potentially counter-productive, on a grand scale. The RCD enjoyed a measure of genuine popularity that the PSD had forfeited (if, indeed, it had ever enjoyed it) long before the "Historic Change."

In 1989, the electorate enthused over the leaders who had shouldered Bourguiba aside, committed themselves to strengthening the economy and supporting social development programs, and dug in against political Islam. Five years later the success of the campaign against the Islamists, an economy growing at a sustained rate of more than 4 percent a year, and discernible progress in alleviating some of the country's most severe social inequities further enhanced the stature of the party and contributed to the magnitude of its electoral triumph. The Fonds de Solidarité Nationale (FSN – National Solidarity Fund), established in 1992, proved an especially effective weapon in both undermining the Islamists and winning support for the RCD government. Soliciting private contributions (which ultimately comprised a third of its resources) to supplement its base of public funds, the FSN initially targeted 1,100 of the least developed areas of the country (*zones d'ombre*, or shadow zones) as beneficiaries of projects to ensure the availability of electricity, clean drinking water, adequate housing, basic health care, and schooling. In addition to helping to reduce poverty to the lowest level in the Arab world other than in the oil-based economies, the program also deprived Islamist social agencies of the opportunity to attract adherents by supplying basic services in underprivileged areas neglected by the government.

The 1994 vote underscored the impressive power of the RCD, which the Tunisian political tradition of party–state interconnectedness reinforced still further. The man who headed both, Zine al-ᶜAbidine ben ᶜAli, had become at least as powerful as Habib Bourguiba in his heyday. The composition of the elite surrounding him reinforced ben ᶜAli's power. By shouldering aside once influential figures of the old regime, he made room for a younger generation of technocrats that answered to him. Many were modern, well-educated women who had carved out careers in the liberal professions, academia, and business. Their advocacy of progressive social programs and their disdain for the Islamists' agenda, which they viewed as a backward step for Tunisian women, made them ideal RCD recruits and, often, effective spokespersons for the party. Members of the new cadre who attained ministerial rank encountered frequent reshufflings of the government – during the first decade of the ben ᶜAli presidency over one hundred men and women held portfolios – that prevented them from exercising real power. "The ministries and the names change," noted an observer, "but the policy of the president remains and all the cards are in the hands of the Chief of State."[8] At a lower echelon, ben ᶜAli encouraged the infusion of new blood into the party by rejuvenating its urban neighborhood cells, which served as training grounds for young men and women preparing to serve the RCD in more elevated capacities. The results of the 1994 elections bore the imprint of these moves. More than three-quarters of the new legislators were under fifty years of age; more than half had never before held elected office at the national level; and a mere five had sat in the Chamber of Deputies before 1987.

Two critical and related questions faced ben ᶜAli and the RCD after the 1994 elections: could the party indefinitely sustain its popular support, particularly among a middle class that comprised more than 80 percent of the population, without converting its contrived pluralist system into a more genuinely participatory arrangement, and were they willing to pursue a course of action transforming the RCD from the master of the political arena to simply one of many parties vying for influence within it? An indication of high-level thinking on these matters came with the arrest, shortly after the elections, of Moncef Marzouki, on charges that his calls for greater political freedom and the legalization of al-Nahda defamed the state. In 1995, the once compliant MDS secretary-general Muhammad Mouada and Khemais Chammari, who had a long history of LTDH activism, addressed an open letter to the president decrying the restrictive political environment. Both were jailed. With its al-Nahda critics out of the way, the government was cracking down on outspoken secular political opponents and human rights advocates, who now joined al-Nahda militants as political prisoners.

Authoritarianism in the political sphere coexisted with, and frequently expedited, the state's commitment to the economic restructuring tirelessly promoted by the IMF and the World Bank, whose president described Tunisia as the organization's "best student . . . in the region."[9] In 1995 Tunisia entered into an agreement with the European Union (EU – the renamed European Communities) that began the process of putting a free trade zone in place by 2007. Since acquiring EEC associate member status in 1969, Tunisia had received preferential treatment in certain aspects of its trade with Europe. By the mid-1990s the single European market, in being since 1993, supplied 70 percent of the country's imports and purchased 80 percent of its exports, making the EU Tunisia's most important commercial partner. Because the General Agreement on Tariffs and Trade, to which Tunisia had adhered at the urging of the international financial agencies in 1990, banned discriminatory trade practices of the kind from which Tunisia had previously benefited, the free trade agreement represented its only realistic means of breaking into the EU market.

The price, however, was high. To begin with, the immediate loss of the 20 percent of state receipts derived from duties on imports from Europe threatened to decimate social programs essential for the maintenance of stability. To preclude such an outcome, the government imposed an unpopular value added tax in 1996. In the face of intense competition, Tunisian exporters sought to make their products more attractive in Europe even as they searched for new, alternative markets. Planners calculated that as many as two-thirds of all Tunisian businesses, particularly small companies and firms relying on traditional techniques, would either fail or experience serious economic difficulties as the agreement took hold. The enterprises that weathered these short-term adversities would emerge as the core of a more modern, more vigorous, and more globally competitive economy. Inasmuch as an authoritarian regime offered the greatest likelihood of keeping the country on course through this difficult and turbulent process of globalization, the governments of capitalist countries whose economies were poised to reap substantial profits from the expansion of free trade largely overlooked, and often quietly approved of, the autocratic inclinations of the RCD. Within the country, those who opposed the economic policies of the government, like those who criticized its understanding of pluralism, risked harassment or worse if they expressed their views too forcefully. The RCD had evolved into more of a security apparatus than a political party, and the Tunisia of ben ᶜAli had begun to resemble nothing so much as "the Corsican police state managed by hard-line French residents such as Marcel Peyrouton in 1934 and Jean de Hautecloque in 1952."[10]

As the twentieth century drew to a close, the Tunisian cinema overtook the written word as a vehicle for presenting political and social concerns to the public. In keeping with the policy of privatization, SATPEC, whose influence had waned steadily since the 1980s, ceased to function altogether in 1992, its work rendered largely superfluous by production companies such as Ahmad ᶜAttia's Cinétéléfilms. In addition to nurturing the careers of Férid Boughedir and Nouri Bouzid, who had won acclaim as the "father of Tunisian nouveau cinéma," ᶜAttia took another promising director, Moufida Tlatli, under his wing. Within a few years of his triumphant directorial debut in 1986, Bouzid brought two new features to the screen. *Safaʾih min dhahab/Sabots d'or* (1989) told the story of a man broken by long years in prison and ultimately driven to suicide, while the deep inconsistencies and contradictions in Tunisian life provided the underlying theme of *Bezness/Business* (1992), a film that contrasted the personal behavior of a male prostitute with his treatment of his female relatives and friends. After absences of several years, two distinguished directors returned to filmmaking early in the 2000s. Naceur Ktari took third prize at the 2000 Carthage Film Festival with the psychological drama *Sois mon amie*, while Nouri Bouzid won the second prize at the 2002 festival for his recently released *Poupées d'argile*.

Boughedir's first full-length feature film, *ʿUsfur al-stah/Halfaouine: L'Enfant des Terrasses* (1990), was a semi-autobiographical portrait of a child growing up in Tunis' Halfaouine neighborhood in the 1950s. It not only enjoyed a warm reception from Tunisian audiences, but also garnered greater critical acclaim, including the 1990 Tanit d'Or, and achieved greater popularity abroad than had any previous Tunisian film. His next, less critically acclaimed, feature, *Salifan fi Halq al-Wadi/Un Eté à La Goulette* (1995), paid tribute to an aspect of Tunisian diversity more commonly acknowledged in the past. Set in the Tunis suburb of La Goulette in the 1960s and centered on three teen-aged girls – one Muslim, one Jewish, and one a Catholic of Italian ancestry – the film stressed the virtues of religious tolerance at a time of widespread chauvinism, but also revealed, through the attitudes of the girls' fathers, cultural affinities common to all the peoples of the Mediterranean world.

Moufida Tlatli had studied cinema in France in the 1960s and had worked as a film editor for well over a decade prior to her debut as a director. *Samt al-qasr/Les Silences du palais* (1994), a tale of women's repression in the 1950s, was a sympathetic portrayal of an earlier generation of Tunisian women that reinforced the recent efforts of feminists (and others) to safeguard rights guaranteed in the Personal Status Code in the face of Islamist criticisms of the statute. Like *Halfaouine*, Tlatli's film fared well both in Tunisia and abroad, winning first prize at the 1994 Carthage Film Festival. Her second feature, *Mausim al-rijal/La Saison des hommes* (2001), told the story of contemporary women on the island of Jerba whose husbands work for most of the year elsewhere in the country or abroad, leaving them to cope with personal and communal issues within the framework of a society that, despite its exclusively feminine composition, accords women no greater latitude than traditionally restrictive customs allow.

In addition to *Halfaouine* and *Les Silences du palais*, a third important film released in the 1990s had the decade of the 1950s as its setting. ʿAli ʿAbidi's *Redayef 54* (1997), described a confrontation in a southern mining town late in the protectorate era between supporters of Bourguiba and the Yusufists – a subject that could not have been broached prior to ben Yusuf's

Figure 7.2. Tunisian cinema. Like several of her male counterparts, Moufida Tlatli, Tunisia's first female director of major motion pictures, has won international recognition for her films, including *La Saison des hommes* (2001).

rehabilitation, which had occurred in stages after 1987. (At the invitation of ben ᶜAli, the widow of Bourguiba's main rival returned to Tunisia in 1988. Ben Yusuf's remains were brought back three years later for reburial in his native land.) In each of these films, Boughedir, Tlatli, and ᶜAbidi were contributing to a quest by their generation – born in the colonial period, too young at the time of independence and the immediately succeeding years to comprehend the events swirling around them, and now in positions of influence – to preserve an accurate memory, replete with both positive and negative features, of the culture from which they had sprung.

Despite the possibility of interpreting the rehabilitation of ben Yusuf as implicitly sanctioning principled opposition to single party rule, contemporary adversaries of the regime continued to meet with very little success in their efforts to cobble together viable alternatives to the RCD. Following the 1994 elections Mustafa ben Jaᶜfar, an LTDH activist and a former member of the MDS who had broken with the party when Mestiri's successors showed their willingness to cooperate with the government, founded the Forum Démocratique pour le Travail et les Libertés (FDTL – Democratic Forum for Labor and Liberty) in an effort to sustain the pressure for democratization, but the authorities denied the party legal status for more than eight years. With the same goal in mind, ben Jaᶜfar joined other liberals in creating the Conseil National des Libertés en Tunisie (CNLT – National Council for Liberties in Tunisia) in 1998, but this umbrella organization also failed to gain access to the political arena. On the eve of the 1999 elections Najib Chebbi, the leader of the Parti Démocratique Progressiste (PDP – Progressive Democratic Party) – the former RSP, which steadfastly refused to soften its criticisms of the government – noted with disgust that "Tunisia will enter the twenty-first century with an electoral system from the fifties."[11]

During the latter half of the 1990s the government assiduously maintained the appearance of promoting pluralism even as it tightened its hold over the limited opposition that did function legally. After 1997, for example, each party represented in the National Assembly received an annual subvention based on the number of its parliamentarians. Nonetheless, the 1999 legislative elections produced results that differed in no substantive way from the two earlier contests of the ben ᶜAli era. The usual group of opposition parties – the Mouvement des Démocrates Sociales, the Parti d'Unité Populaire, the Union Démocratique Unioniste, the Mouvement de la Rénovation – and one newcomer, the Parti Social Libéral (PSL – Liberal Social Party) – held a meaningless total of just over thirty seats between them. In nationwide municipal elections held the next year, even these "successful" parties proved unable to field candidates in more than a handful of voting districts, most of them in the larger cities.

In the 1999 presidential elections, ben ᶜAli faced opposition – albeit of the most perfunctory nature – for the first time since coming to power. Revisions in the election law permitted the heads of political parties represented in the outgoing parliament, who also met qualifications based on age and the length of their service as party leaders, to stand for the presidency. Both Muhammad Bel Hadj ᶜAmor of the PUP and ᶜAbd al-Rahman Tlili, secretary-general of the UDU, satisfied these requirements and both mounted uninspired campaigns against ben ᶜAli. In the end, most opposition voters preferred to support ben ᶜAli's inevitable victory rather than to cast a vote for the leader of a rival party – a clear indication of the opposition's resistance to pooling their meager resources against an entrenched power no one of them could hope to defeat by itself. As a result, ben ᶜAli received 99.44 percent of the votes cast. Less than three years later, Tunisians again went to the polls, this time to vote on a constitutional amendment enabling ben ᶜAli to continue as president at the end of his third term in 2004. Of those who participated 99.52 percent gave their assent. The outcome of the referendum, while entirely predictable, left a particularly bitter taste in the mouths of those who had hailed, as the first step in a desperately needed political opening, the removal of the country's first "president for life" a mere fifteen years earlier, at a time when there had been virtually universal agreement that granting such tenure in so critical an office had been an act of folly.

Tunisia's strong economy throughout most of the ben ᶜAli era helped to neutralize political opposition. Around the turn of the millennium, strong economic indicators reflected a sustained period of growth: since the mid-1990s, the overall economy had expanded at an average rate in excess of 5 percent a year, exports were increasing by more than 7 percent annually despite the challenges of globalization, and foreign investors, most of them Europeans, were injecting as much as a billion dinars a year into the economy. Some of that investment was linked to privatization, an important aspect of the original structural adjustment plan that was intended to fortify an enfeebled private sector but received limited attention until the IMF and the World Bank insisted on its more rigorous application in the late 1990s. As a result, almost as many state enterprises were privatized between 1997 and 2001 (seventy-eight) as in the entire preceding decade. Inflation, the budget deficit, and the ratio of external debt to gross domestic product all stood at manageable, if still improvable, levels. The thriving economy made it possible to continue building upon earlier progress in the social sphere. Education, health care, and other similar services regularly commanded more than half of the state's annual budget. Population growth leveled at 1.1 percent a year, literacy, nationwide, reached 75 percent, and life expectancy rose to almost seventy-three years.[12] Amid the prevailing prosperity, individual financial success, access to consumer goods, and a share in the "good life" assumed greater importance for many middle-class Tunisians than did the mechanics of the political process. Sustaining Tunisia's economic vitality was, therefore, of the utmost importance to the government and the RCD.

For that reason, the impact of the September 11, 2001, terrorist attacks in the United States on the international tourist trade on which Tunisia so heavily depended posed a grave danger. Even as government officials and private citizens who worked in the tourist industry – one in eight Tunisians depended, directly or indirectly, on this sector for their livelihoods – were taking steps to contain the fallout from the events of September and the subsequent war in Afghanistan, an act of terrorism on Tunisian soil severely compounded matters. In April 2002 a bomb blast at a historic synagogue on the popular resort island of Jerba killed twenty-one people, fourteen of them German tourists. Although Tunisia hosted five million international visitors during 2002, that figure constituted a decline of 6 percent from the previous year, while revenues from tourism fell by 13 percent. Travelers' concerns about security were the most obvious cause of this downturn, but economic setbacks in Germany, which accounted for roughly one-fifth of Tunisia's tourists, also played a part. The situation underscored the problems of reliance on an industry subject to vicissitudes over which its beneficiaries exercised no control. Implicitly acknowledging ben ᶜAli's record of vigorous action against threats to national security, the Tunisian minister of tourism attributed the relatively modest decline (in comparison with much harder hit destinations such as Morocco and Egypt) to the "sure and stable image of our country in the world."[13] Nonetheless, tourism officials set to work devising campaigns to reduce the industry's heavy reliance on Europeans and to develop new markets in the Middle East and the Arabian Peninsula. They also targeted the neighboring North African countries, since a substantial increase in visitors from Algeria and Libya during 2002 had been a major factor in offsetting the decline in Western visitors. Just as recovery appeared assured, however, the invasion of Iraq by the United States and the United Kingdom in March 2003 again plunged the international tourism industry into a period of uncertainty.

REFLECTIONS ON AUTHORITARIANS, WARTS AND ALL

Following Habib Bourguiba's death on April 6, 2000, the government decreed a week-long period of official mourning, but the ex-president's passing occasioned none of the outpouring of emotion that marked the demise of such other twentieth-century Arab political luminaries as Jamal ᶜAbd al-Nasser of Egypt, King Husain of Jordan, or King Hassan of Morocco, all of whom had dominated their states as Bourguiba had his. Whereas Nasser and the two monarchs were in power at the time of their death, the nearly thirteen years since Bourguiba had left office (and the eleven since his last public political appearance in 1990, when he received ben ᶜAli in Monastir on the eve of the Rassemblement Constitutionnel Démocratique party congress) constituted a considerable span of time for a citizenry whose median age was less than twenty-five. Obituaries in the Western press, no doubt written years earlier – speculation about the state of Bourguiba's health dated from the early 1970s – and last updated in 1987, tended to echo a national mythology fostered at the highest levels of party and government during the fifty-three years that Bourguiba stood astride Tunisia like the proverbial Colossus. This narrative cast the nation's modern history exclusively in terms of Bourguiba and the Neo-Dustur, downplaying, marginalizing, and sometimes entirely ignoring, events and personalities that would have required its formulators to revise their partisan interpretations. Within the country, however, such a reading of the past had begun to lose its appeal even before Bourguiba was ushered out of the presidential palace. By 2000, it had yielded to a "history" more in line with the needs of Bourguiba's successors.

The most influential architect of the Bourguibist construction of the past was Muhammad Sayah, a prominent member of the PSD political bureau from 1964 to 1987 and a frequent holder of ministerial portfolios in the latter half of that period. In 1969, Sayah took over the editorship of a project, initiated several years earlier, to produce the official history of the nationalist movement as embodied in the Neo-Dustur. Under his supervision, *Histoire du Mouvement National Tunisien*, the fifteenth and final volume of which appeared in 1979, evolved into a collection that was at least as much Bourguiba hagiography as it was (highly subjective) party history. Sayah carried the account beyond independence in two additional books, *Le Nouvel état aux prises avec le complot youssefiste, 1956–1958* (1983) and *La République délivrée de l'occupation étrangère, 1959–1964* (1986). The final contribution of the industrious compiler, which appeared in 1986 and 1987, was a four-volume compendium of Bourguiba's letters and documents entitled *Ma vie, mon oeuvre,* covering the years from 1934 to 1956. School history texts naturally privileged Bourguiba as well, customarily linking his name with the abstraction of "the Nation."[14]

Because Bourguiba's success in subverting the colonial political structure had not been matched by a similar triumph in creating one to replace it, Sayah (and others engaged in enhancing the presidential image) concentrated their efforts on the years prior to independence. In the mid-1970s, however, only a third of the population, at most, was old enough to have even a childhood memory of the nationalist campaign, and by 1987 that fraction had fallen to less than a quarter. Many younger Tunisians dismissed the protectorate era as "ancient history," viewing Bourguiba and his contemporaries as fossilized remnants of a time they did not remember and did not regard as relevant to their lives. Nor did they think that the relics who controlled the government understood, or even cared about, the debilitating social and economic problems they confronted on a daily basis. But far more potentially destructive than the unwillingness of Tunisian youth to accept the national mythology at face value or to concede Bourguiba's right to rule the state by virtue of feats accomplished years before their births was the fact that, in the 1980s, the entire country was awash with doubts about the president's physical and mental fitness that no amount of partisan praise could lay to rest. Well attuned to these sentiments and fearful that Bourguiba's vindictive, erratic behavior would sooner or later cause irreparable damage to the state, those positioned to effect a leadership change judged, correctly, that the Tunisian people would support them. The transfer of power elicited no protests on behalf of a restoration. Nor were there jubilant celebrations. Rather, the prevailing mood was one of relief that the transition had occurred constitutionally, peacefully, and seamlessly.

By the time of Bourguiba's death in 2000, most ordinary Tunisians, if they had not entirely forgotten him, had largely put him out of mind. The new government expedited this process by removing or altering some of the more obvious superficial vestiges of the old regime – the statues of Bourguiba that were commonplace in town squares; the postage stamps, coins, and banknotes that bore his image; and the names of the myriad streets honoring him. Within a short time of his removal from office, the most conspicuous, if morbid, public evocation of the former president was the grandiose mausoleum in Monastir that he had ordered to be built years earlier as his final resting place. In the reworking of the national mythology that inevitably accompanied this process, ben ᶜAli's accession to power emerged as the new central focus of Tunisian history. November 7 assumed pride of place among the country's holidays, while "Avenue du 7 Novembre 1987" became the preferred designation of the streets that had formerly been "Avenue Habib Bourguiba."

In the early days of his presidency, ben ʿAli often reminded Tunisians that Bourguiba's contributions to the nation entitled him to their respect. Nevertheless, the new regime did not muzzle critics of the old. Pointing out the deficiencies of Bourguiba and the failure of policies pursued at his direction served, after all, to underscore the legitimacy of those who had shouldered him aside. Some enemies of the former president availed themselves of the opportunity to take the offensive without fear of retribution primarily to avenge real or imagined slights. Others, however, were chiefly concerned with disclosing information that made possible the establishment of an accurate account of events. Revelations about the Bourguiba years continued to trickle out through the 1990s, with his death stimulating renewed efforts to come to grips with his life and times. This cathartic process highlighted the alienation and isolation that had developed between Bourguiba and the Tunisian people during his years in power. While so complex a phenomenon obviously cannot be explained solely by reference to personality traits, Bourguiba's narcissistic arrogance and egotism – the *hubris* of Greek tragedians – do shed helpful light on the disjunction between a leader who believed that the people of his country owed him a great debt of gratitude even as they viewed him as a distant, uncaring authoritarian responsible for most of the problems in their daily lives.

Years of study in French schools of the Third Republic endowed the young Bourguiba with an appreciation for such concepts as secularism, rationalism, and modernism, all of which became core components in his belief system. His successful navigation of this alien educational system reinforced an already healthy measure of self-confidence and fueled a conviction that his ideas, judgments, and interpretations of events had inherently greater worth than those of others, even others with credentials that matched his own and who worked in concert with him. Consequently, from the beginning of his political career, he rarely gave more than pro forma consideration to advice that ran counter to his own views, and tolerated dissent grudgingly, if at all. In a contemplative essay written shortly after Bourguiba's death, the historian L. Carl Brown asserted that he could interact only with subordinates, never with equals. A factor contributing to this flaw, Brown suggests, was his certainty that even his closest associates could not be trusted to stay the course or to remain unwaveringly loyal, but would "let him down" time after time.[15] Lesser mortals could not bring to the analysis of complex issues the same acumen that he possessed and they could not understand them with the same clarity. During the nationalist struggle, this mind-set drove a wedge between Bourguiba and the other co-founders of the Neo-Dustur. Later, it opened the more dramatic and destructive break with ben Yusuf. Although Bourguiba's assessments of the circumstances surrounding these rifts may have been more accurate than those of his colleagues (as Brown maintains), his systematic denigration of alternative viewpoints poisoned the post-independence political environment.

In the matter of dissent, Bourguiba established the tone for the next thirty years in a speech to the Chamber of Deputies a month after independence. "It is," he told the legislators, "essential to put an end to the activity of elements of anarchy and destruction that seek to counteract our work."[16] His audience correctly linked these remarks to the still smoldering Yusufist movement, but in reality they had a much broader implication. The Manichean dichotomy between "our work" and elements that "seek to counteract [it]" left scant ground for other perspectives. It clearly did not invite them. Bourguiba's superiority complex fostered his absolute certainty in the perfection and, therefore, the indispensability of the course he had charted for the future of Tunisia – a conviction that validated his authoritarian inclinations and enabled him to conflate dissent with treason.

Thereafter, in his capacity as the chief executive of the Republic of Tunisia, Bourguiba's self-importance manifested itself in many destructive ways: his tendency to formulate policy unilaterally or in consultation only with a coterie of cronies, giving short shrift to government ministers and party officials; his reluctance to acknowledge or express appreciation for the contributions and ideas even of this shifting inner circle; his resistance to institutionalizing a succession process or even designating a political heir, despite his own poor health; and his determination to stifle opposing views, initially repressing them, later rendering them ineffectual by permitting them to be aired only within the tightly controlled framework of the PSD (*pluralité monopartisane*),[17] and, when even that stratagem failed, creating a superficially multiparty system in which the government resolutely stacked the deck against the opposition parties. Such practices turned many members of the elite against Bourguiba. Their exclusion from meaningful engagement in political affairs frequently prevented them from realizing their ambitions and often lay behind their alienation, although others simply feared that Bourguiba was leading the country down a path fraught with danger. Nevertheless, disillusioned elites and their followings represented only a tiny minority of the population. The alienation of the Tunisian masses stemmed primarily from the consequences flowing from the president's inability to come to terms with, or even acknowledge, his shortcomings. As social and economic problems intensified in the late years of his presidency, so also did their resentment of the regime.

This state of affairs rendered government espousals of Tunisian democracy increasingly hollow. *"Démocratie à la tunisienne"* frequently glossed over principles as basic as "liberty, equality, and fraternity" – ideals that had informed Bourguiba's education and with which he had browbeaten the French authorities during the protectorate. It drew sufficiently on the trappings of democratic government – regular (if not necessarily free or fair) elections and a representative (if not necessarily empowered) legislature – to keep up appearances, but overarching these symbolic nods in the direction of popular sovereignty, and trumping them as deemed necessary, was an authoritarian ruler prepared to brook neither interference with nor evasion of his will. *Démocratie à la tunisienne* gave citizens the opportunity to endorse the work of their government, but not to set its agenda. Bourguiba shaped this system, positioned himself squarely at its center, and rarely missed an opportunity to point out that he alone could ensure its smooth functioning. Although the monarchy had been abolished soon after independence, in all but title Bourguiba became the bey, exercising his authority, working and residing in his palaces, and reveling in the pageantry and rituals once reserved for the Husainid rulers. The elections that confirmed him in office resembled nothing so much as the *bai'a*, the oath of fealty sworn to the bey by his retainers.

Somewhat paradoxically for a person who expected others to accept without challenge the wisdom of his views and the soundness of his decisions, Bourguiba placed a high premium on education. He believed that his own schooling, by exposing him to a culture based on principles and practices vastly different from those of his ancestral society and teaching him how to function in it, capitalize on its assets, and turn them to his advantage, had liberated him from traditional restraints. Making a similar education available to the Tunisian population at large was, in his view, the sine qua non for sustained national development. The independent government's emphasis on education did succeed in greatly enlarging the number of citizens equipped to appreciate the social and economic programs then transforming Tunisia into a nation with all the accoutrements of modernity. The tangible improvements in the quality of life that these programs produced in the early years of the republic brought the vast majority of Tunisians into line behind their president. Those who did dare to criticize Bourguiba's policies fell into the perilous category of "elements of anarchy and destruction."

Conservative Muslim leaders, disturbed by the state's cavalier interference in deeply entrenched social, educational, legal, and religious practices, were the first to mount an organized protest. Seeing their disapproval primarily as a challenge to the secularism that he valued so highly, Bourguiba dismissed their objections out of hand, going so far as to insist that his intellectual prowess enabled him to interpret Islam with as much authority as any religious scholar. This show of contempt, along with a callous disregard for Muslim sensibility – exemplified by such provocative acts as the public consumption of orange juice during Ramadan or the mean-spirited remark that "if the Prophet were alive, he would not give you what I have given you"[18] – horrified religious leaders and rendered any accommodation all but impossible. Thereafter, conservative Muslims, thoroughly alienated from the regime, sullenly despised it, convinced that the abandonment of traditional values and practices lay at the root of all subsequent political, social, and economic troubles. When a religiously based opposition movement reappeared in the last decade of the Bourguiba era, his disdain proved even more virulent than before and he furiously lashed out at the Muslim activists. But by then the curtain was coming down on his political career. His instinctive intolerance of opposition had degenerated into a parody of single party governance. His attempts to continue ruling unilaterally and with an iron fist, despite his worsening health and increasingly erratic behavior, reduced him to an object of widespread ridicule. *Hubris* had given way to *pathos*. Bourguiba's physical and mental degeneration played into the hands of the Muslim activists as surely as did the economic and social malaise pervading the country.

At least in part, ben ᶜAli invoked the constitutional provisions on presidential incapacity to halt Bourguiba's pursuit of measures against the Islamists that were certain to incite serious strife. His command of the Gendarmerie National during his military career and his appointment, on several subsequent occasions, to key positions in the ministry of national security, had made the new chief executive an advocate of law and order, but a prudent one. In his mind, the repressive measures favored by Bourguiba were counterproductive – a significant factor in converting a small minority of politically discontented Tunisians into a much larger and more dangerous contingent. The release of many political detainees hinted at the new regime's readiness to sanction pluralism; the legalization of several political parties seemed to confirm that stance; the holding of multiparty elections put it to the test. It failed. To most Tunisians, the *pluralisme contrôlé*[19] that proved to be the extent of ben ᶜAli's commitment to diversity retained the most objectionable features of the past. The exclusion of the Islamists

continued and the secular opposition, although permitted to organize in a
way unimaginable under Bourguiba, had no chance of mounting a viable
challenge to the ruling party. The "Historic Change" changed very little
insofar as the impact of elections was concerned. Indeed, in this regard,
Tunisia's second president came to look increasingly like a repackaged version of its first.

Ben ᶜAli did, however, distinguish himself from his predecessor with
triumphs in two fields where success had ultimately eluded Bourguiba. The
first was the economy. Its revitalization under his leadership translated into
an annual per capita income equivalent to $2,100 by 2001 – higher than any
country in North Africa except for its thinly populated, oil-rich neighbor,
Libya. Upper- and middle-class Tunisians fared better still, enabling them
to enjoy a standard of living approximating to that of many southern and
eastern European countries. Although the earnings of the lower class fell
short of the average, and often by a considerable amount, it was nonetheless
true that even the poorest Tunisians experienced an improvement in the
quality of their lives as the twentieth century drew to a close. Mirroring the
process by which economic travail had turned Tunisians against Bourguiba
in droves, the prosperity of the 1990s shored up ben ᶜAli and the RCD.

The defining moment of ben ᶜAli's rule came in the confrontation with
Tunisian Islamists following the resort to violence by al-Nahda radicals.
The president's decision to treat the movement as a threat to national
security and, accordingly, to destroy it as a viable political enterprise, won
him the gratitude of those (primarily upper- and middle-class) citizens,
who believed that any advancement of the Islamist agenda jeopardized the
non-traditional lifestyles they had cultivated under the aegis of the secular
state championed by both Bourguiba and ben ᶜAli. Countless Tunisians
who preferred protecting personal privileges to safeguarding the rule of law
looked the other way as the repression of the Islamists proceeded, often with
scant respect for legal formalities. Their tacit acceptance of the suspension
of some citizens' civil and human rights bound them to the regime and
added to its already considerable potency. Having once unleashed their fury
on an element of the body politic they had designated as "beyond the pale"
without encountering significant objections, the authorities found that very
little stood in the way of their turning on other groups or individuals that
offended them. The treatment meted out to the Islamists put every would-
be adversary of the ben ᶜAli government on notice and smothered, at least
in the short term, public manifestations of dissent.

Later, as open criticism resumed, memories of al-Nahda's fate inspired
a certain prudence and wariness in opponents of the regime, who by then

included many former supporters of the repression of the Islamists. The fear of arrest had a similarly inhibiting effect. The government has always denied holding prisoners of conscience, but laws regulating the press, the nature of organizations and associations (political and other), and the composition and content of public meetings give it the power to detain individuals for a wide range of offenses amounting to lese-majesty. More so than in the Bourguiba era, prison sentences have been imposed on both secular and religious antagonists of ben ᶜAli. And yet, despite the vigorous disparagement of alternative views and courses of action, "multiparty" elections took place in 1994 and 1999, and are scheduled for 2004. Moncef Marzouki, an outspoken and articulate critic of the president, has accused him of "establishing laws in order to violate them and . . . proclaiming democracy in order to mask his totalitarian regime." Ben ᶜAli's Tunisia, he laments, has become "schizophrenic."[20]

In 1989 ben ᶜAli and the RCD ran on a commitment to guide the country out of the morass in which it had become mired during Bourguiba's last years in power. In 1994 and 1999, they ran on their records of having done so and particularly of having saved the country from Islamic radicalism and substantially improved the material well-being of its people. In an interview with a foreign journalist in 2002, Faïza Kéfi, the minister of professional training and employment, boasted that

No one is hungry in Tunisia; there are no people sleeping under bridges. Tunisians have a roof over their head and a decent income that allows them to handle their basic expenses.[21]

The hyperbole of politicians aside, her remarks reflected RCD pride in satisfying Tunisians' most urgent needs and paving the way for the fulfillment of their longer term aspirations which, in turn, accounted for the party's spectacular successes at the polls. Given the top-down, essentially one-way, relationship between the party-government and the people, the former imposed its policies on the latter without prior consultation – the conceit of the authoritarian ruler intuiting the best interests of the population that had characterized Tunisia since 1956.

Seemingly broad acceptance of the decisions of the party-government during the 1990s shielded it from the need to make concessions to critics calling for a more open and participatory political process. In 2000, however, a well-informed French observer of Tunisian politics argued that obliging citizens to barter political apathy for material prosperity had created "a silent, and perhaps sullen, majority [of persons hostile to ben ᶜAli], largely persuaded of democratic ideals and political pluralism, but thwarted in their application."[22] In the absence of reliable public opinion data or other solid evidence of the strengthening of the opposition, it cannot be said for certain that this assessment is correct. In any event, as the weak and fragmented opposition prepared for the autumn 2004 parliamentary and presidential elections, it faced the daunting task of doing what, until this point in Tunisian history, only the Neo-Dustur and its later incarnations have done – galvanize and mobilize a disillusioned population. Taking advantage of the 2002 referendum enabling him to seek an additional term in 2004, ben ʿAli seems certain to win, in effect becoming Tunisia's second "president for life." If the results of the legislative elections also replicate those of the past, the prospects for democratizing the political system, at least by non-violent means, might well be more dismal than at any time since independence.

Notes

1 THE MARCH TO THE BARDO, 1835–1881

1. Mohamed Hedi Chérif, "L'Incident des Khmirs de 1881, d'après les sources tunisiennes," *Cahiers de Tunisie*, 45:162–163 (1992), p. 150.
2. According to Hachemi Karoui and Ali Mahjoubi, *Quand le soleil s'est levé à l'ouest. Tunisie 1881 – Impérialisme et Résistance* (Tunis: CERES Productions, 1983), p. 24, the decline was from 750,000 hectares in 1840 to 150,000 in 1855. The high taxes of the era, peasant conscription, and widespread corruption in rural regions help to explain so dramatic a drop. For an overview of pre-modern Tunisian agriculture, see Lucette Valensi, *Fellahs tunisiens: l'économie rurale et la vie des compagnes aux 18è et 19è siècles* (Paris and The Hague: Mouton, 1977), or its English translation *Tunisian Peasants in the Eighteenth and Nineteenth Centuries* (Cambridge: Cambridge University Press, 1985).
3. Mezri Bdira, *Relations internationales et sous-développement: la Tunisie 1857–1864* (Stockholm: Almqvist and Wiksell, 1978), presents an excellent study of the troubled reign of Muhammad Bey and forms the basis of the account herein. Noting (p. 47) that shortly before the Sfez incident, Muhammad had imposed the death sentence on a Muslim soldier who had killed a Jew, Bdira suggests that the bey may have seen Sfez's punishment as a means of restoring balance to intercommunal relations.
4. This figure is based on an estimate of fewer than 25,000 Jews at the start of the French protectorate that appears in Jacques Taieb, "Evolution et comportement démographiques des juifs de Tunisie sous le protectorat français (1881–1956)," *Population*, 37:4–5 (1982), p. 953, and a percentage breakdown of the two groups in the same period in Mohammed Larbi Snoussi, "Aux origines du mouvement sioniste en Tunisie à la veille de la Grande Guerre: Création de l'Aghoudat-Sion et sa première scission (1887–1914)," *Cahiers de Tunisie*, 44:157–158 (1991), p. 227.
5. Janice Alberti Russell, "The Italian Community in Tunisia, 1861–1961: A Viable Minority," unpublished Ph.D. dissertation, Columbia University, 1977, p. 39. The estimate of the Maltese population is from Julia Clancy-Smith, "Marginality and Migration: Europe's Social Outcasts in Pre-colonial Tunisia, 1830–1881," in Eugene Rogan (ed.), *Outside In: On the Margins of the Modern Middle East* (London: I. B. Tauris, 2002), p. 150.

6. The best study of the issues raised by the presence of European women is Julia Clancy-Smith, "Gender in the City. Women, Migration and Contested Spaces in Tunis, c. 1830–1881," in David M. Anderson and Richard Rathbone (eds.), *Africa's Urban Past* (Oxford: James Curry, 2000), pp. 189–204.

7. *Ibid.*, p. 200. A growing body of literature has also brought to light important material concerning the lives of Tunisian women in the precolonial period. See, for example, Abdelhamid Largueche and Dalenda Largueche, *Marginales en terre d'Islam* (Tunis: Centre d'Etudes et de Recherches Economiques et Sociales, 1992); Adelhamid Largueche, *Les Ombres de la ville: Pauvres, marginaux et minoritaires à Tunis* (Tunis: Centre de Publications Universitaires, 1999); and Dalenda Bouzgarrou-Largueche, *Histoire des femmes au Maghreb: Culture matérielle et vie quotidienne* (Tunis: Centre de Publications Universitaires, 2000).

8. Andreas Tunger-Zanetti, *La Communication entre Tunis et Istanbul, 1860–1913. Province et métropole* (Paris: L'Harmattan, 1996), pp. 18–19, describes nineteenth-century Tunis as having two external metropolises, Paris and Istanbul. He argues that, for Tunisia's leaders, the former took precedence over the latter in the 1850s. For the country's bourgeoisie, the shift took another two decades, and for ordinary Tunisians, the European city never supplanted the Muslim one.

9. Anne-Marie Planel, "Etat réformateur et industrialisation au XIXe siècle: les avatars d'une manufacture (1837–1884)," *Maghreb-Machrek Monde Arabe*, 157 (1997), p. 103, observes that because the Ottoman Empire had taken out six major loans in Europe between 1854 and 1862 and because Mexico, Peru, and the Confederate States of America were seeking loans in the early 1860s, the cost of borrowing on European markets at the time was quite high. While this is true, the terms of the Tunisian loan must be considered excessive.

10. Cited in Noureddine Sraieb, "Elite et Société: l'invention de la Tunisie de l'état-dynastie à la nation moderne," in Michel Camau (ed.), *Tunisie au présent: une modernité au-dessus de tout soupçon?* (Paris: CNRS (Centre National de la Recherche Scientifique), 1987), p. 83. Translations throughout this volume are by the author.

11. With the money came renewed demands for obeisance. The ambassador chided the bey for his attitude towards Istanbul, reminding him that the sultan had never recognized the Husainid claim to hereditary rule as he had, for example, for the descendants of Muhammad ʿAli in Egypt. The exasperated Muhammad al-Sadiq responded, "If the Porte recognized the hereditary power of my family . . . why would I not be obedient, as the Egyptians are?" Quoted in Abdeljelil Temimi, "Considérations nouvelles sur la révolution d'Ali ben Gadehem," *Revue de l'Occident Musulman et de la Méditerranée*, 7 (1970), p. 181.

12. *Ibid.*, p. 176.

13. For insights about the importance of fishing for the Italian community in Tunisia, and a discussion of some fishermen's roles as cultural mediators,

especially outside the region of Tunis, see Hassine Raouf Hamza, "Les Pêcheurs saisonniers italiens à Mahdia (1871–1945)," in Institut de Recherches et Etudes sur le Monde Arabe et Musulman (IREMAM), *Etre marginal au Maghreb* (Paris: CNRS, 1993), pp. 155–159.

14. Khair al-Din's appeal found a particularly responsive audience among ulama who had come to Tunis from the provinces. Because of their origins, many of these men were relegated to a second tier in the religious establishment of the capital and saw reform as an avenue of personal advancement. Moreover, some of them, or their families, had been victims of Ahmad Zarruk's rampage through the Sahil, which persuaded them of the necessity of reform. The prime minister also enjoyed stronger support from ulama of the Hanafi *madhhab* (school of legal interpretation) than from the more numerous followers of the Maliki *madhhab*. See Arnold Green, "Political Attitudes and Activities of the ᶜUlama in the Liberal Age: Tunisia as an Exceptional Case," *International Journal of Middle East Studies*, 7 (1976), p. 230.

15. This incentive was particularly important because of the lengthy period – often as long as ten years – between planting and first harvest. A similar inducement applied to date palms, most of which were cultivated in regions other than the Sahil.

16. Quoted in François Arnoulet, "Les Rapports tuniso-ottomans de 1848 à 1881: d'après les documents diplomatiques," *Revue de l'Occident Musulman et de la Méditerranée*, 47 (1988), p. 148.

17. Hachemi Karoui, "La résistance populaire à l'occupation française (1881) chez les élites tunisiennes, désavoue et oubli," in Jean-Claude Vatin (ed.), *Connaissances du Maghreb: Sciences sociales et colonisation* (Paris: CNRS, 1984), p. 415. Despite the provisions of the Bardo Treaty, France made no effort to shore up Muhammad al-Sadiq's credibility. Through an intermediary, Roustan counseled one leader of the revolt that his overtures to the bey to end hostilities were pointless because matters were entirely in the hands of the French. Mohamed-Hedi Chérif, "Les Mouvements paysans dans la Tunisie du XIXe siècle," *Revue de l'Occident Musulman et de la Méditerranée*, 30 (1980), p. 43. Even so, until his death in 1882, Muhammad al-Sadiq rarely passed up an opportunity to obstruct, however feebly, French policy.

2 WHOSE TUNISIA?, 1881–1912

1. Cambon's boast that ᶜAli would do nothing without his approval is reported in Moncef Dellagi, "L'Avènement d'Ali Bey en octobre 1882," *Revue d'Histoire Maghrébine*, 17–18 (1980), p. 18, which is also the basis for this account of ᶜAli's investiture.

2. Jean-François Martin, *La Tunisie de Ferry à Bourguiba* (Paris: Editions L'Harmattan, 1993), p. 58.

3. These policies bore strong similarities to those introduced by Khair al-Din a decade earlier. For a description of the tax system in the early years of the protectorate, see Richard A. Macken, "The Indigenous Reaction to the French

Protectorate in Tunisia, 1881–1900," Ph.D. dissertation, Princeton University, 1973, pp. 146–161.

4. Using the unusually rich records of the Nabeul municipality, Yahya al-Ghoul has captured the essence of a typical council, with its mixed membership but European domination, in a series of micro-studies: "Colonisation et vie municipale: Nabeul à la fin du 19ème siècle," *Cahiers de Tunisie*, 45:159–160 (1992), pp. 25–45; "Colonisation et vie municipale: La Fiscalité et les recettes municipales à Nabeul à la fin du XIXe siècle," *Revue de l'Institut des Belles Lettres Arabes*, 176 (1995), pp. 261–288; and "Colonisation et vie municipale: Les Services et les dépenses municipales à Nabeul à la fin du 19e siècle," *ibid.*, 177 (1996), pp. 3–31.

5. Hachemi Karoui and Ali Mahjoubi, *Quand le soleil s'est levé à l'ouest. Tunisie 1881 – Impérialisme et Résistance* (Tunis: CERES Productions, 1983), p. 31.

6. Crispi is quoted in Arthur Marsden, *British Diplomacy and Tunis, 1875–1902* (Edinburgh: Scottish Academic Press, 1971), p. 228. Janice Alberti Russell, "The Italian Community in Tunisia, 1861–1961: A Viable Minority," Ph.D. dissertation, Columbia University, 1977, p. 115, cites the Tunis newspaper.

7. Russell, "The Italian Community," p. 43. The size of the Italian population, both in absolute terms and relative to the number of French citizens in Tunisia, caused protectorate officials great anxiety over the next fifty years.

8. For a study of Lavigerie's important role in the protectorate, see J. Dean O'Donnell, *Lavigerie in Tunisia: The Interplay of Imperialist and Missionary* (Athens, Ga.: University of Georgia Press, 1979). François Arnoulet, "Le Cardinal Lavigerie et le clergé italien en Tunisie, 1881–1891," *Revue d'Histoire Maghrébine*, 71–72 (1993), pp. 375–386, presents a more narrowly focused examination of the prelate's dealings with the Italian clergy.

9. On the Jewish community in the early years of the protectorate, see Mohammed Larbi Snoussi, "Aux origines du mouvement sioniste en Tunisie à la veille de la Grande Guerre: Création de l'Aghoudat-Sion et sa première scission (1887–1914)," *Cahiers de Tunisie*, 44:157–158 (1991), pp. 229–233. For the population of the Jewish community throughout the protectorate period, see Jacques Taieb, "Evolution et comportement démographique des juifs de Tunisie sous le protectorat français (1881–1956)," *Population*, 37:4–5 (1982), pp. 952–958.

10. Mohamed Dabbab and Tahar Abid, *La Justice en Tunisie: Un siècle d'histoire judiciaire (essai): de 1856 jusqu'à la veille de l'indépendance* (Tunis: Ministère de la Justice, 1998), pp. 164–166. Other portions of this official publication provide useful overviews of changes in the judicial system during the protectorate.

11. Ali Mahjoubi, *L'Etablissement du protectorat français en Tunisie* (Tunis: Publications de l'Université de Tunis, 1977), p. 309.

12. Macken, "The Indigenous Reaction," pp. 303, 330, and 332; Russell, "The Italian Community," p. 43.

13. The description of "official" colonization that follows draws on Macken, "The Indigenous Reaction," pp. 303–336. On this topic see also Charles C. Harber,

"Tunisian Land Tenure in the Early French Protectorate," *Muslim World,* 63:4 (1973), pp. 307–315; Carmel Sammut, "Régimes de terres collectives de tribus," *Revue d'Histoire Maghrébine,* 6 (1976), pp. 195–202; and Byron Cannon, "Le Marché de location des habous en Tunisie: Dialectique de développement agricole, 1875–1902," in Byron Cannon (ed.), *Terroirs et sociétés au Maghreb et au Moyen Orient* (Lyon: Maison de l'Orient, 1988), pp. 79–108.

14. It continued to rise steadily, if less dramatically, thereafter, as French vintners used the generally potent Tunisian wines to add alcohol content to their own. For cultivation figures see Martin, *La Tunisie,* p. 74.

15. A good study of this convoluted process – whose author maintains that "the franc was not introduced into Tunisia, but the monetary unit of Tunisia became the franc" – is Carmel Sammut, "L'Installation du protectorat français et la reforme du système monétaire tunisien," *Revue d'Histoire Maghrébine,* 4 (1975), pp. 184–194.

16. Macken, "The Indigenous Reaction," p. 354; Mahjoubi, *L'Etablissement du protectorat,* p. 41.

17. Macken, "The Indigenous Reaction," p. 387.

18. Quoted in *ibid.,* p. 328.

19. Jacques Taieb, "La Tunisie des premiers temps coloniaux," *Revue de l'Institut des Belles Lettres Arabes,* 141 (1978), p. 68.

20. These tax statistics appear in Mahjoubi, *L'Etablissement du protectorat,* pp. 61–65.

21. Quoted in Moncef Dellagi, "Une Campagne sur l'insécurité des colons de Tunisie en 1898," in *Revue d'Histoire Maghrébine,* 7–8 (1977), p. 101.

22. *Ibid.,* p. 104.

23. Carmel Sammut, *L'Impérialisme capitaliste français et le nationalisme tunisien (1881–1914)* (Paris: Publisud, 1983), pp. 125–130. On the company's role in exploiting Tunisia's minerals, see Mohamed Lazhar Gharbi, "La Compagnie Bône-Guelma et son reseau minier tunisien (1900–1914)," *Revue de l'Institut des Belles Lettres Arabes,* 164 (1989), pp. 227–254. After World War I, the company dropped the Algerian cities from its name, becoming the *Compagnie Fermière des Chemins de Fer Tunisiens.*

24. For the formation of the company, see Noureddine Dougui, "La Naissance d'une grande entreprise coloniale: la compagnie des phosphates et chemins de fer de Gafsa," *Cahiers de Tunisie,* 30:119–120 (1982), pp. 123–164. The same author discusses the railroad component of the concession in "La Construction et l'exploitation du reseau de chemin de fer Sfax-Gafsa (1897–1914)," *Cahiers de Tunisie,* 31:123–124 (1983), pp. 13–46.

25. Noureddine Dougui, "Sociétés capitalistes et investissements coloniaux en Tunisie (1881–1920): Quelques éléments d'approche," *Cahiers de Tunisie,* 33:131–132 (1985), p. 77.

26. Julia Clancy-Smith, "L'Ecole Rue du Pacha, Tunis: L'Education de la femme arabe et 'La Plus Grande France' (1900–1914)," in *Clio: Histoire, Femmes, et Société,* 12 (December 2000), pp. 33–55. See also Souad Bakalti, "L'Enseignement féminin dans le primaire au temps de la Tunisie coloniale,"

Revue de l'Institut des Belles Lettres Arabes, 166 (1990), p. 260, for enrollment figures.

27. Patrick Cabanel, "L'Ecole laïque française en Tunisie (1881–1914): La Double utopie," in Jacques Alexandropoulos and Patrick Cabanel (eds.), *La Tunisie mosaïque: Diasporas, cosmopolitanisme, archéologies de l'identité* (Toulouse: Presses Universitaires du Mirail, 2000), p. 266.

28. Carmel Sammut, "La Genèse du nationalisme tunisien: le mouvement Jeunes-Tunisiens," *Revue d'Histoire Maghrébine*, 2 (1974), p. 158, quoting Bashir Sfar.

29. De Canières is quoted in Pierre Soumille, "L'Idée de race chez les européens de Tunisie dans les années 1890–1910," *Revue de l'Histoire Maghrébine*, 5 (1976), p. 63, and in Charles-André Julien, "Colons français et Jeunes Tunisiens (1892–1912)," *Revue française d'histoire d'outre-mer*, 54 (1967), p. 131.

30. Cited in Macken, "The Indigenous Reaction," p. 414.

31. Quoted in Cabanel, "L'Ecole laïque," p. 278. Cabanel uses this statement to buttress his assertion that French educators accepted a "Tunisophile myth" – that Tunisians were particularly cultured and well disposed to education – parallel to the Algerian "Kabyle myth" of the inherently greater receptivity to assimilation of Berbers than Arabs.

32. Noureddine Sraieb, "Le Collège Sadiki de Tunis et les nouvelles élites," *Revue de l'Occident Musulman et de la Méditerranée*, 72 (1994), p. 51.

33. Charles-André Julien, "Colons français et Jeunes Tunisiens (1882–1912)," in *Revue Française d'Histoire d'Outre-Mer*, 54 (1967), p. 136. For an account of the proceedings of the congress, see pp. 134–141.

34. Noureddine Sraieb, "L'Idéologie de l'école en Tunisie coloniale (1881–1945)," *Revue de l'Occident Musulman et de la Méditerranée*, 68–69 (1993), p. 248.

35. A good account of the Jellaz incident appears in Taoufik Ayadi, "Insurrection et religion en Tunisie: l'exemple de Thala-Kasserine (1906) et du Jellaz (1911)," in Direction des Archives de France, *Révolte et Société* (Paris: Histoire au Présent, 1989), pp. 170–173.

3 SQUARING OFF, 1912–1940

1. Ali Mahjoubi, *Les Origines du mouvement national en Tunisie (1904–1934)* (Tunis : Université de Tunis, 1982), pp. 151–152.

2. *Ibid.*, pp. 150 and 185.

3. *Ibid.*, p. 174.

4. For a discussion of the controversy over the book's authorship, see Adnan Zmerli, "*La Tunisie Martyre, ses revendications*: Oeuvre collective ou oeuvre individuelle?," *Revue de l'Institut des Belles Lettres Arabe*, 187 (2001), pp. 25–38. Thaᶜalbi asserted that his claim was intended to shield others from prosecution but that, in any event, he had substantially revised the earlier material before the publication of *La Tunisie Martyre*.

5. Quoted in Mustapha Kraiem, "Le Parti réformiste tunisien (1920–1926)," *Revue de l'Histoire Maghrébine*, 4 (1975), p. 152.

6. For several estimates of Dustur numbers between 1922 and 1925, see Mahjoubi, *Les Origines*, p. 260. Puaux's concerns are cited on p. 261.

7. Robert Raymond, *La Nationalisme tunisienne* (Paris: Comité Algérie-Tunsie-Maroc, 1925), p. 21.

8. Quoted in Kraiem, "Le Parti réformiste," p. 157.

9. Juliette Bessis, "A propos de la question des naturalisations dans la Tunisie des années trente," in Moncef Chenoufi (ed.), *Les Mouvements politiques et sociales dans la Tunisie des années trente* (Tunis: Le Ministère de l'Education, de l'Enseignement et de la Recherche Scientifique, 1985), pp. 602–603.

10. The standard history of the theatre in colonial Tunisia, on which this paragraph draws, is Hamadi Ben Halima, *Un demi siècle de théâtre arabe en Tunisie (1907–1957)* (Tunis: Publications de l'Université de Tunis, 1974).

11. Hassine-Raouf Hamza, "Eléments pour une réflexion sur l'histoire du mouvement national pendant l'entre-deux-guerres: la scission du Destour de mars 1934," in Chenoufi, *Les Mouvements politiques et sociales*, pp. 51–78.

12. Cited in Mahjoubi, *Les Origines*, p. 469.

13. Mustapha Kraiem, "Le Néo-Destour: cadres, militants et implantations pendant les années trente," in Chenoufi, *Les Mouvements politiques et sociales*, pp. 24–25, argues that, far from stagnating after 1926, the Dustur actually expanded its membership, particularly in the Sahil – the region from which Bourguiba and his closest allies hailed. In 1933, the Sahil accounted for 59 percent of the party's members.

14. Mahjoubi, *Les Origines*, p. 563.

15. Quoted in Lisa Anderson, *The State and Social Transformation in Tunisia and Libya, 1830–1980* (Princeton: Princeton University Press, 1986), p. 171.

16. Kraiem, "Le Néo-Destour," p. 37, quoting Salah ben Yusuf. Because it was to the advantage of the party to inflate them, and of the protectorate authorities to trim them, records of the Neo-Dustur's membership vary significantly. The 70,000 figure, attributed to Mahmoud Matatri and judged reasonably accurate by Kraiem, appears on p. 46.

17. On these early examples of the politicization of Tunisian women, see Ilhem Marzouki, "La voile des colonisées: Tunisie, 1924–1936," *Revue de l'Institut des Belles Lettres Arabes*, 161 (1988), pp. 59–89, and two articles by Lilia Labidi, "Circulation des femmes musulmanes dans l'espace public et politique formel: le cas de la Tunisie en période coloniale," and "L'Emergence du sentiment politique chez les féministes dans la première moitié du XXème siècle: le cas de la Tunisie," both in Lilia Labidi (ed.), *Participation des femmes à la vie politique* (Tunis: Centre de Recherche et de Formation Pédagogique, 1990), pp. 19–43 and 44–62.

18. Ahmad Kassab, "La communauté israélite de Tunis entre la francisation et le sionisme (1930–1940)," in Chenoufi, *Les Mouvements politiques et sociales*, p. 546.

19. Tahar Chikhaoui, "Les Journées d'avril 38 à travers les mémoires de Mahmoud Materi. Mouvance et Obliquité," *Cahiers de Tunisie*, 47–48:145–148

(1988–1989), pp. 214–215. Matari also believed, in retrospect, that a Franco-Tunisian accommodation would have occurred before World War II had it not been for the events of 1938. Matari's recollections are not without a self-serving aspect. Bourguiba later accused him of deserting the Neo-Dustur at a critical moment and Matari was defending himself. But others have also laid responsibility for the events of April 1938 at Bourguiba's feet. See, for example, Georges Adda, "Quelques souvenirs et réflexions à propos des événements du 9 avril 1938," in *ibid.*, pp. 201–210. The conference marking the fiftieth anniversary of the 1938 riots, for which both these articles were prepared, met a few months after Bourguiba's removal from the presidency, which undoubtedly facilitated the presentation of perspectives that did not accord with the standard nationalist mythology. For a well-balanced assessment of the responsibility for the rioting, see Hassine-Raouf Hamza, "Les émeutes du 9 avril 1938 à Tunis: Machination policière, complot nationaliste ou mouvement spontané?," in Direction des Archives de France, *Révolte et Société*, II (Paris: Publications de la Sorbonne, 1988), pp. 185–191.

4 REDEFINING THE RELATIONSHIP, 1940–1956

1. Quoted in Abdelhamid Hassen, "Moncef Bey et le mouvement moncefiste (1942–1948)," *Revue d'Histoire Maghrébine*, 49–50 (1988), p. 25.
2. Mokhtar Ayachi, "Le Mouvement zeitounien dans le contexte de la seconde guerre mondiale," in *La Tunisie de 1939 à 1945* (Tunis: Ministère de l'Education, de l'Enseignement Supérieur et de la Recherche Scientifique et Technique, 1989), p. 291.
3. Annie Rey-Goldzeiguer, "L'Opinion publique tunisienne, 1940–1944," *ibid.*, p. 155.
4. Hassine-Raouf Hamza, "Le Néo-Destour, dès lendemains d'avril 1938 à la veille de l'indépendance: hégémonie et institutionalisation," *ibid.*, p. 212.
5. Selwa Zangar, "La Tunisie et l'Union Française: Position nationaliste et positions coloniales, 1946–1951," *Revue d'Histoire Maghrébine*, 67–68 (1992), pp. 313–314.
6. Mustapha Kraiem, "Les Evénements du 5 août 1947 à Sfax," *Revue d'Histoire Maghrébine*, 9 (1977), p. 319, cites government figures based on a retail price index of 100 for the year 1940 that showed an increase from 512 in 1945 to 1280 in 1947. Lazhar Gharbi, "La Politique financière de la France en Tunisie au lendemain de la Deuxième Guerre: contraintes mondiales et exigences nationalistes" in *La Tunisie de l'après-guerre (1945–1950)* (Tunis: Faculté des Sciences Humaines et Sociales, 1991), pp. 29–31, discusses the impact of the 30 percent devaluation of the franc in December 1945. In the following year, protectorate officials dismissed the Grand Council's attempt to detach the Tunisian franc from the French currency as a purely political endeavor.
7. Hamza, "Le Néo-Destour," p. 212.
8. *Ibid.*, p. 213.

9. For accounts of political activity at Zaituna in the 1930s, see Ayachi, "Le Mouvement zeitounien," pp. 272–284 and Mokhtar Ayachi, "Le Néo-Destour et les étudiants zeytouniens: de l'alliance à l'affrontement," in *La Tunisie de l'après-guerre*, pp. 232–236.

10. Noureddine Sraieb, "Le Problème franco-tunisien est un problème de souveraineté. Traduction et présentation de la lettre de Bourguiba à la beyya," *Revue de l'Occident Musulman et de la Méditerranée*, 1 (1966), p. 206.

11. Charles-Robert Ageron, "La parti colonial face à la question tunisienne (1945–1951)," in *La Tunisie de l'après-guerre*, p. 199, quotes both Schuman's charge to his resident general and Périllier's less sweeping description of his mission. Charles-André Julien, *Et la Tunisie devint indépendante . . . (1951–1957)* (Paris: Les Editions Jeune Afrique, 1985), p. 27, suggests that Schuman made his remark off-handedly, without "considering its impact."

12. Khaled Ben Fredj Abid, "Le Conflit Bourguiba-Thameur en Egypte et ses incidences: vers une vision 'jugurthienne' de l'histoire bourguibienne, 1947–1950," *Revue d'Histoire Maghrébine*, 102–103 (2001), pp. 247–248. Identifying Bourguiba with unremitting resistance to foreign rule, the pamphlet praised him as a new Jugurtha, the Berber leader who had rebelled against Rome in the second century BCE. His associates betrayed Jugurtha, causing him to fail in his mission – disloyalty that the new Jugurtha would not tolerate.

13. Hautecloque was a protégé of Gabriel Puaux, whom he served as secretary general of the Syrian mandate while Puaux was high commissioner. Puaux held the Damascus post after his assignment as secretary general of the Tunisian protectorate in the 1920s, during which he had encouraged Resident General Saint's hard line towards Nasir Bey and the Dustur (see above, p. 81). After the war, Puaux enjoyed considerable influence in French right-wing circles. In 1951, his son François headed the Ministry of Foreign Affairs office that oversaw all the protectorates. At its upper echelons, the "parti colonial" consisted of a closely knit collection of "insiders."

14. Julien, *Et la Tunisie*, p. 47.

15. Abdesslem Ben Hamida, "Le Rôle du syndicalisme tunisien dans le mouvement de libération nationale (1946–1956)," *Cahiers de Tunisie*, 29:117–118 (1981), p. 242.

16. Julien, *Et la Tunisie*, p. 124.

17. Jean-François Martin, *La Tunisie de Ferry à Bourguiba* (Paris: Editions L'Harmattan, 1993), p. 163.

18. For a survey of right-wing settlers' attitudes in the final years of the protectorate, see Amira Aleya Shgaier, "Les Groupements politiques français de droite en Tunisie et la décolonisation, 1954–1956)," in *Actes du IXe colloque international sur processus et enjeux de la décolonisation en Tunisie (1952–1956)* (Tunis: Institut Supérieur d'Histoire du Mouvement National, 1999), pp. 205–236. The figure of 20,000 demonstrators appears on p. 226.

19. On Mendès-France and the autonomy talks, see Mohammed Lotfi Chaibi, "Les Enjeux d'une décolonisation négociée: l'exemple tunisien (1954–1956)," *Revue de l'Institut des Belles Lettres Arabes*, 186 (2000), pp. 191–211.

20. Clement Henry Moore, *Tunisia Since Independence. The Dynamics of One-Party Government* (Berkeley: University of California Press, 1965), p. 62.
21. Susan Waltz, *Human Rights and Reform: Changing the Face of North African Politics* (Berkeley: University of California Press, 1995), p. 57.

5 THE INDEPENDENT STATE SETS ITS COURSE, 1959–1969

1. Clement Henry Moore, *Tunisia since Independence: The Dynamics of One-Party Government* (Berkeley: University of California Press, 1965), p. 74.
2. *Ibid.*, p. 151, and Charles Debbasch, "Du Néo-Destour au parti socialiste destourienne: le congrès de Bizerte," *Annuaire de l'Afrique du Nord*, 3 (1964), p. 37.
3. Driss Abassi, "La Conception de l'Histoire selon Bourguiba," in Abdeljelil Temimi (ed.), *Habib Bourguiba et l'établissement de l'état national: approches scientifiques de bourguibisme* (Zaghouan: Fondation Temimi pour la Recherche Scientifique et l'Information, 2000), p. 22. Abassi also notes Bourguiba's references to the Pakistani philosopher and reformer Muhammad Iqbal's belief in the importance of rethinking Islam without at the same time breaking with the past.
4. Mounira M. Charrad, *States and Women's Rights: The Making of Postcolonial Tunisia, Algeria, and Morocco* (Berkeley: University of California Press, 2001), p. 223. For a general discussion of the code, see pp. 219–231.
5. For a survey of women's roles in the national liberation movement, see Souad Bakalti, "Mouvement et organisations féminines de lutte de libération nationale en Tunisie," in *Actes du IXe; colloque international sur processus et enjeux de la décolonisation en Tunisie (1952–1964)*. (Tunis: Institut Supérieur d'Histoire du Mouvement National, 1999), pp. 187–204. Membership statistics appear on p. 194.
6. Defining the political elite as members of the government or of key bodies within the Neo-Dustur, Noureddine Sraieb, "Le Collège Sadiki de Tunis et les nouvelles élites," *Revue de l'Occident Musulman et de la Méditerranée*, 172 (1994), p. 51, notes that, between 1955 and 1969, 65 percent of them were graduates of the Sadiki College, while 14 percent studied at the Lycée Carnot and 15 percent more at other lycées and colleges offering a European education.
7. Souad Bakalti, "L'Enseignement féminin dans le primaire au temps de la Tunisie coloniale," *Revue de l'Institut des Belles Lettres Arabes*, 166 (1990), p. 267.
8. Zakya Daoud, "Les femmes tunisiennes: Gains juridiques et statut économique et social," *Maghreb-Machrek*, 145 (1994), p. 31, and Kenneth J. Perkins, *Tunisia: Crossroads of the Islamic and European Worlds* (Boulder, Co.: Westview Press, 1986), p. 120.
9. Statistics on European demography in the latter half of the 1950s are drawn from Habib Kazdaghli, "Communautés européennes de Tunisie face à la décolonisation (1955–1962)," in *Actes du IXe colloque international*, pp. 332–334; Lilia Ben Salem, "Stratégies politiques et formation d'une élite: les premiers

cadres de la Tunisie indépendante," *ibid.*, pp. 348–351; and Lisa Anderson, *The State and Social Transformation in Tunisia and Libya, 1830–1980* (Princeton: Princeton University Press, 1986), p. 236.

10. Statistics on Jewish population movements at this time appear in Abdelkrim Allagui, "La Minorité juive de Tunisie face à la décolonisation au cours des années 50," in *Actes du IXe colloque international*, pp. 306–309; Jacques Taieb, "Evolution et comportement démographiques des juifs de Tunisie sous le protectorat français (1881–1956)," *Population*, 37:4–5 (1982), p. 955; and Moore, *Tunisia since Independence*, p. 10 n.

11. On Bourguiba's contacts with the World Jewish Congress, see Abdeljelil Temimi, "La Question palestinienne et les relations de Bourguiba avec le Congrès Juif Mondial," in Temimi, *Habib Bourguiba et l'établissement de l'état national*, pp. 109–127.

12. Moore, *Tunisia since Independence*, p. 195.

13. Jean Poncet, "L'Economie tunisienne depuis l'indépendance," *Annuaire de l'Afrique du Nord*, 8 (1969), p. 104. For the heavy reliance on foreign aid, see Samir Radwan, Vali Jamal, and Ajit Ghose, *Tunisia: Rural Labor and Structural Transformation* (London: Routledge, 1990), pp. 30–31. On investment levels and national debt, see Karen Pfeiffer, "Between Rocks and Hard Choices: International Finance and Economic Adjustment in North Africa," in Dirk Vandewalle (ed.), *North Africa: Development and Reform in a Changing Global Economy* (New York: St. Martin's Press, 1996), p. 43.

14. Stephen J. King, "Economic Reform and Tunisia's Hegemonic Party: The End of the Administrative Elite," in Ali Abdullatif Ahmida (ed.), *Beyond Colonialism and Nationalism in the Maghrib: History, Culture, and Politics* (New York: Palgrave, 2000), p. 175. On the shrinkage of the European population, see Kazdaghli, "Communautés européennes," p. 336.

15. Alaya Allani, "Bourguiba et le courant 'libéral' au sein du parti destourien: 1970–1971," in Temimi, *Habib Bourguiba et l'établissement de l'état national*, p. 51.

16. Poncet, "L'Economie tunisienne," p. 110.

17. Alexander Graham and H. S. Ashbee, *Travels in Tunisia* (London: Dulau & Co., 1887, p. 149.

18. T. Wemyss Reid, *The Land of the Bey, Being Impressions of Tunis under the French* (London: Sampson Low, Marston, Searle & Rivington, 1882), p. 53.

6 REGIME ENTRENCHMENT AND THE INTENSIFICATION OF OPPOSITION, 1969–1987

1. Kenneth J. Perkins, *Tunisia: Crossroads of the Islamic and European Worlds* (Boulder, Co.: Westview Press, 1986), p. 136; Karen Pfeiffer, "Between Rocks and Hard Choices: International Finance and Economic Adjustment in North Africa," in Dirk Vandewalle (ed.), *North Africa: Development and Reform in a Changing Global Economy* (New York: St. Martin's Press, 1996), p. 43; and Stephen J. King, "Economic Reform and Tunisia's Hegemonic Party: The End

of the Administrative Elite," in Ali Abdullatif Ahmida, *Beyond Colonialism and Nationalism in the Maghrib: History, Culture, and Politics* (New York: Palgrave, 2000), p. 181.

2. Samir Radwan, Vali Jamal, and Ajit Ghose, *Tunisia: Rural Labor and Structural Transformation* (London: Routledge, 1990), pp. 10 and 25–26.

3. Zakya Daoud, "Les femmes tunisiennes: Gains juridiques et statut économique et social," *Maghreb-Machrek*, 145 (1994), p. 31.

4. Pfeiffer, "Between Rocks and Hard Choices," p. 44.

5. Radwan *et al.*, *Tunisia: Rural Labor*, p. 4. Lisa Anderson, *The State and Social Transformation in Tunisia and Libya, 1830–1930* (Princeton: Princeton University Press, 1986), p. 244, estimates that the number of Tunisians working abroad in the late 1970s exceeded that of the entire industrial workforce in the country.

6. Perkins, *Tunisia*, p. 139.

7. For a biography of one of the MTI's founding fathers and most influential leaders, see Azzam Tamimi, *Rachid Ghannouchi: A Democrat Within Islamism* (New York: Oxford University Press, 2001). The percentage of persons living in poverty is based on Anderson, *The State and Social Transformation*, p. 244, citing a criterion established by the World Bank.

8. Clifford Geertz, as quoted in King, "Economic Reform," p. 183.

9. Quoted in Lisa Anderson, "Political Pacts, Liberalism and Democracy: The Tunisian National Pact of 1988," *Government and Opposition*, 26:2 (1991), p. 249. The estimate of the strength of the Tunisian Communist Party appears in Kenneth Perkins, *Historical Dictionary of Tunisia*, 2nd edn (Lanham, Md.: The Scarecrow Press, 1997), p. 143.

10. Emma C. Murphy, *Economic and Political Change in Tunisia: From Bourguiba to Ben Ali* (London: Macmillan, 1999), p. 90.

11. Vincent Geisser, "Tunisie: des élections pour quoi faire? Enjeux et 'sens' du fait électoral de Bourguiba à Ben Ali," *Maghreb-Machrek*, 168 (2000), p. 41

12. Murphy, *Economic and Political Change*, p. 94. Figures on the annual average growth rate of the economy appear in *Jeune Afrique/L'Intelligent*, 2180–2181 (2002), p. 76.

13. Lisa Anderson, "Democracy Frustrated: The Mzali Years in Tunisia," in Reeva Simon (ed.), *The Middle East and North Africa: Essays in Honor of J. C. Hurewitz* (New York: Columbia University Press, 1990), p. 201, quoting an MTI official.

14. Murphy, *Economic and Political Change*, p. 96.

15. Geisser, "Tunisie: des élections pour quoi faire?" p. 42.

16. Clement Henry Moore, "Tunisia and Bourguibisme: Twenty Years of Crisis," *Third World Quarterly*, 10:1 (1988), p. 186.

17. Ingram later returned to North African locales, shooting *Garden of Allah* in Algeria in 1927 and *Baroud* in Morocco in 1932. For an overview of Tunisian cinema, a filmography of its most important productions, and biographies of key filmmakers, see the section on Tunisia in Roy Armes, "Cinema in the Maghreb," in Oliver Leaman (ed.), *Companion Encyclopedia of Middle Eastern and North African Film* (London: Routledge, 2001), pp. 490–511. Much of the

material that follows is drawn from this source and from earlier unpublished essays by Professor Armes.

7 CONSTANCY AND INNOVATION IN THE "NEW" TUNISIA, 1987–2003

1. This argument is developed in Vincent Geisser, "Tunisie: des élections pour quoi faire? Enjeux et 'sens' du fait électoral de Bourguiba a Ben Ali," *Maghreb-Machrek*, 168 (2000), pp. 24–26. The author points out that the Islamists' success in the 1989 elections may have done them more harm than good. By giving them the appearance of being the sole opposition worthy of notice, the election results encouraged the government to focus its attention on them.
2. Abdelbaki Hermassi, "The Rise and Fall of the Islamist Movement in Tunisia," in Laura Guazzone (ed.), *The Islamist Dilemma: The Political Role of Islamist Movements in the Contemporary Arab World* (London: Ithaca Press, 1995), p. 120.
3. *Tunisia: Basic Data* (Tunis: Tunisian External Communication Agency, 1993), pp. 79, 82–83; "Une destination toujours prisée," *Jeune Afrique/L'Intelligent*, 2194 (2003), p. 81.
4. Kenneth J. Perkins, *Historical Dictionary of Tunisia*, 2nd edn (Lanham, Md.: The Scarecrow Press, 1997), pp. 64–65 and 185.
5. Hermassi, "Rise and Fall," p. 125. Not coincidentally, the restoration of significant levels of United States aid to Tunisia came as the situation in Algeria deteriorated.
6. Michel Camau, "D'une république à l'autre: Refondation politique et aléas de la transition libérale," *Maghreb-Machrek*, 157 (1997), p. 10. In 1994, the RCD operated 6,800 cells.
7. Perkins, *Historical Dictionary*, p. 117.
8. Camau, "D'une république à l'autre", p. 9.
9. Guilain Denoeux, "La Tunisie de Ben Ali et ses paradoxes," *Maghreb-Machrek*, 166 (1999), p. 51.
10. Clement Henry Moore, "Post-Colonial Dialectics of Civil Society," in Yahya H. Zoubir (ed.), *North Africa in Transition: State, Society, and Economic Transformation in the 1990s* (Gainesville, Fl.: University Press of Florida, 1999), p. 12. The author argues that the Islamists' effort to carve out a role for themselves in civil society replicates the nationalist struggle against French colonialism.
11. Geisser, "Tunisie: des élections pour quoi faire?" p. 19.
12. These statistics appear in "L'économie: ouverture et partenariat," *Jeune Afrique/L'Intelligent*, 2197 (2003), p. 59. On privatization, see "Changement de tempo," *ibid.*, 2180–2181 (2002), pp. 79–80.
13. Quoted in "Tunisie: Une destination toujours prisée," *ibid.*, 2194 (2003), p. 80.
14. For a discussion of the content of Tunisian textbooks in secondary schools and professional training institutes, see Driss Abassi, "La Conception de l'histoire selon Bourguiba," in Abdeljelil Temimi (ed.), *Habib Bourguiba et l'établissement de l'état national: approches scientifiques à*

Bourguibisme (Zaghouan: Fondation Temimi pour la Recherche Scientifique et l'Information, 2000), pp. 26–29.

15. L. Carl Brown, "Bourguiba and Bourguibism Revisited: Reflections and Interpretation," *Middle East Journal*, 55:1 (2001), p. 50.

16. Abassi, "La Conception de l'histoire," p. 21.

17. This apt term is used by Geisser, "Tunisie: des élections pour quoi faire?" p. 15.

18. Quoted in Fathi Kacemi, "La Deuxième conférence internationale sur Bourguiba et les bourguibiens: Prélude d'une polémique politique," in *Revue d'Histoire Maghrébine*, 102–103 (2001), p. 241.

19. Geisser, "Tunisie: des élections pour quoi faire?" p. 15.

20. Danny Braün, "Tunisie: Le pays muselé," *L'Actualité*, August 2002, p. 62.

21. *Ibid.*, p. 63.

22. Geisser, "Tunisie: des élections pour quoi faire?" p. 16. The author draws a contrast with Bourguiba, who, he asserts, confronted "an active, but minority, opposition."

Suggestions for further reading

Until 1956, scholarship on Tunisia was largely a French preserve. Since then, other European and North American and Asian historians and social scientists have conducted extensive research in the country and published their findings in their own languages. Nevertheless, fifty years after independence, the bulk of publication on Tunisian topics continues to appear in French, although it is increasingly the work of Tunisian scholars, some of whom also publish in Arabic (while others write exclusively in that language). The French- and English-language sources cited in what follows do not, by any means, constitute an exhaustive bibliography. For a more thorough compilation that was up to date at the time of its publication, see the relevant sections of Kenneth J. Perkins, *Historical Dictionary of Tunisia*, 2nd edn (Lanham, Md.: The Scarecrow Press, 1997).

Two books in English that provide useful overviews of modern Tunisia, but which are less sharply focused than this study, in one instance chronologically and in the other geographically, are Lisa Anderson, *The State and Social Transformation in Tunisia and Libya, 1830–1980* (Princeton, NJ: Princeton University Press, 1986), and Kenneth J. Perkins, *Tunisia: Crossroads of the Islamic and European Worlds* (Boulder, Co.: Westview Press, 1986). A similar survey in French is Jean-François Martin, *Histoire de la Tunisie contemporaine: de Ferry à Bourguiba*, 2nd edn (Paris: L'Harmattan, 2003).

Like all of those books, many other of the suggested readings contain material germane to more than a single chapter of this work. Such entries are indicated by an asterisk following the citation.

1 THE MARCH TO THE BARDO, 1835–1881

A survey of political, social, and economic conditions in early nineteenth-century Tunisia, along with an account of the changes introduced by Ahmad Bey, make up the focus of L. Carl Brown, *The Tunisia of Ahmad Bey, 1837–1855* (Princeton, NJ: Princeton University Press, 1974). Mezri Bdira, *Relations internationales et sous-développement, la Tunisie 1857–1864* (Uppsala: Almqvist & Wiksell International, 1978), explores the growth of European influence that confronted Ahmad's successors. Studies of the role of non-Muslim minority communities in precolonial Tunisia include Claude Hagege, "Communautés juives de Tunisie à la veille du

227

protectorat français," *Le Mouvement Social*, 110 (1980), pp. 35–50; Julia Clancy-Smith, "Marginality and Migration: Europe's Social Outcasts in Pre-colonial Tunisia, 1830–1881," in Eugene Rogan (ed.), *Outside In: On the Margins of the Modern Middle East* (London: I. B. Tauris, 2002), pp. 149–182; Andrea L. Smith, "Les Maltais en Tunisie à la veille du protectorat: Une population intermédiaire," in Jacques Alexandropoulos and Patrick Cabanel (eds.), *La Tunisie mosaïque: Diasporas, cosmopolitanisme, archéologies de l'identité* (Toulouse: Presses Universitaires du Mirail, 2000), pp. 115–27; and a doctoral dissertation by Janice Alberti Russell, "The Italian Community in Tunisia, 1861–1961: A Viable Minority," Columbia University, 1977. The marginalization experienced by these minorities also extended to some Tunisians, particularly by virtue of gender or social class. Many of them are discussed in a collection of essays edited by Fanny Colonna and Zakya Daoud, *Etre marginal au Maghreb* (Paris: Centre National de la Recherche Scientifique, 1993)* and in Abdelhamid Largueche and Dalenda Largueche, *Marginales en terre d'islam* (Tunis: Centre d'Etudes et de Recherches Economiques et Sociales, 1992)*.

Abdelmajid Kraiem and Hédi Jellab, *Le Mouvement réformiste en Tunisie, 1815–1920* (Tunis: Institut Supérieur d'Histoire du Mouvement National, 1994)*, presents an overview of the political reform efforts that began in the nineteenth century. L. Carl Brown, *The Surest Path. The Political Treatise of a Nineteenth-Century Muslim Statesman* (Cambridge, Ma.: Harvard University Press, 1967), is an English translation of Khair al-Din's influential book that includes an intro-duction providing a useful contextualization of the work. The spread of modern education figured prominently among Khair al-Din's objectives. Laroussi Mizouri, "La Pénétration de l'enseignement européen dans la Tunisie précoloniale: origine et répercussions," in *Cahiers de Tunisie*, 44:157–158 (1991), pp. 177–196, places the prime minister's educational reforms within an already existing trend, while Noureddine Sraieb, *Le Collège Sadiki de Tunis, 1875–1956* (Paris: Centre National de la Recherche Scientifique, 1995)*, devotes considerable attention to the early history of one of the most important legacies of his administration. The role of the religious leadership at a time when traditional patterns of life were in great flux is documented in Arnold H. Green, *The Tunisian Ulama, 1873–1915. Social Structure and Response to Ideological Currents* (Leiden: Brill, 1978)*. Reform from above sometimes met with opposition at the local level, particularly in the less prosperous rural regions. For an overview of nineteenth-century rural resistance, see Mohamed Hédi Chérif, "Les Mouvements paysans dans la Tunisie du XIXe siècle," *Revue de l'Occident Musulman et de la Méditerranée*, 30 (1980), pp. 21–55. An extremely valuable, and broader, survey of Tunisian rural life is Lucette Valensi, *Tunisian Peasants in the Eighteenth and Nineteenth Centuries* (Cambridge: Cambridge University Press, 1985). The importance of developments in rural areas is also explored by F. Robert Hunter, "Capital Appreciation and Provincial Power in Pre-Protectorate Tunisia (1850–1881): Notes from the Tunis Archives," *Middle Eastern Studies*, 23 (1987), pp. 108–115.

Despite its age and conventional approach, Jean Ganiage, *Les Origines du protectorat francais en Tunisie (1861–1881)* (Paris: Presses Universitaires de France, 1959), remains an important source for the diplomatic and financial events leading to the

French occupation of Tunisia. British policy prior to the inauguration of the protectorate and during its early decades is discussed in Arthur Marsden, *British Diplomacy and Tunis, 1875–1902* (Edinburgh: Scottish Academic Press, 1971)*. Tunisia's linkages with the Ottoman Empire are the subject of several studies, including Pierre Bardin, *Algériens et tunisiens dans l'empire ottoman de 1848 à 1914* (Paris: Centre Nationale de Recherche Scientifique, 1979)*; Andreas Tunger-Zanetti, *La Communication entre Tunis et Istanbul, 1860–1913. Province et métropole* (Paris: L'Harmattan, 1996)*; and Kenneth J. Perkins, "'The Masses Look Ardently to Istanbul': Tunisia, Islam, and the Ottoman Empire, 1837–1931," in John Ruedy (ed.), *Islamism and Secularism in North Africa* (New York: St. Martin's Press, 1994), pp. 23–36*.

The 1881 French incursion into Tunisia and the resistance that it sparked are the subjects of Hachemi Karoui and Ali Mahjoubi, *Quand le soleil s'est levé à l'ouest. Tunisie 1881 – Impérialisme et Résistance* (Tunis: Centre d'Etudes et de Recherches Economiques et Sociales, 1983); Mohamed Hédi Chérif, "L'Incident des Khmir de 1881, d'après les sources tunisiennes," *Cahiers de Tunisie*, 45:162–163 (1992–3), pp. 149–155; and Byron Cannon, "Tribal Polities on the Algero-Tunisian Border before 1881: The Kroumir Problem Reexamined," *Cahiers de Tunisie*, 45:105–6 (1978), pp. 49–77.

2 WHOSE TUNISIA?, 1881–1912

The mechanics of imposing French control over Tunisia lie at the core of a study by Ali Mahjoubi, *L'Etablissement du protectorat français en Tunisie* (Tunis: Publications de l'Université de Tunis, 1977). The most detailed account of this process in English is an unpublished doctoral dissertation by Richard Macken, "The Indigenous Reaction to the French Protectorate in Tunisia, 1881–1900," Princeton University, 1972. A third useful work covering a similar period is Carmel Sammut, *L'Imperialisme capitaliste français et le nationalisme tunisien (1881–1914)* (Paris: Publisud, 1983). The responses of one especially important segment of the Tunisian population, the religious leadership, form the basis of Arnold H. Green, "The Tunisian Ulama and the Establishment of the French Protectorate, 1881–1892," *Revue d'Histoire Maghrébine*, 1 (1974), pp. 14–25. Gabriel Payre, "Les Origines et le rôle du contrôle civil dans la régence de Tunis (1881–1956)," *Revue d'histoire diplomatique*, 98 (1984), pp. 267–288*, describes the formation and operation of the corps of civilian agents representing French authority in the Tunisian countryside. The impact of the protectorate on the Italian population is considered in Laura Davi, "Entre Colonisateurs et colonisés: Les Italiens de Tunisie (XIXè–XXè siècle)," in Jacques Alexandropoulos and Patrick Cabanel (eds.), *La Tunisie mosaïque: Diasporas, cosmopolitanisme, archéologies de l'identité* (Toulouse: Presses Universitaires du Mirail, 2000)*, pp. 99–113. Jewish Tunisians and the growing attraction of some members of their community to Zionism are examined in Mohamed Larbi Snoussi, "Aux origines du mouvement sioniste en Tunisie à la veille de la Grande Guerre: Création de l'Aghoudat-Sion et sa première scission (1887–1914)," *Cahiers de Tunisie*, 44:157–8 (1991), pp. 225–274. Two broad surveys that comment on changes introduced by the French into the judicial system are Mohamed Dabbab and Tahar Abid, *La Justice en Tunisie: Un siècle d'histoire judiciaire (essai): de 1856 jusqu'à la veille de l'indépendance* (Tunis: Ministry of Justice, 1998)* and Adnen Mansar, "Pouvoir colonial et justice tunisienne," *Rawafid*, 4 (1998), pp. 39–57.

Several of the above works touch on the question of *colon* land acquisition, but more sharply focused essays appear in numerous articles, among them Byron Cannon, "Le Marché de location des habous en Tunisie: Dialectique de développement agricole, 1875–1902," in Byron Cannon (ed.), *Terroirs et Sociétés au Maghreb et au Moyen Orient* (Lyon: Maison de l'Orient, 1988), pp. 79–108; Charles C. Harber, "Tunisian Land Tenure in the Early French Protectorate," *Muslim World*, 63:4 (1973), pp. 307–315; and Pierre Voizard, "Paul Bourde et l'olivier de Tunisie," *Comptes Rendus des Séances Trimestriels de l'Académie des Sciences Outremer*, 34 (1974), pp. 205–219. Jean Poncet, *La Colonisation et l'agriculture européenne en Tunisie depuis 1881* (Paris and The Hague: Mouton, 1962)*, is a sweeping study of the kinds of crops and methods of cultivation employed by settler farmers. Tunisian resentment over the loss of agricultural land is evident in Moncef Dellagi, "Une Campagne sur l'insécurité des colons de Tunisie en 1898," *Revue d'Histoire Maghrébine*, 7–8 (1977), pp. 99–106, as well as in Taoufik Ayadi, "Insurrection et religion en Tunisie: l'exemple de Thala-Kasserine (1906) et du Jellaz (1911)," in Direction des Archives de France, *Révolte et Société* (Paris: Publications de la Sorbonne, 1989), pp. 166–175. A good picture of *colon* life in provincial Tunisia emerges in a series of articles by Yahya al-Ghoul on Nabeul, the most general of which is "Colonisation et vie municipale: Nabeul à la fin du 19è siècle," *Cahiers de Tunisie*, 45:159–160 (1992), pp. 25–45.

The Tunisian scholar Noureddine Dougui has written extensively on French capital investment and particularly the development of the phosphate industry. On the broader theme, see "Sociétés capitalistes et investissements coloniaux en Tunisie (1881–1920): Quelques éléments d'approche," *Cahiers de Tunisie*, 33:131–132 (1985), pp. 73–105, and "Etat colonial et entreprise concessionnaires en Tunisie (1890–1940)," *Cahiers de Tunisie*, 46:161 (1992), pp. 3–23*. On the phosphate mines and the railroad that transported the ore to the coast, see Noureddine Dougui, "La naissance d'une grande entreprise coloniale: la compagnie des phosphates et chemin de fer de Gafsa," *Cahiers de Tunisie*, 30:119–120 (1982), pp. 123–164, and "La Construction et l'exploitation du réseau de chemin de fer Sfax–Gafsa (1897–1914)," *Cahiers de Tunisie*, 31:123–124 (1983), pp. 13–46. The importance of other railroads is shown in Mohamed Lazhar Gharbi, *Impérialisme et réformisme au Maghreb: Histoire d'un chemin de fer algéro-tunisien* (Tunis: Centre d'Etudes et de Recherches Economiques et Sociales, 1994).

For many Tunisians, education represented the surest, and often only, method of advancement. As a supplement to the sections on education included in many of the works previously cited for this chapter, see François Arnoulet, "Les problèmes de l'enseignement au début du protectorat français en Tunisie (1881–1900)," *Revue de l'Institut des Belles Lettres Arabes*, 167 (1991), pp. 31–62; Patrick Cabanel, "L'Ecole laïque française en Tunisie (1881–1914): La Double utopie," in Jacques

Alexandropoulos and Patrick Cabanel (eds.), *La Tunisie mosaïque: Diasporas, cosmopolitanisme, archéologies de l'identité* (Toulouse: Presses Universitaires du Mirail, 2000), pp. 216–285; and two articles by Noureddine Sraieb, "L'Idéologie de l'école en Tunisie coloniale (1881–1945)," *Revue de l'Occident Musulman et de la Méditerranée*, 68–69 (1993), pp. 239–254*, and "Le collège Sadiki de Tunis et les nouvelles élites," *Revue de l'Occident Musulman et de la Méditerranée*, 72 (1994), pp. 37–52*. Women's education is the theme of Souad Bakalti, "L'Enseignement féminin dans le primaire au temps de la Tunisie coloniale," *Revue de l'Institut des Belles Lettres Arabes*, 166 (1990), pp. 249–274*, as it is of Julia Clancy-Smith, "L'Ecole Rue du Pacha, Tunis: L'Education de la femme arabe et 'La Plus Grande France,' (1900–1914)," *Clio: Histoire, Femmes, et Société*, 12 (2000), pp. 33–55.

The turn to political activism by Tunisians disillusioned with the shortcomings of the protectorate administration also receives attention in many of the works previously cited. A more detailed account appears in Ali Mahjoubi, *Les Origines du mouvement national en Tunisie (1904–1934)* (Tunis: Université de Tunis, 1982)*. Taoufik Ayadi, *Mouvement réformiste et mouvements populaires à Tunis (1906–1912)* (Tunis: Université de Tunis, 1986), focuses squarely on the Young Tunisian movement. Charles-André Julien, "Colons français et Jeunes Tunisiens (1892–1912)," *Revue Française d'Histoire d'Outre-mer*, 54 (1967), pp. 87–150, a study by one of the giants of French North African scholarship, remains authoritative despite its age. Another lengthy article that has also stood the test of time well is Bechir Tlili, "Socialistes et Jeunes-Tunisiens à la veille de la grande guerre (1911–1913)," *Cahiers de Tunisie*, 22:85–86 (1974), pp. 49–134. Little has been written in English on the Young Tunisians. Byron Cannon, "Rural Social Justice Rhetoric and the Young Tunisian Movement, 1907–1912," *Revue d'Histoire Maghrébine*, 59–60 (1990), pp. 63–71, links questions of rural unrest with this early period of political activism.

3 SQUARING OFF, 1912–1940

In addition to Ali Mahjoubi, *Les Origines du mouvement national en Tunisie (1904–1934)* (Tunis: Universite de Tunis, 1982)*, two older books on nationalist movements across North Africa offer good points of departure for an understanding of the formation of the Dustur party. These are Charles-André Julien, *L'Afrique du nord en marche: nationalismes musulmanes et souveraineté français* (Paris: Julliard, 1972)*, and Roger Le Tourneau, *L'Evolution politique de l'Afrique du nord musulmane, 1920–1961* (Paris: Armand Colin, 1962)*. The evolutionary process leading from the Young Tunisians to the Dustur provides the topic for Noureddine Sraieb, "Aux Origines du Destour ou une continuité exemplaire," *Revue d'Histoire Maghrébine*, 65–66 (1992), pp. 71–79. Daniel Goldstein, *Libération ou annexion aux chemins croisés de l'histoire tunisienne (1914–1922)* (Tunis: Maison Tunisienne de l'Edition, 1978), discusses the impact of World War I on Tunisian and French thinking about the protectorate. A study of Dustur efforts to gain support in France at the end of the war is Mohammed Dabbab, *Les Délégations destouriennes à Paris ou la "Question tunisienne" dans les années 1920* (Tunis: Maison Tunisienne de l'Edition, 1980). A study of the Parti Reformiste, which competed with the Dustur for a time in the early 1920s, appears in Mustapha Kraiem, "Le parti réformiste tunisien (1920–1926)," *Revue d'Histoire Maghrébine*, 4 (1975), pp. 150–162. For the linkages between the Dustur and organized labor, see Béchir Tlili, "Des Rapports entre le Parti Libéral et Constitutionnaliste Tunisien et la Confédération Générale Tunisienne du Travail (1924–1925)," *Cahiers de Tunisie*, 28:113–114 (1980), pp. 115–164. Ahmed Ben Miled, *Mhamed Ali. La Naissance du mouvement ouvrier tunisien* (Tunis: Editions Salammbo, 1984), surveys the life and times of the founder of the first Tunisian labor union. A shorter sketch of his life, in English, is Eqbal Ahmad and Stuart Schaar, "Mhamed Ali: Tunisian Labor Organizer," in Edmund Burke III (ed.), *Struggle and Survival in the Modern Middle East* (Berkeley, Ca.: University of California Press, 1993), pp. 191–204.

The devastation visited on Tunisia by the Great Depression contributed to a resurgence of nationalist activity after a period of relative quiescence. Various aspects of the Depression's impact are explored in Abdesslem Ben Hamida, "Les Bourgeois tunisiens face à la crise économique de 1929," *Cahiers de la Méditerranée*, 45 (1992), pp. 129–136; Claude Liauzu, "Un Aspect de la crise en Tunisie: la naissance des bidonvilles," *Revue Française d'Histoire d'Outre-mer*, 63:232–233 (1976), pp. 607–621; and André Nouschi, "La Crise de 1930 en Tunisie et les débuts du Néo-Destour," *Revue de l'Occident Musulmane et de la Méditerranée*, 8 (1970), pp. 113–123. The consequences of hard economic times for European settlers form the core of Jean Poncet, "La Crise des années 30 et ses répercussions sur la colonisation française en Tunisie," *Revue Française d'Histoire d'Outre-mer*, 63:232–233 (1976), pp. 622–627.

The surveys of North African nationalism cited above include accounts of the split in the Dustur that led to the founding of the Neo-Dustur in 1934 and the new party's subsequent strategies in mobilizing resistance to French control. Analyses of many critical political and social occurrences of the 1930s have been collected in Moncef Chenoufi (ed.), *Les Mouvements politiques et sociales dans la Tunisie des années trente* (Tunis: Ministère de l'Education, de l'Enseignement et de la Recherche Scientifique, 1987). Many contributors to this work are Tunisian scholars, some well established and others relative newcomers to the writing of their country's history. The schism in the nationalists' ranks is reviewed in Hassine Raouf Hamza, "Eléments pour une réflexion sur l'histoire du mouvement national pendant l'entre-deux-guerres: la scission du destour de mars 1934," pp. 51–78. Two chapters deal with the politically charged question of naturalization, Juliette Bessis, "A propos de la question des naturalisations dans la Tunisie des années trente," pp. 597–609, and Abdelmajid Kraiem, "L'Echec de la politique de naturalisation en Tunisie (1933/1937)," pp. 623–651. Mustapha Kraiem, "Le Néo-Destour: Cadres, militants et implantation pendant les années trente," pp. 17–49, assesses the early work of the party, while Mohamed Hédi Chérif, "Composition sociale des mouvements de rue en Tunisie dans les années trente," pp. 611–621, considers the background of Tunisians engaged in public protests. Other especially useful chapters are Ahmad Kassab, "La communauté israélite de Tunis entre la francisation et le sionisme (1930–1940)," pp. 525–548; Mokhtar Ayachi, "La politique coloniale et la question zeitounienne dans les années trente," pp. 817–835, and Mohamed

Larbi Snoussi, "Le mouvement national et les régimes totalitaires à la veille de la seconde guerre mondiale (1934–1939)," pp. 365–383. Although not part of the same volume, Hassine Raouf Hamza, "Les émeutes du 9 avril 1938 à Tunis: Machination policière, complot nationaliste ou mouvement spontané?" Direction des Archives de France, *Révolte et Société* (Paris: Publications dela Sorbonne, 1988), pp. 185–191, is an important attempt to evaluate the causes of the April 1938 disorders that temporarily crippled the Neo-Dustur. A general overview of the party in the decade after its founding is Samya el-Méchat, *Le Nationalisme tunisien: scission et conflits, 1934–1944* (Paris: L'Harmattan, 2002)*. Hamadi Ben Halima, *Un demi siècle de théâtre arabe en Tunisie (1907–1957)* (Tunis: Université de Tunis, 1974)*, surveys the theatre, of which the nationalists occasionally made highly effective use.

Among the articles that look specifically at the role of women in the nationalist movement are Ilhem Marzouki, "La voile des colonisées: Tunisie, 1924–1936," *Revue de l'Institut des Belles Lettres Arabes*, 161 (1988), pp. 59–89; Souad Bakalti, *La Femme tunisienne au temps de la colonisation: 1881–1956* (Paris: L'Harmattan, 1996); and two essays by Lilia Labidi, both in a volume edited by her, *Participation des femmes à la vie publique* (Tunis: Centre de Recherche et de Formation Pédagogique, 1990), "Circulation des femmes musulmanes dans l'espace publique et politique formel: le cas de la Tunisie en période coloniale," pp. 19–43, and "L'Emergence du sentiment politique chez les féministes dans la première moitié du XXè siècle: le cas de la Tunisie," pp. 44–62. The writings of Tahar Haddad, an outspoken advocate of women's rights, are discussed in Zeineb Ben Said Cherni, *Les Dérapages de l'histoire chez Tahar Haddad. Les Travailleurs, dieu et la femme* (Tunis: Ben Abdallah, 1993), and in Noureddine Sraieb, "Tahar Haddad, une pensée au service de l'action émancipatrice en Tunisie," in Charles-André Julien (ed.), *Les Africains* (Paris: Editions Jeune Afrique, 1977), VII, pp. 73–97.

Two volumes of letters and other documents produced by Habib Bourguiba, *Ma vie, mon oeuvre, 1934–1938* (Paris: Plon, 1986), and *Ma vie, mon oeuvre, 1938–1943* (Paris: Plon, 1986)*, are useful sources of primary material, as is a collection of newspaper articles, Habib Bourguiba, *Articles de presse, 1929–1933* (Tunis: Dar al-Amal, 1982). The editor of these compendia was Bourguiba's longtime colleague Mohamed Sayah, who also compiled the fifteen-volume *Histoire du mouvement national tunisien* (Tunis: Ministère de l'Information, 1967–1979)*, a work whose subjectivity necessitates cautious usage. A political memoir by a close associate of Bourguiba throughout much of the 1930s is Mahmoud Materi, *Itinéraire d'un militant (1926–1942)* (Tunis: Centre d'Etudes et de Recherches Economiques et Sociales, 1992)*.

4 REDEFINING THE RELATIONSHIP, 1940–1956

The brief reign of Moncef Bey and the deposed ruler's continuing impact on Tunisian political life are at the center of Abdelhamid Hassen, "Moncef Bey et le mouvement moncefiste (1942–1948)," *Revue d'Histoire Maghrébine*, 49–50 (1988), pp. 25–45; Omar Khlifi, *Moncef Bey: roi martyr* (Tunis: Editions Kahia, 1994); and Rachid Driss, "Résistance du Néo-Destour. Contribution de Moncef Bey à l'action nationale (1941–1943)," *Cahiers de Tunisie*, 28:113–114 (1980), pp. 255–288. A concise account of the military campaign that ended in the Allied victory that preceded Moncef's removal can be found in "North African Campaign," in I. C. B. Dear and M. R. D. Foot (eds.), *The Oxford Companion to the Second World War* (Oxford: Oxford University Press, 1995), pp. 813–818. Other important events of the World War II period are treated in *La Tunisie de 1939 à 1945* (Tunis: Ministère de l'Education, de l'Enseignement Supérieur et de la Recherche Scientifique and Centre National Universitaire de Documentation Scientifique et Technique, 1989). As in its companion volume (cited above) focused on the 1930s, the authors of this collection of essays are primarily Tunisian historians. Among its chapters are Mohamed Hédi Chérif, "Mouvement national et occupation germano-italienne de la Tunisie (novembre 1942–mai 1943)," pp. 157–169, and Mokhtar Ayachi, "Le Mouvement zeitounien dans le contexte de la seconde guerre mondiale," pp. 271–309.

The creation of the UGTT and its role in the revival of Neo-Dustur fortunes after the war have been the subject of numerous studies. Abdesselem Ben Hamida, *Le Syndicalisme tunisien de la deuxième guerre mondiale à l'autonomie interne* (Tunis: Université de Tunis I, 1989), examines both the objectives of the union and its connections with the nationalist movement. Two articles by Mustapha Kraiem offer a detailed account of the rivalries among fledgling labor organizations in the postwar era. They are "La Question de l'unité syndicale entre l'UGTT et l'USTT," *Revue d'Histoire Maghrébine*, 12 (1978), pp. 271–285, and "L'Adhésion de l'UGTT à la Fédération Syndicale Mondiale," *Revue d'Histoire Maghrébine*, 1 (1974), pp. 26–34. Also by the same author is "1952, l'année ultime de la vie de Hached: son action de résistance et son assassinat," in *Actes du IXè Colloque International sur Processus et Enjeux de la Décolonisation en Tunisie (1952–1964)* (Tunis: Institut Supérieur d'Histoire du Mouvement National, 1999), pp. 149–186, a review of political and labor questions in the year that saw the assassination of Farhat Hached, the UGTT leader and a key figure in the Neo-Dustur. An older but still useful source, in English, on union activities in the 1940s and 1950s is Willard A. Beling, "WFTU and Decolonization: A Tunisian Case Study," *Journal of Modern African Studies*, 2:4 (1964), pp. 551–564.

The reassertion of Neo-Dustur prominence and its dealings with other components in the anti-French camp are treated in yet another volume of collected essays concerning a narrow chronological period of nationalist history, *La Tunisie de l'après-guerre (1945–1950)* (Tunis: Faculté des Sciences Humaines et Sociales, 1991). See, for example, Hassine Raouf Hamza, "Le Néo-Destour, des lendemains d'avril 1938 à la veille de l'indépendance: hégémonie et institutionalisation," pp. 209–229, and Mokhtar Ayachi, "Le Neo-Destour et les étudiants zeytouniens: de l'alliance à l'affrontement," pp. 231–250. The activities of the Tunisian Communist Party are developed in detail in Hassine Raouf Hamza, *Communisme et nationalisme en Tunisie de la "Libération" à l'indépendance* (Tunis: Université de Tunis, 1994). The nationalists' decision to take the Tunisian case for the termination of the protectorate to the United Nations is explored in Samya El-Machat, "L'indépendance de la Tunisie gagnée à l'ONU? (1952–1954)," in *Actes du IXè Colloque*

International sur Processus et Enjeux de la Décolonisation en Tunisie (1952–1964) (Tunis: Institut Supérieur d'Histoire du Mouvement National, 1999), pp. 27–38, and in greater detail in the same author's *Tunisie: Les Chemins vers l'indépendance (1945–1956)* (Paris: L'Harmattan, 1992). Mohammed Lotfi Chaibi, "Les Enjeux d'une décolonisation négociée: l'exemple tunisien (1954–1956)," *Revue de l'Institut des Belles Lettres Arabes*, 186 (2000), pp. 191–211, focuses on the closing stages of the negotiations. Some of the problems arising at that point are also examined in Juliette Bessis, "La Crise d'autonomie et de l'indépendance tunisienne, classe politique et pays réel," in René Gallissot (ed.), *Mouvemenet ouvrier, communisme et nationalismes dans le monde arabe* (Paris: Les Editions Ouvrières, 1978), pp. 265–292. An account of the decade leading to independence by a French scholar who personally knew many of the figures involved on both sides of the table is Charles-André Julien, *Et la Tunisie devint indépendante, 1951–1957* (Paris: Editions Jeune Afrique, 1985).

5 THE INDEPENDENT STATE SETS ITS COURSE, 1956–1969

Clement Henry Moore, *Tunisia since Independence: The Dynamics of One-Party Government* (Berkeley, Ca.: University of California Press, 1965), the first English-language study of politics and governance in independent Tunisia, remains a superb source for the early postcolonial period. Despite being of similar vintage, a second work on Tunisian politics, Lars Rudebeck, *Party and People: A Study of Political Change in Tunisia* (London: C. Hurst & Co., 1969), also remains a useful source for this period. Habib Bourguiba has been the subject of numerous biographies, most of them in French or Arabic. The best in English is Derek Hopwood, *Habib Bourguiba of Tunisia: The Tragedy of Longevity* (New York: St. Martin's Press, 1992)*. The second of a two-volume account by Sophie Bessis and Souhayr Belhassen, *Bourguiba: Un si long règne (1957–1989)* (Paris: Jeune Afrique, 1989)*, largely avoids either the excessive fawning or bitter polemics that characterize many accounts written primarily for political purposes. An attempt to assess the place of Bourguiba in the overall scheme of modern Tunisian history, made soon after his demise in 2000, is L. Carl Brown, "Bourguiba and Bourguibism Revisited: Reflections and Interpretation," *Middle East Journal*, 55:1 (2001), pp. 43–57*.

Two articles addressing quite different points of contention with the former colonial power in the 1950s appear in *Actes du IXe Colloque International sur Processus et Enjeux de la Décolonisation en Tunisie (1952–1964)* (Tunis: Institut Supérieur d'Histoire du Mouvement National, 1999). They are Gian Paolo Calci Novati, "Le bombardement de Sakiet Sidi Youssef et les péripéties de la politique tunisienne face à la guerre d'Algérie," pp. 55–75, and Habib Kazdaghli, "Communautés européennes de Tunisie face à la décolonisation (1955–1962)," pp. 321–338. The same volume also has a parallel article on the Jewish community, Abdelkrim Allagui, "La minorité juive de Tunisie face à la décolonisation au cours des années 50," pp. 305–319. The conflict with France over the naval base at Bizerte is the subject of Werner Ruf, "The Bizerte Crisis: A Bourguibist Attempt to Resolve Tunisia's

Border Problem," *Middle East Journal*, 25 (1971), pp. 201–211. Bourguiba's unorthodox (for an Arab head of state) approach to the problem of Palestine is outlined
in Yaroslav Bilinsky, "Moderate Realism in an Extremist Environment: Tunisia
and the Palestine Question (1965–1970)," *Revue de l'Occident Musulmane et de la
Méditerranée*, 13–14 (1973), pp. 109–123, and discussed further in Abdeljelil Temimi,
"La Question palestinienne et les relations de Bourguiba avec le Congrès Juif
Mondial," in Abdeljelil Temimi (ed.), *Habib Bourguiba et l'établissement de l'état
national: approches scientifiques de bourguibisme* (Zaghouan: Fondation Temimi
pour la Recherche Scientifique et l'Information, 2000), pp. 109–127.

General surveys of the Tunisian economy that treat the immediate post-
independence efforts to formulate a viable economic approach include Allan
Findlay, "Tunisia: The Vicissitudes of Economic Development," in Richard
Lawless and Allan Findlay (eds.), *North Africa: Contemporary Politics and Economic Development* (London: Croom Helm, 1984), pp. 217–240*, and the more
recent Emma C. Murphy, *Economic and Political Change in Tunisia: From Bourguiba to Ben Ali* (London: Macmillan, 1999)*. The shift from a liberal economy to
Neo-Dustur socialism is reviewed in Charles Debbasch, "Du Néo-Destour au parti
socialiste destourien: le congrès de Bizerte," *Annuaire de l'Afrique du Nord*, 3 (1964),
pp. 27–43, while Jean Poncet, "L'Economie tunisienne depuis l'indépendance," in
Annuaire de l'Afrique du Nord, 8 (1969), pp. 93–114, presents an overview of economic issues facing the country during its first decade of independence. Tahar
Haouet, "L'Expérience tunisienne de développement agricole," in Jean Cuisenier
(ed.), *Problèmes du développement économique dans les pays méditerranéens* (Paris
and The Hague: Mouton, 1963), pp. 65–116, focuses specifically on the agricultural sector, while C. Zarka, "L'Economie tunisienne à l'heure de la planification
impérative," *Annuaire de l'Afrique du Nord*, 1 (1962), pp. 207–241, is an early illustration of the case for economic planning. Key aspects of Ahmad Ben Salah's
thinking become apparent in Marc Nerfin, *Entretiens avec Ahmed ben Salah sur la
dynamique socialiste dans les années 1960* (Paris: Maspero, 1974), while a sample in
English of the Planning Minister's ideas can be found in his essay "Tunisia: Endoge-
nous Development and Structural Transformation," in Marc Nerfin (ed.), *Another
Development: Approaches and Strategies* (Uppsala: The Dag Hammarskjold Foundation, 1977), pp. 242–262. John Simmons, "Agricultural Cooperatives and Rural
Development," *Middle East Journal*, 24 (1970), pp. 455–465, and 25 (1971), pp. 45–
57, assesses Ben Salah's policies, and Mouldi Lahmar, "La Réforme agraire dans les
années soixante en Tunisie: le PSD contre ses assises rurales," *Revue de l'Institut
des Belles Lettres Arabes*, 52, 163 (1989), pp. 39–68, is a later critique by a Tunisian
scholar. An early study on tourism that highlighted serious problems emerging in
regions where the industry was heavily concentrated is Hafedh Sethom, "Agriculture et tourisme dans la région de Nabeul–Hammamet, co-existence féconde ou
déséquilibre croissant?" *Cahiers de Tunisie*, 24:93–94 (1976), pp. 101–111*.

Relevant sections of Mounira M. Charrad, *States and Women's Rights: The
Making of Postcolonial Tunisia, Algeria, and Morocco* (Berkeley, Ca.: University
of California Press, 2001)*, give a good overview of changes in the legal status of
Tunisian women and especially of the impact of the Personal Status Code of
1956, as does Mark Tessler, Janet Rogers, and Daniel Schneider, "Women's

Emancipation in Tunisia," in Lois Beck and Nikki Keddie (eds.), *Women in the Muslim World* (Cambridge, Ma.: Harvard University Press, 1978), pp. 141–158*. Women's mobilization efforts, extending into the precolonial era, are discussed in Ilhem Marzouki, *Le Mouvement des femmes en Tunisie au XXè siècle: féminisme et politique* (Paris: Maisonneuve et Larose, 1993)*. Mohamed Ennaceur, "La Politique sociale de la Tunisie depuis l'indépendance et sa place dans le développement," in Abdelwahab Bouhdiba (ed.), *Le Développement en question* (Tunis: Centre d'Etudes et de Recherches Economiques et Sociales, 1990), pp. 335–392*, explores the use of social policies, including those targeting women, as instruments of development. James Allman, *Social Mobility, Education and Development in Tunisia* (Leiden: Brill, 1977)*, looks specifically at the role played by education in fostering development following independence.

6 REGIME ENTRENCHMENT AND THE INTENSIFICATION OF OPPOSITION, 1969–1987

Demands for reforms within the Socialist Dustur Party in the early 1970s provide the backdrop for Alaya Allani, "Bourguiba et le courant 'libéral' au sein du parti destourien: 1970–1971," in Abdeljelil Temimi (ed.), *Habib Bourguiba et l'établissement de l'état national: approches scientifiques du bourguibisme* (Zaghouan: Fondation Temimi pour la Recherche Scientifique et l'Information, 2000), pp. 51–57. More research on the events of the past thirty years has been published in English than is true of any earlier period in Tunisia's history. A contemporary evaluation of the reform movement is John Entelis, "Ideological Change and an Emerging Counter-Culture in Tunisian Politics," *Journal of Modern African Studies*, 12 (1974), pp. 543–568. Jon Marks, "Tunisia," in Tim Niblock and Emma Murphy (eds.), *Economic and Political Liberalization in the Middle East* (London: British Academic Press, 1993), pp. 166–176*, surveys the changes that marked the 1970s and 1980s. A second such overview is Asma Larif-Beatrix, "L'évolution de l'état tunisien," *Maghreb-Machrek*, 116 (1987), pp. 35–44. Possible explanations for the political leadership's survival, despite its resistance to anything more than superficial manifestations of pluralism, emerge in Dirk Vandewalle, "Bourguiba, Charismatic Leadership and the Tunisian One Party System," *Middle East Journal*, 34 (1980), pp. 149–159. Clement Henry Moore, "Tunisia and Bourguibisme: Twenty Years of Crisis," *Third World Quarterly*, 10:1 (1988), pp. 176–190, summarizes the many difficulties that plagued Bourguiba in the later years of his rule. Fitting within that period is the sharply focused study by Lisa Anderson, "Democracy Frustrated: The Mzali Years in Tunisia," in Reeva Simon (ed.), *The Middle East and North Africa: Essays in Honor of J. C. Hurewitz* (New York: Columbia University Press, 1990), pp. 185–203.

The public disturbances triggered by economic policies beginning in the late 1970s are compared to similar outbreaks of violence by David Seddon, "Riot and Rebellion in North Africa: Political Responses to Economic Crisis in Tunisia, Morocco, and Sudan," in Berch Berberoglu (ed.), *Power and Stability in the Middle East* (London: Zed Press, 1989), pp. 114–135. Along the same lines, see Mouldi Lahmar, "La 'Révolte du pain' dans la campagne tunisienne: notables, ouvriers et fellahs," *Esprit*, 100 (1985), pp. 9–19. A memoir by Habib Achour, *Ma Vie politique et syndicale. Enthousiasme et déception (1944–1981)* (Tunis: Alif, 1989)*, sets forth the veteran labor leader's views on these events and places them within the broader context of the relationship between the party and the union. An analysis of the attack on Gafsa in 1980 is Pierre Robert Baduel, "Gafsa comme enjeux," *Annuaire de l'Afrique du Nord*, 19 (1980), pp. 485–511.

Much has been written on the restructuring of the Tunisian economy that began in the waning days of the Bourguiba presidency. An introduction to the issues involved is provided by Mahmoud Ben Romdhane, "Fondements et contenu des restructurations face à la crise économique en Tunisie: Une Analyse critique," *Annuaire de l'Afrique du Nord*, 26 (1987), pp. 149–176. Other helpful surveys include Stephen J. King, "Economic Reform and Tunisia's Hegemonic Party: The End of the Administrative Elite," in Ali Abdullatif Ahmida (ed.), *Beyond Colonialism and Nationalism in the Maghrib: History, Culture, and Politics* (New York: Palgrave, 2000), pp. 165–193, and Karen Pfeiffer, "Between Rocks and Hard Choices: International Finance and Economic Adjustment in North Africa," in Dirk Vandewalle (ed.), *North Africa: Development and Reform in a Changing Global Economy* (New York: St. Martin's Press, 1996), pp. 25–63*. Samir Radwan, Vali Jamal, and Ajit Ghose, *Tunisia: Rural Labour and Structural Transformation* (London: Routledge, 1990)*, probe some of the specifically rural dimensions of restructuring. Efforts to promote privatization are examined in Iliya Harik, "Privatization and Development in Tunisia," in Iliya Harik and Dennis J. Sullivan (eds.), *Privatization and Liberalization in the Middle East* (Indianapolis, In.: Indiana University Press, 1992), pp. 210–232*, and in Abdelsatar Grissa, "The Tunisian State Enterprises and Privatization Policy," in I. William Zartman (ed.), *Tunisia: The Political Economy of Reform* (Boulder, Co.: Lynne Rienner, 1991), pp. 109–127*. Also in the latter collection is Eva Bellin, "Tunisian Industrialists and the State," pp. 45–65*, that explores the links between powerful business interests and the government.

The emergence of an Islamist movement posing a serious challenge to the Bourguiba presidency also spawned great scholarly interest. Among the many articles that discuss the early activity of the movement are two by Abdelbaki Hermassi, "La société tunisienne au miroir islamiste," *Maghreb-Machrek*, 103 (1984), pp. 39–56, and "The Rise and Fall of the Islamist Movement in Tunisia," in Laura Guazzone (ed.), *The Islamist Dilemma: The Political Role of Islamist Movements in the Contemporary Arab World* (London: Ithaca Press, 1995), pp. 105–127*, which, as the title suggests, presents a more comprehensive picture of the movement. Also helpful for the early period is Patrick Bannerman, "The Mouvement de la Tendance Islamique in Tunisia," in R. M. Burrell (ed.), *Islamic Fundamentalism* (London: Royal Asiatic Society, 1989), pp. 67–74. Several other articles that posit theories on the popularity of the Islamist cause are Abdelkader Zghal, "Le Retour du sacré et la nouvelle demande idéologique des jeunes scholarisés: le cas de Tunisie," *Annuaire de l'Afrique du Nord*, 18 (1979), pp. 41–64; Susan Waltz, "Islamist Appeal in Tunisia," *Middle East Journal*, 40 (1986), pp. 651–670; and Norma Salem, "Islam and the Politics of Identity in Tunisia," *Journal of Arab Affairs*, 2 (1986), pp. 194–216. Abdelbaki Hermassi, "The Islamist Movement and November 7," in Zartman,

Tunisia: The Political Economy of Reform, pp. 193–204, looks into the Islamists' role in bringing down the Bourguiba government.

The history of the Tunisian cinema and vignettes of many of its most important productions are in Roy Armes, "Cinema in the Maghreb: Tunisia," in Oliver Leaman (ed.), *Companion Encyclopedia of Middle Eastern and North African Film* (London and New York: Routledge, 2001), pp. 490–512 ; in Mohamed Salah Rassaa, *35 ans de cinéma tunisien* (Tunis: Sahar, 1993); and in Sonia Chamkhi, *Cinéma tunisien nouveau* (Tunis: Sud Editions, 2002). Férid Boughedir, "Le Cinéma en Tunisie (1966–1986). Vingt ans de cinéma tunisien: la société tunisienne vue par ses films," *Revue Tunisienne de Communication*, 9 (1986), pp. 88–113, writes as both a Tunisian critic and the director of some of the country's most successful films. The work of a pioneer in Tunisian cinema and photography is examined in Guillemette Mansour, *Cinéma et photographie en Tunisie – Samama Chikly – Un tunisien à la rencontre de XXè siècle* (Tunis: Simpact, 2000). Badra Bchir, *Eléments du fait théâtral en Tunisie* (Tunis: Centre d'Etudes et de Recherches Economiques et Sociales, 1993), and Mohamed Masood Driss, "L'Activité théâtrale en Tunisie, 1970–1980: essai de bilan," *Revue de l'Institut des Belles Lettres Arabes*, 156 (1985), pp. 313–329, deal with stage productions. The first venture into private commercial theater is described by Jean Fontaine, "Le 'Nouveau Théâtre' de Tunis, 1976–1982," *Revue de l'Institut des Belles Lettres Arabes*, 151 (1983), pp. 123–133. Fontaine is also the author of *La Littérature tunisienne contemporaine* (Paris: Centre Nationale de Recherche Scientifique, 1990); *Le Roman tunisien de langue arabe, 1956–2001* (Tunis: Centre d'Etudes et de Recherches Economiques et Sociales, 2002); *Ecrivaines tunisiennes* (Tunis: Gai Savoir, 1990), on women writers; and, in English, "Arabic Language Tunisian Literature (1956–1990)," *Research in African Literatures*, 23 (1992), pp. 183–193. Sophie el-Goulli, "Les Arts plastiques en Tunisie," *Europe*, 702 (1987), pp. 49–56, focuses primarily on painting. On modern Tunisian music, see Ali Racy, "Music of Tunisia: A Contemporary Perspective," *Arabesque*, 5:1 (1979), pp. 18–24 and 28.

7 CONSTANCY AND INNOVATION IN THE "NEW" TUNISIA, 1987–2003

Early assessments of the "Historic Change" of 1987 are Mohsen Toumi, *La Tunisie de Bourguiba à Ben Ali* (Paris: Presses Universitaires de France, 1989), Clement Henry Moore, "La Tunisie après vingt ans de crise du succession," *Maghreb-Machrek*, 120 (1988), pp. 5–22, and two articles in *Middle East Journal*, 42 (1988), Dirk Vandewalle, "From the New State to the New Era: Towards a Second Republic in Tunisia," pp. 602–620, and Lewis B. Ware, "Ben Ali's Constitutional Coup in Tunisia," pp. 587–601. Guilain Denoeux, "La Tunisie de Ben Ali et ses paradoxes," *Maghreb-Machrek*, 166 (1999), pp. 32–52, and Michel Camau, "D'Une république à l'autre: Refondation politique et aléas de la transition libérale," *Maghreb-Machrek*, 157 (1997), pp. 3–16, both survey the political terrain in the decade after the transition. An account of the new regime's initial attempt to build a broad base of support appears in Lisa Anderson, "Political Pacts, Liberalism and Democracy: The Tunisian National Pact of 1988," *Government and Opposition*, 26 (1991), pp. 244–260. Mohamed Abdelhaq and Jean-Bernard Heumann, "Opposition et élections en Tunisie," *Maghreb-Machrek*, 168 (2000), pp. 29–40*, analyzes the results of several ostensibly multiparty national elections.

The role played by labor organizations since 1987 is examined in Riadh Zghal, "Nouvelles orientations du syndicalisme tunisien," *Maghreb-Machrek*, 162 (1998), pp. 6–17, and in Christopher Alexander, "State, Labor, and the New Global Economy in Tunisia," in Dirk Vandewalle (ed.), *North Africa: Development and Reform in a Changing Global Economy* (New York: St. Martin's Press, 1996), pp. 177–202 . The ties between labor and the Islamist movement are outlined in Christopher Alexander, "Opportunities, Organizations, and Ideas: Islamists and Workers in Tunisia and Algeria," *International Journal of Middle East Studies*, 32 (2000), pp. 465–490. Clement Henry Moore, "Post-Colonial Dialectics of Civil Society," in Yahya H. Zoubir (ed.), *North Africa in Transition: State, Society, and Economic Transformation in the 1990s* (Gainesville, Fl.: University Press of Florida, 1999), pp. 11–28, describes the emergence of other components of civil society in the post-Bourguiba era. The growth of a human rights association and its engagement in the political process provide the subject matter for Susan Waltz, *Human Rights and Reform: Changing the Face of North African Politics* (Berkeley, Ca.: University of California Press, 1995).

Delphine Henry, "Le Président Ben Ali et les islamistes," *L'Afrique et l'Asie Moderne*, 164 (1990), pp. 135–149, treats the new chief executive's initial approach to the Islamist movement. The deteriorating situation brought about by the failure of the movement and the government to reach a modus vivendi is described in Michael C. Dunn, "The al-Nahda Movement in Tunisia: From Renaissance to Revolution," in John Ruedy (ed.), *Islam and Secularism in North Africa* (New York: St. Martin's Press, 1994), pp. 149–165*, but perhaps the most interesting account in English of the political role played by Tunisian Islamists is by a former activist, Mohamed Elhachmi Hamdi, *The Politicization of Islam: A Case Study of Tunisia* (Boulder, Co.: Westview Press, 1998)*. Concerns that Islamist successes might jeopardize advances secured in the past by Tunisian women constitutes an undercurrent in Zakya Daoud, "Les femmes tunisiennes: Gains juridiques et statut économique et social," *Maghreb-Machrek*, 145 (1994), pp. 27–48*.

The national economy receives treatment in Hachemi Alaya, *Les Nouvelles règles du jeu économique en Tunisie: principes et mécanismes de l'économie de marché* (Tunis: Centre de publication universitaire, 1999). A broader perspective on recent economic developments is afforded by André Wilmots, *De Bourguiba à Ben Ali: L'Etonnant parcours économique de la Tunisie, 1960–2000* (Paris: L'Harmattan, 2003)*. Addressing the challenges posed by globalization lies at the core of Hakim Ben Hammouda, *Tunisie, ajustement et difficulté de l'insertion internationale* (Paris: L'Harmattan, 1995), and of a study by the World Bank, *Tunisia's Global Integration and Sustainable Development: Strategic Choices for the 21st Century* (Washington, DC: World Bank, 1996). The economic consequences for Tunisia of its formal relationship with the European Union are discussed in Jean-Pierre Cassarino, "The EU–Tunisian Association Agreement and Tunisia's Structural Reform Program," *Middle East Journal*, 53:1 (1999), pp. 59–74.

Index